BREAKING INTO COMMERCIALS

THE COMPLETE GUIDE TO MARKETING YOURSELF, AUDITIONING TO WIN, AND GETTING THE JOB

3rd Edition, Revised and Updated

Terry Berland and Deborah Ouellette

SILMAN-JAMES PRESS   LOS ANGELES

10 9 8 7 6 5 4 3 2 1

Library of Congress Cataloging-in-Publication Data

Berland, Terry.
Breaking into commercials : the complete guide to marketing
yourself, auditioning to win, and getting he job / by Terry Berland
and Deborah Ouellette. – Third Edition, updated and revised.
pages cm
Includes index.
ISBN 978-1-935247-09-8 (alk. paper)
1. Television acting–Vocational guidance. 2. Television advertising–
Vocational guidance. I. Ouellette, Deborah. II. Title.
PN1992.8.A3B47 2014
791.4502'8023–dc23

2013042608

Cover design by Wade Lageose for Lageose Design

Printed and bound in the United States of America

Silman-James Press, Inc.
www.silmanjamespress.com

Commercials Are a Hot Commodity

Working in commercials is one of the most exciting careers in showbiz, and the hunt for performers with special magic never ends. The market for talent is huge—and so are the rewards. And now two of the top names in the business have written the most complete and practical guide to breaking into commercials and making the most of the many professional opportunities the business provides. The wealth of expert advice answers such questions as:

- How do I pursue a career acting in commercials from start to success?
- How do I find work in major and regional markets?
- How do I get a great headshot (your calling card)?
- Who are the key players in the commercial industry—and what part do they play in my career?
- What seven qualities give me the winning edge in an audition?
- How does a parent both promote and protect a child in the fast commercial track?
- How do models cross over into acting in commercials?
- How can I win the high-stakes game of BREAKING INTO COMMERCIALS?

TERRY BERLAND, award-winning casting director and former head of casting for the third largest ad agency in the world, BBDO/New York, heads her own casting company, Berland Casting, and teaches the workshop "Acting in Television Commercials" around the nation. *www.berlandcasting.com*

DEBORAH OUELLETTE is an award-winning photographer and writer in the entertainment industry who serves as a judge and guest speaker at regional and national modeling and talent competitions. *www.deborahouellettephotography.com*

"If you're looking for the bible on getting into commercials, this is it! This book will teach you how to successfully break into this very lucrative field. It logically and thoroughly covers all the basics—from headshots through bookings. If you follow these tips, you're halfway there."—**Daisy Sinclair, former Head of Casting, Ogilvy & Mather advertising agency, New York City**

"In an industry changing as rapidly as ours, actors need to read as much as possible. I learned from this book. You will too."—**Jerre Hookey, Former National Director of Organizing and Southwest Regional Chief, Screen Actors Guild**

"This book is filled with insight, information, and inspiration for all aspiring actors."—**Professor Ellen Faith Brodie, Director of Theatre, Eastern Connecticut State University**

"The wisdom of a veteran casting director and the viewpoint of a photographer-writer mix well to give newcomers to commercial acting all the how-tos, tips, and references to break in. . . . On the basis of their collective experience and interviews with more than 75 industry pros, Berland and Ouellette completely debunk some of the myths surrounding success: that talent is the only quality that matters; that you can pay to get on camera; and that all you need for voice-overs is a great demo tape. . . . A good reality check about acting for both kids and adults."—**Barbara Jacobs, *Booklist***

"The most comprehensive book on the how-tos of doing commercials, this book is the bible for all actors. It gives them all the tools they need to help them help themselves."—**Liz Lewis, Casting Director, Liz Lewis Casting Partners, New York City**

"You can't get the part unless you get the audition. *Breaking Into Commercials* tells you how to get them and book them."—**Nancy Vines, Director of New Business Development, Mr. Wonderful/Northern Lights/Bodega Studios, former commercial television and radio producer, New York City**

"The book will teach you about getting your commercial headshots, how to put together an acting résumé, and what training you will need. There is also a valuable chapter on avoiding scams. If you want to know what to expect on a commercial audition and how the casting of commercials is done—this book is for you. A very useful resource for any commercial actor."—**Donna Grayson, Actress, Los Angeles**

"This book is dead-on."—**Cynthia St. John, Actress, Aspen, CO**

"What a wonderful book for newcomers. . . . The sections for regional actors, models moving into talent careers, and children in the business make for a well-rounded look at the industry and how it works."—**Tom Persing, Actor, Detroit, MI**

"My agent had Terry Berland on a list of recommended acting coaches, so I bought her book. It's great! What's unique about the book is the in-depth advice on space work and beats. . . . Great advice!"—**Susan Lee-Bustamante, Actress**

"This book is fabulous! . . . After reading it, I found myself recommending it to every new actor that came into the agency. . . . Simple, concise language. Helpful photographs and illustrations. A MUST for the beginning actor!"—**Lisa Staton, Russell Langley Model Talent Agency, Tulsa, OK**

"I used the section that suggested playing to things that don't exist *off* camera, left and right, incorporating the whole room. Thanks to that, I booked my very next audition as a principal in a commercial."—**Peter Louis, Actor, Los Angeles**

Contents

SECTION 3: Wrapping It All Up

Acknowledgments

Jason Alexander, Bob Lasky, Michael D'Ambrosia, Robert Kazandjian, Kenneth Dapper, Wylie Small, Vanessa Marshall, Karman Kruschke, Joseph Perlman, Sharon Chatten, Laura Fogelman, Sarah Carpenter, Traci Danielli, Robert Schroeder, Nancy Johnson, Carol Ingber, Al Onorato, Angela Peri, Heather Laird, Lori Wyman, Tom Jourden, Julene Renee-Preciado, Barbara Goldman, Nick Omana, Charlie Adler, Bob Bergen, Vincent Cirrincione, Elle Macpherson, Carmen, Tim Saunders, Patrick Johnson, Carol Lyn Sher, Judy Savage, Sue Schacter, Alan Simon, Debbie Boyd, Jennifer Arens, Karen Tank, Kimberlee Lucas, Robin Carus, Susan Maizner, David Reivers, Steve Guilmette, Peter Trencher, Forbes Riley, Michael Helms, Lazarus Jackson, Victoria Hoffman, John Jennens, Michael Roud Photography, Brett Ericson, Kim DiFederico, Aiden Andrews, Joanna Holden, Kelsey Edwards, Jenna Boyd, Cody Arens, Aaron Berger, Dr. Glenn Berger, Morgan Thrush, Rich Hogan, Old School Photography, Studio D. Photography, Hayden Tank, Shultz Bros. Photography, Gary Tice, Jack "Bean" Lucas, Corbin Bleu, Nancy Jo Gilchrist, Paul Doherty, Vicki Weiss, Harriet Greenspan, Jeff Danis, Conrad Bachmann, Ellen Brodie, Gwen Feldman.

Foreword
by Jason Alexander

When asked how I got started as an actor, I tell people I "fell" into the business . . .

I can't remember a time when I wasn't performing. I don't know where my interest came from, but it was entrenched by the time I was six. When I was twelve or thirteen, I was taking it seriously enough to do everything I could do locally—in New Jersey, where I grew up.

I was doing school plays, community theater, and children's theater. One of the children's shows we were doing was seen by a television producer who thought it would be a neat idea to film it as a children's special for television.

In order to do it, we all had to join the union. The show aired in New York, New Jersey, and Connecticut. The day after it aired, a manager (Neiderlitz & Steele) called me up and asked if I would like to be a client. I stayed with them for the next nine years, and they guided me into the business.

Throughout college, all I did was commercial work, which was great. I always thought of commercials as thirty-second movies. I was working with people who really knew what they were doing. It had all the excitement of doing film work with none of the tedium because it moved so fast.

Fortunately, my career was always progressive. The work I did always begat other work, and I was lucky that it stayed of a certain quality. Even though some things flopped, the people I got to work with were spectacular.

There was my Broadway debut, *Merrily We Roll Along*, written by Stephen Sondheim and George Furth and directed by Hal Prince. The show was not a success for them but it sure was for me.

My next show, *The Rink*, was only a moderate success, but with stars like Chita Rivera and Liza Minnelli, the composer John Kander and lyricist Fred Ebb, and the playwright Terrence McNally, I was surrounded by brilliant people.

Then I worked with Neil Simon, which was a tremendous opportunity. Some years later, I won a Tony for *Jerome Robbins' Broadway*, which, ironically, was a show I never wanted to do. I thought it was going to be a humongous dance review, and I could move but not dance . . . certainly not like that. I finally got dragged into that show, which turned out to be a great experience.

I also started doing little teeny roles in film, and every now and then, I'd be out in LA doing a series.

I was never one to sit back and let things happen. It's very important for actors to take charge of their careers and always work at fine-tuning their craft.

When asked what advice I would give to actors who have taken one weekend workshop and feel they have mastered some technique, I always say that in my experience, the craft of acting is something that comes with age, maturity, and insight. People without training think that all you have to do is learn your lines and show up; professionals know that it takes a long time to learn the tools, techniques, and skills that are as important to an actor as color is to a visual artist or theory is to musicians.

Some of these tools are very technical. Others are instinctual. The technical skills came very easily to me, which is not necessarily the norm for most people. Most people struggle with the technical skills.

What I had trouble with was what we call the emotional life of the character. For some actors it comes naturally, and, in fact, that's all they can do. They're emotional as hell, but they don't know how to craft it or shape it.

So, no matter which end of the fence you come down on, I think it takes a lifetime of work to bring the other half up to snuff.

There are very successful, well-known actors who have never taken a class in their lives. They don't believe in it. They don't do any homework. They just show up on the set and do what comes naturally. And they do it very, very well. But my feeling is that without a technique or craft, there's no way to prepare. You can only cross your fingers and hope for the best.

I don't think you can study enough. The trick is to find someone who speaks your language and techniques you understand. It's a very delicate situation, being in class, because you're using your own ego and your own imagination as tools. And your tools are often criticized.

How do you find a good coach? Word of mouth. By observing. The best way is to talk to someone whose work you admire. Find out if they're studying and where. Go check them out. It's really trial and error. You'll know if someone is speaking your language and if it's an atmosphere you think you'd like to work in.

If you don't know any actors, call a local university that has an acting program and see if any of the teachers or professors teach outside the school, or call the local unions to see if they have any recommendations.

Anyone who reads my story is going to think that this is the easiest business in the world. Unfortunately, nothing could be further from the truth. *The first thing you're going to find when you get into the business is the biggest Catch-22 in the world:* Do you want to work as a professional or as an amateur? If you want to work as a professional, you have to get into the unions, and you can't get into the unions without a professional job. One way to get into the union is to audition for a union job and to get booked.

Challenge number two is, how do you market yourself? Nobody knows how to market him/herself. Actors have a very unrealistic idea of what they are about. Homely people think they are leading men and leading ladies. I've seen very funny people try to be dramatic actors. I've seen people who have no sense of humor try to do comedy. Old people try to play young, young people try to play old.

Certainly you have to believe that you can do anything. You should believe that, but on a realistic, commercial level, you have to know what it is that you present.

Are you going to New York, LA, or Chicago? Are you going to London? Are you going to go to good regional theater? Are you going to focus on theater? On television? On commercials?

Challenge number three is learning to control your career. Actors have to try and do career planning. Many actors tend not to do this, and nobody seems to tell them that they have to.

Actors have to go and read, and when they find material that's right for them that can be developed, they should develop it. Buy it. Get into improvisational theater groups and get up on stage with people. If you sing, develop a sort of cabaret act. Form theater groups within your community. See what kind of theater thrives in your area and have something special ready that will get you noticed. This way, you're not always going to them and begging for a job. They will come to you at work and say they like what you do.

You have to own your career. It's the hardest thing to do, but if you don't do it, you are just waiting . . . and waiting *kills* talent. Waiting kills careers.

What it takes to make it in this business is a certain level of *desperation.* I always tell people, particularly young acting students, "If there's anything else you could do and be happy—not even exquisitely happy but just happy—pursue it, because, in my observation, this business is only for people who have no other option." If it is not your end-all, be-all, something you really must have or you'll jump off a bridge, then don't get on the bridge. It's not for you.

However, if you decide it *is* for you, you need a sense of bravura. You need a thick hide that's only thick on the outside. It has to be very thin on the inside or your vulnerability, your compassion, will die. And no actor can survive without them.

I don't know how to tell you to develop that hide. I don't think anyone does, but it is an absolute job requirement. You're going to hear "No!" a hell of a lot more than you'll hear "Yes!"

What's the best way to deal with the inevitable frustration and rejection that goes along with a career in this business? Have a life beyond the business.

Find other things you love to do. Have people outside the profession in your life. Don't get stuck with acting as your only realm.

Stay involved with your community. Stay involved with current events. Learn other things. Learn a skill. I once spent months learning to roller-skate, then got a job because I knew how to roller-skate.

Learn a language. Learn a new business. Go someplace you've never been before, even if it's only ten miles away. Observe people. Talk to people in other professions so if you ever play a stockbroker, for instance, you've done your research already. Just don't get stuck. You have to stay in motion.

It's a real didactic profession because it comes down to "I got it" or "I didn't get it." It's that hot and cold.

Actors always crack me up because they'll do an audition and they'll ask the agent to call and get feedback. What good is the feedback? It's only one person's opinion. "Did I get the job?" "Yes or no." If I did, then I did good. If I didn't get it, for whatever reason, it didn't happen.

The only reason you need feedback is if somebody says, "He comes in with a real chip on his shoulder," or "He comes in and his hygiene is not good." This is the only kind of feedback you want to get. Other than that, you took your shot and it did or didn't happen.

I think, in the business, there's an illusion that everything has to happen very quickly. There are a lot of young stars. The movies in particular right now are youth-oriented and there's a feeling that if you haven't participated in this business by the time you are twenty-five or thirty, it's too late.

My feeling is that anyone who is supposed to be doing this and who has real ability, real commitment, will find success. And success is defined very individually.

There are some people who will feel successful laying the classics at the Seattle Repertory. There are other people who will feel extraordinarily successful making six figures a year doing commercials, even if they've never performed elsewhere. Others will not be happy until they are box-office stars.

Success comes in many forms and you have to decide as an actor, "What do I want?" "Where will I be happy?"

Success is not always about making money. It's not always about being in a big theater. It's not about being in front of a camera. And it doesn't have to happen fast.

You may not get a particular job. You may not do well at an audition, but you are working on your craft. The craft gets better. You perform the craft and you do it over and over and over again . . . and you *love* it.

You enjoy doing it. You love studying it. You like displaying it.

Actors get better every year they're living. It's a craft about maturity. So live. And grow. And stop knocking your brains out trying to succeed on somebody else's terms.

Succeed on your own terms and in your own time.

Good luck!

Introduction

Our goal in creating this book is to help you break into commercials with a clear, concise sense of how the industry works. People all around the country from every walk of life are exposed to commercials. Many people who watch commercials, hear them on the radio, and see them in print aspire to do commercials as a full- or part-time career.

Commercials seem more accessible than parts in film or TV shows—and they *are*. More people have been able to break into the business and join the actor's union SAG-AFTRA (one union made up of Screen Actors Guild and American Federation of Television and Radio Artists) through commercial work than through any other medium in the industry. Roles in commercials are cast for performers of all ages, types, and ethnicities. According to union figures, over a five-year period, union members averaged approximately $600 million per year for commercial work. All over the country, advertising agencies, producers, directors, and casting people view thousands of headshots and résumés daily, searching for new faces to use in the next ad campaign.

Commercials have changed lives. With the earnings from commercial work, actors have financed college educations, purchased homes, underwritten family businesses, and supported themselves while making the transition into film and television.

Commercial work is big business, but it is not easy. Everyone can think about being in a commercial, but not everyone knows how to go about entering the field. Competition is fierce. To make it in this industry, you have to be better prepared than the person sitting next to you at the audition. Talent alone won't do it. It takes a combination of talent, business savvy, training, the ability to audition effectively, and a lot of hard work. To get to the point where you have the competitive edge, you must invest the time and energy necessary to fine-tune your skills to razor-sharp precision.

Our travels around the country and involvement in the educational development of talent have given us firsthand information on the wants, needs, dreams, aspirations, and misconceptions of today's performers. Our combined professional experience of over forty years (Terry as a casting director and Deborah as an industry photographer and writer) gives us an everyday, hands-on perspective on what it takes to make it in the business.

This is the first book of its kind to acknowledge that most actors who make it to the "ivory tower" (major markets) start out in secondary, regional areas. We have interviewed professionals in every state who either represent, cast, or book talent— individuals who enjoy developing actors, care about their talent, and are interested in maintaining a high level of professionalism.

This book will provide clear guidance from a collaboration of professional insights all over the country to those of you who are just breaking into the business, as well as to seasoned professionals. We want you to find the highest degree of professionalism in your own market.

You must be aware that there will be trials and tribulations, frustration, and rejection. And then there are the scams—rip-offs by unsavory individuals or groups who make their living preying on unsuspecting people who desperately want to break into the business. A virtual gauntlet of obstacles and disappointments awaits you if you tread unknowingly into a world where both magical and tragic events can occur. The more you know and understand about the business beforehand, the more likely you are to avoid the pitfalls, *and* the better your chances of launching a successful career.

Your commitment to reading *Breaking Into Commercials* and applying its concepts are major steps toward developing a career in commercials. You'll learn to create a winning promotional package, write a strong résumé and cover letter, set goals, and network effectively. You'll discover how to meet the right people in the industry. You'll develop the competitive edge needed to become the next "new face," and you'll learn how to give a winning audition so that you will be considered for the job regularly.

By collaborating with some of the most respected names in the industry, we have been able to create a complete framework for making a serious move into commercial work. *Breaking Into Commercials* takes you step-by-step through the entire process of becoming a commercial actor. We'll take you into the audition room, teach you how to read a commercial script, and show you what to expect on the set after you book a job. Special summary pages and commercial exercises will help keep you on track and focused on your goals.

By the time you get to the final chapter of *Breaking Into Commercials*, you will have a strong base from which to expand your career. To reinforce some of the most important concepts necessary to create a successful commercial career, we conclude the book with invaluable advice from industry professionals from markets across the country. You'll learn the common misconceptions fledgling actors have about the business, industry "pet peeves," and what it takes to really make it as a performer. You'll close the book feeling prepared, well-informed about the industry and how it works, and confident that you know enough to get out there and go for it.

To get the most from this book, read each chapter thoroughly (and keep the book handy as a quick reference), then act on any exercises or activities suggested. Doing so will help keep you on track and ready for the next step. This book was meant to be an "active" reference. By doing each exercise and reviewing the special summary pages at the end of the chapters, you'll be well on your way to getting your commercial act together.

Our best wishes go with you as you make your way through what we hope will be an exciting, fulfilling, lucrative career.

Terry Berland
& Deborah Ouellette

SECTION 1

PUTTING TOGETHER A WINNING PROMOTIONAL PACKAGE

1.

Getting Headshots

The Makings of a Good Commercial Headshot

In this business, to really go out and sell yourself, you need a calling card, and that calling card is your commercial headshot.

The commercial headshot is your most important marketing tool. Getting the right shot is essential to finding work in the industry and represents an initial opportunity to (a) introduce yourself, (b) show a dimension of your personality, (c) arouse the interest of the viewers, and (d) make them want to meet you. A great headshot can literally make or break your chances of getting called in for work.

It helps to know something about commercial technique *before* having a commercial photo session. Take a workshop from a professional to explore commercial technique and discover who you are. Also, watch commercials on TV. This will begin to give you a point of reference—a point of view as to attitude and an understanding of the energy required for commercial shoots.

You should have a realistic idea of what type you are commercially (age range, physical look, and personality traits). Examples of physical "looks" include:

- *Character:* This is someone with extreme features (large nose, bushy eyebrows, puffy cheeks, heavy, etc.), likeable, or even funny-looking. It could be someone with tattoos, piercings, or extreme hair styles. If you fit into the character category, a chipped tooth or a space between the teeth could add to or be natural for the character.

- *P&G* (Procter & Gamble look): A generic, middle-American look with well-proportioned, middle-of-the-road, attractive features. Extremely beautiful people or character types do not fit this category.

- *Pretty or handsome* (but not a model, not glamorous): This is someone who is natural and approachable.

- *Model type:* Some with above-average looks, beautiful or handsome. Model types generally have high cheekbones, strong jaw line, perfect teeth, and excellent skin, can be exotic-looking, and have a well-proportioned, toned body. Prototype: Charlize Theron.

- *Slightly offbeat/slightly quirky:* Individuals who are specifically different from the average, middle-American look. Prototypes: Ben Stiller, Benedict Cumberbatch, and Jonah Hill.

- *Quirky/good-looking and funny:* Prototypes: Emma Stone, Paul Rudd, Joseph Gordon-Levitt, and Zooey Deschanel.

- *Urban/city type:* Someone with a stylish edge, with an intense, trendy look.

- *Suburban type:* Plainer, casual, relaxed, sporty, rugged, outdoorsy looking.

- *Ethnic/Multicultural* Caucasian, African-American, Asian, Latino/Hispanic, Indian, Native American, Jewish, European, dark hair and olive skin tones, ethnically ambiguous, or a mix.

- *Slacker:* Age about 16–25, lazy, laid-back, unruffled by anything.

- *Scruffy:* Male—unkempt, couple of days' beard growth, ripped jeans.

- *Aspirational:* Good-looking or successful-looking with an intelligent feel.

When viewing commercials, study the actors. Make note of the types of people being featured in various commercials and which products they are used for. What are their energies? What are they wearing? What hairstyles do they have? Which products use humor? Where might you fit in? Could you be the "mom" or "dad"? A seasoned executive? A student? A construction worker? Don't box yourself into one type.

Notice all the opportunities available to you. The more you know about commercials, the more comfortable you will be at your photo shoot.

Commercials are generally energetic and upbeat. People in commercials are friendly and approachable. No one is evil-looking, scary, or really angry. Instead, they are frustrated in a manner that invokes humor and are approachable.

Your commercial headshot should show the depths and layers of your personality. You should have a spark of attitude. Most of the time, it has a degree of playfulness to it. There should be a spark of energy in your eyes. A smile is always good. It allows the viewer to see your clean, white teeth.

A good headshot is generally taken straight on (so the camera can capture all your features and the viewer can look straight into your eyes). If you are the alternative character type, show it. Do not homogenize or neutralize yourself. Anything goes.

Your headshot exists in a casting director's hands or is viewed on a computer screen for about five seconds. You'll either be chosen or not. The eyes have to speak to the casting director, producer, or director. And very important: Your picture needs to look like you. A great headshot is not about perfect makeup or hair; it's about communication and openness that invite the viewer into the photograph.

Differences between a Commercial Headshot, a Theatrical Headshot, and a Commercial Composite

An actor might have three different photographs with three different looks that he or she uses to get work.

Your *commercial headshot* (figs. 1, 3 & 5) is used to get work in commercials. Commercial headshots are always in color. Be aware that even though your photo is in color, depth and layers of your personality must be captured.

Your commercial headshot should be well-illuminated and have an overall bright appearance, showing depth and layers of your personality. Let the happy, upbeat side of your personality shine through. You should look very warm and approachable, "pleased to be here."

Most important is for the casting director, when viewing your photograph, to see the subtle attitudes, and depth, and layers of your personality in your face and eyes.

Headshots should either be head-and-shoulder type (figs. 1, 3, 4 & 8), three-quarter length shots (figs. 5 & 6), or horizontal (fig. 2). Headshots may be printed with borders (figs. 1–5) or borderless (fig. 8). Headshots can be creative as long as the photographer makes sure the focus stays on you and not on his work. Headshots submitted on the Internet on any breakdown service are thumbnail size, horizontal, and will have no borders.

The hard copy finish should be semi-matte, not glossy. There are excellent labs available for making lithographic copies (lithos) as well.

Simple, clean-looking makeup and hairstyling as well as careful attention to wardrobe selection are important for these photos. Open-necked collars and medium tones set the right ambiance for a successful commercial photograph. Clothing and jewelry should not distract the viewer's eyes from moving directly to the face and eyes of the photo.

Theatrical headshots (figs. 2, 4 & 8) are more serious, showing strong eye contact and dramatic attitudes. Hair, makeup, and wardrobe choices may be more dramatic. Deeper-toned backdrops may be used along with subtle-to-rich variations in lighting. Actors use these shots to get parts in theater, television, film, and daytime drama. For work in industrial films or corporate videos, actors may use either their commercial or theatrical headshot.

Commercial composites (fig. 6) are in color and generally consist of three to four photographic images, each of which shows a unique facet of one's personality, a different energy, or a different character type. They are used for commercial print work, which consists of magazine ads, brochures, and catalogs.

How to Get the Best Headshot

FIND A GOOD PHOTOGRAPHER

Locating a good photographer can involve a considerable amount of research, but the results will be well worth the effort. Word of mouth is always the best referral. Talk to agents, casting directors, coaches, and other actors to secure leads.

If you have none of these resources, the next step is to do an online search and check out local and regional trade publications.

In New York and Los Angeles you can refer to *Back Stage* either online or in newsstands. In Chicago, refer to *Performink.com.* Photographers also post ads at local drama clubs and in bookstores. In major markets like New York, Los Angeles, and Chicago, there are plenty of professional resources.

An online search makes it easy to find information (good or bad) on industry photographers. Not only can you view samples of a photographer's work online; some photographers post session fees, wardrobe suggestions, and other helpful information on their websites. Once you have narrowed your choices down a bit, consider meeting each photographer. It is important to find someone who makes you feel comfortable, someone whom you connect with in a way that will result in a good headshot.

QUESTIONS TO ASK

- How far in advance are you booked?
- Is a deposit required to hold the booking?
- What happens if I have to cancel? How much notice is required to cancel? Is there a cancellation fee?
- What is your session fee?
- How many shots do you take during a typical headshot session?
- Is a hair/makeup person available? If so, is there an extra charge for this service?
- How many changes of clothing are allowed?
- How much time should I put aside for the shoot?
- Do you shoot standard head-and-shoulder shots? Three-quarter body shots? Both?
- Do you prefer to shoot in studio? On location? Both?
- How do you present your proofs? Online? Showing images on a monitor as you go (during the shoot)? Shipping proofs on a CD?
- How long between shooting and being able to view proofs?
- Do you help me decide which images to invest in?

- Does the session fee include any enlargements? If not, what do you charge for enlargements? How long does it take to get enlargements made? Do you print yourself or outsource print work?

- Is retouching included in the print fees? If not, how much to have images touched up? Do you do the retouching yourself? Or do you outsource retouching services? How long does it generally take for the retouching part of the job?

- Who owns the digital images? Under what conditions do you release or sell copies of the digital files? How long do you archive client images?

- What happens in the event images are lost or damaged? What types of backup do you have in place to protect against loss/damage of client images?

- Do you recommend printers for mass reproductions of headshots?

- What happens if I am not happy with the results of the session, retouching, or enlargements?

After hearing what each photographer has to say concerning these issues, decide which ones you still want to pursue and view each photographer's work before you make a choice. Most photographers post samples of their work online. If you prefer, set up an appointment to view each photographer's portfolio in person. Look carefully at each professional's portfolio (sample photographs), then ask yourself:

- *Do the headshots all look the same, or can you see each actor's individual personality shining through?* You should not be able to identify the photographer by any one specific image. The photograph needs to be about the subject, not about the photographer.

- *Are the photographs well lit, sharp, and in crisp focus?* The lighting should clearly separate the subject from the background and, if the setting is outside, the background should be out of focus. The colors in the image should complement your eyes, hair color, and complexion. Nothing in the picture should distract from the subject. There should be no obvious, unflattering shadows. Any hard copies (enlargements) should be printed on high-quality, matte-finished photographic paper.

After viewing each photographer's work on line, take time to go over your notes (you should have a lot to work with by now), meet each photographer, decide which photographer you're most comfortable with, and make your appointment for your headshot session.

NOTE: Although it's important to take price into consideration, don't let that be the key factor in selecting a photographer. Your commercial headshot can open (or shut) doors for you, so it pays (literally) to work with the best photographer within your budget.

Prepare for the Shoot

Once you decide on a photographer, it's time to get together everything you will need at the shoot. Most photographers will discuss wardrobe, hair, and makeup dos and don'ts either at the initial consultation or when you call to book your shoot. Clothing should direct all attention to your face. V-necks do that naturally and are great choices for photo shoots. Solid colors work best— avoid busy patterns or polka dots. Textures are wonderful—sweaters and jackets work well. Bring lots of casual stuff. If you have a doubt about it, bring it; the photographer can help you decide which things to wear once she sees it. If you are any character type, as discussed previously, your wardrobe should reflect your character.

Bring in as many changes of clothing as possible. You won't use them all, but it is much better to go through everything with the photographer and decide what would be best to wear.

Bring your favorite clothes. Textures are good; perhaps a sweater with nooks and crannies. Fabrics like wool, cotton, and denim work well. Avoid logos, turtlenecks, and busy patterns. Stick with medium tones, simple styles, and open necklines.

WARDROBE CHECKLIST

- Make sure your clothing is clean, fitted, in good condition, and well-pressed. Choose simple styles with open necklines.

- If you want to wear glasses in the shoot, make sure they have "no glare" lenses or purchase a set of frames in your favorite style without the glass. This will prevent glare from the photographer's lights and reflectors.

- Leave your hats at home. Agents and casting people want to see your hair. If you are bald, they need to see that too.

- Don't wear busy patterns, logos, distracting ruffles, bows, or jewelry. Men, if you wear gold chains and earrings, know it puts you into a definite character category. Don't expect to get a call to audition for the wholesome dad, boyfriend, or guy-next-door based on this particular photo.

- Avoid wearing white. When viewing a photograph, the eye naturally goes to the lightest area of the image first. Your goal is to have the viewer focus immediately on your face and, more specifically, your eyes (some photographers whiten the whites of the subject's eyes a bit to draw the viewer's attention to them). If you wear white, the viewer's eye will go to your clothing first, then travel to the face and eyes.

- Consider wearing medium-toned clothing, which, with a medium-toned background (in studio or on location), will wrap around the subject and draw the viewer's eye to the most important part of the print—you! NOTE: *An exception to the "avoid wearing white" rule would be if you are being photographed wearing white against a high-key (white or very light) background. The photographer you choose needs to know how to use the clothing and background colors properly.*

Your hair should be clean and healthy, in an attractive, contemporary style (no "big" hair). If you can also be extremely trendy, style yourself as such. Don't fight against who you are. If you are edgy, let your clothing and hair reflect that fact. You can have about three looks. If you have too many looks, the wide range can backfire on you. You do not want to portray the feeling that you don't know who you are. You cannot please all of the people all of the time. Make a choice as to how you want to market yourself.

Younger guys should decide on the image they want to market. If you are young and trendy, your photo should reflect that. You might want to come to the shoot with a day or two scruff for some shots. Then shave for a more conservative look. If you think you might be the full-beard type and also the no-beard type, come to the shoot with your beard for some shots and shave during the shoot. Discuss this choice with the photographer before the shoot. But watch the new blades— nicking yourself can create serious complications at the shoot.

NOTE: Commercially, there is usually not enough time between the call and the shoot to grow a beard. Know that the way you present yourself at the audition is how you would be cast.

Females should not look like you are wearing makeup in your commercial headshot. The look for commercials is clean, fresh, and energetic. Women often have a tough time getting a good commercial shot because the photographer (or the women themselves) wants to capture their pretty side instead of bringing out the depths and layers of their personality. Commercial shots are not glamorous. Make sure you end up with a "personality" shot, not a beauty shot, unless you are truly the model type.

Los Angeles makeup artist Karman Kruschke notes, "The stylist's goal is to make people look as they will look when they go into the audition, so I try to get some history on their experience in putting on their own makeup. If someone doesn't wear a lot of makeup, it's important not to put a lot on them—at least, the look is not very made-up. The skin should look nice and smooth. No heavy lip or eyeliner. This is not a fashion shoot. It's not about how beautiful you can be for a day. It's about looking and being who you are."

Some photographers have the make-up artist do some corrective work as needed to minimize heavy circles under the eyes. Others photographers prefer the makeup artist go for a simple, clean look and let the retoucher minimize distractions like under-eye bags/circles, minor stray hairs and blemishes, etc., in postproduction. If minimizing distractions with makeup, there may be a need to highlight or darken specific areas of the face to bring out cheekbones or play down other features. That's why you'll hear, "Oh, God. I would never wear this [makeup] out in public." And you never would—except for a photo shoot.

Men generally require only a bit of powder to tone down overly shiny skin. Most corrective work is done in postproduction. Trust your photographer and the stylist to do whatever is necessary to make you look good in front of the camera. You want to look totally natural.

Aside from the obvious benefits of having a hair/makeup person available at the shoot, having a stylist there also means you don't have to worry about anything (like whether your makeup is shiny or if your hair is out of place, or whether your clothing needs adjusting). This goes for the photographer, too, so both of you are free to do what you do best—you to act and the photographer to take pictures.

Below are a few more suggestions for preparing for your photo shoot:

■ Get a good night's sleep before the shoot. It is important to arrive at the session well-rested, in a positive frame of mind, and ready to give your best.

■ Have everything you need for the shoot laid out the night before to avoid rushing to get it all done the next morning. This will save a *lot* of unnecessary stress.

■ Bring some of your favorite music to the shoot—something lively and upbeat to help set the mood for a pleasant, comfortable session.

■ Do not schedule anything important directly after the shoot. It will be hard to keep your mind on the task at hand if you are thinking about whatever you've scheduled next.

■ If for any reason you feel that you cannot give one hundred percent to the shoot, call and try to reschedule. The camera doesn't lie. If you have a headache or are in a negative mood, you *will* see it in the pictures.

Giving careful consideration to the planning and preparation of your photo session will help guarantee successful results.

What to Expect the Day of the Shoot

Plan to arrive at the photographer's studio approximately fifteen to twenty minutes prior to your scheduled appointment (allow yourself plenty of time to shower and dress). When you arrive you'll be told where to stand (and change) your clothes. The photographer will go through your wardrobe, helping you select the best pieces for the shoot.

At some point during the process, you'll be expected to pay the photographer. You may be asked to sign a release or agreement of some form, outlining the specific conditions of the shoot—price, services rendered, plus any specific considerations.

Be sure you read the document before signing it. Pay special attention to any part of the agreement that deals with the photographer's claims concerning copyright. Some controversy arises here with regard to copyright (who owns control of the images created during your headshot session). It could be argued that when an actor pays the photographer to create a headshot, this becomes "work for hire" giving the talent control over image use. If you sign an agreement giving the photographer total control over use of the pictures, you may find yourself in a pickle when you try to get—for example ~ mass reproductions of your pictures without getting explicit permission from the creator of the images.

When you negotiate your contract, keep in mind that you want to:

■ Deal with the printer of your choice, without going through the photographer.

■ Use your originals for publicity without paying an extra fee to the photographer. Most agreements give the photographer the right to use your likeness in their advertisements and other publicity—you paid for the shoot, it's only fair that you be free to do the same.

Negotiating a fair agreement allows both you and the person who creates your commercial headshot to utilize the results in a manner that enhances both parties' career interests.

After you've paid the photographer and agreed to the terms of the shoot, it's time to let the hair/makeup person (if available) work his magic. Then you'll get into your first outfit and you're ready to shoot.

What happens during the actual shoot is as individual as each photographer's style. Some photographers suggest specific scenarios to help draw out the subject's personality. Others are naturally comedic and charming, using their own personality to entice you to reveal yours. Any successful shoot is a collaborative effort in which photographer and actor work together to create an image that will attract the eye of casting directors.

Selecting the Right Shot

Many photographers are set up to show proofs on a computer monitor—during or immediately after the session. Others prefer to go over the results first, then burn and ship the proofs on CD. Some post proofs online. Others prefer to make an appointment to show proofs later on. Be sure to ask your photographer how (and when) they will present the proofs from your headshot session.

Generally, photographers indicate which images they prefer. Miami headshot photographer Bob Lasky burns a CD containing contact sheets of his favorite images from each session, which, he says, "agents love." It's a good idea to go over the proofs, look them over carefully, and then give yourself a bit of time before making a final selection. Don't ask your best friends or relatives. If you have access to other industry professionals (agents, casting directors, acting coaches, other actors), you may want to ask which ones they think represent you best.

Select a couple of shots that best capture your personality. After choosing the best shots, take a critical look at each image. Check for expressive eyes, and that you look relaxed and are portraying positive body language. Many times, your agent will want to decide which shot they want you to use. After deciding which images to invest in, consider anything you may want retouched. Take one last look to see that all the qualities you want for your final shot (which seemed to be there when you looked at the proofs or contact sheets) are indeed there.

Retouching

Be sure to discuss with your photographer any touch-up work that needs to be done. For example:

■ Are there any temporary blemishes or dark areas under the eyes?

■ Are there any distracting features in the photograph, such as stray hairs or unwanted reflections in the eyes (or glasses)?

■ Would the image be enhanced by lightening the white areas of the eyes?

If the answer to any of these questions is yes, then the photo retouch artist is your next stop before going to the printer (if having paper prints/enlargements made) and/or before submitting your digital headshots to agents and casting directors. With skillful retouching, only the trained eye can tell that the work has been done.

NOTE: Depending on the skill level of the digital retouch artist, almost anything you can imagine (and are willing to pay for) can be done. There is literally no end to what can be done to an image when a gifted digital artist is at the helm. You can swap out body parts, lose weight without dieting (finally!), grow taller, even get a digital nose job.

Steve Guilmette

FIG. 1: Commercial headshot.

Steve Guilmette

FIG. 2: Theatrical headshot.

FIGS. 1 AND 2: Two shots illustrating the difference between commercial and theatrical headshots. PHOTO CREDIT: Michael D'Ambrosia Photography.

FIG. 3: Commercial shot.

PETER TRENCHER

FIG. 4: Theatrical shot.

FIGS. 3 AND 4: Another example illustrating the difference between commercial and theatrical headshots. PHOTO CREDIT: Robert Kazandjian.

PETER TRENCHER

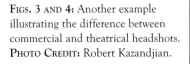

Forbes Riley

FIG. 5: Commercial three-quarter body shot. PHOTO CREDIT: Michael Helms.

FIG. 6: Commercial composite. PHOTO CREDIT: Printed with permission from Lazarus Jackson.

SET YOUR TIVO!!!

for my
Guest Starring Role on

SHE SPIES
"MANHUNT"

Sunday, October 6th,
Midnight on NBC
———★ Check local listings ★———

check out my recent appearance on

MONK
"Mr. Monk Goes to the Theatre"
———★ In Re-runs ★———

Victoria's people are:

AAA - Mark Measures: 310- 859-1417
WMA Animation & Voiceover: 310-859-4085

Victoria Hoffman

FIG. 7: Headshot postcards are an excellent way to keep in touch with people in the industry and to show some individuality and personality. PHOTO CREDIT: Karmen Kruschke.

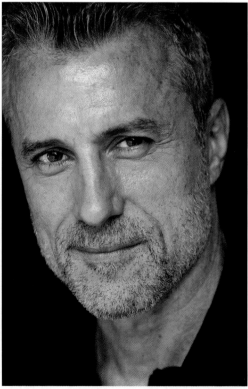

FIG. 8: Borderless commercial or theatrical shot.
PHOTO CREDIT: Ken Dapper Photography.

At the hands of the right artist, reality can be created from scratch or completely altered— the digital darkroom can create sheer magic.

However tempting it may be to go overboard, remember that when you walk into the audition room, you *must* look like your photo. For your commercial headshot, resist any temptation to overwork a print. You don't want to misrepresent yourself. A light touch goes a long way in retouching commercial headshots.

Unless the photographer has indicated otherwise, the cost of retouching is generally not included in the price of the print. Most photographers prefer to maintain control over the work being done to their images, so they will either do the touch-ups themselves or hire the work out.

The cost of retouching varies, depending on the job being done and the caliber of the artist doing the work. Always get a quote before having the work done and be very specific when communicating about what to do and how much is enough. Some retouchers charge by the amount of time it takes to do the job; others have a flat rate based on the type of work being done. Complex retouching jobs cost more than those with simple, basic enhancements. Assuming you have a headshot you're happy with, the extra investment to fine-tune your presentation makes good business sense.

Retouching an image is a one-time investment. As long as nothing happens to the original image—or the version of the original that was retouched—any enhancements should last a lifetime.

One last reminder about retouching: *Don't overdo it!* The purpose of retouching is to enhance the print, not to change the way you look. Remember, when you walk through the door, the casting director expects you to look like your pictures. If, for instance, you have the artist straighten your teeth in the picture, and then come to an audition with crooked teeth, you have misrepresented yourself. You do not look like your picture. What happens if the call is for a toothpaste commercial, which requires you to have perfect teeth? Do you think a casting director would ever call you again after you deliberately misrepresented yourself? Probably not.

Trust your photographer and the retoucher when it comes to deciding whether or not to touch up an image (and how much). Don't try to make everything look perfect. Just have the artist minimize anything that takes away from your personality.

Working with Printers

Many photographers are set up to deliver the entire job from shoot to finished mass reproductions. Others prefer to supply high resolution copies of the final, retouched images for you to take to a printer who specializes in mass-producing photographs for actors.

It pays to shop around. A quick online search provides easy access to a variety of printers who specialize in mass productions of talent headshots. It is not unusual to use a printer from another state. Get referrals from other actors and agents. Do your homework. Printers across the country vary in price and in what you get for the money. (If you're really on top of things, you took care of this while waiting for your images to come back from the retoucher.)

Again, while price is a consideration with most people, make your final decision based on quality of service. If two or more companies produce work of equal quality, but one gives significantly more reproductions for the money, it's easier to narrow your selections.

When placing your order for mass reproductions, be sure to indicate exactly how you want your copies produced. Judging how many to reproduce will depend on the area you live in. In some markets most of your submissions will be online and you will need less hard copies on hand, while other markets may use more hard copies. The preferred format is 8×10 reproductions on matte (non-glossy) double-weight stock. Have your name printed on the front (see sample headshots included in this chapter). Avoid fancy type styles and oversized or undersized letters. Also, expect to pay in full at the time you place your order.

Picture Postcards as a Marketing Tool

Picture postcards (see fig. 7) are a great way to keep in touch with the industry. You can send postcards to announce something you're currently appearing in, just to say hello, or to remind casting directors that you're still out there. Some actors even use them for thank-you notes.

Some people have their postcards printed horizontally, placing two headshots side-by-side, showing two different aspects of their personality. Others take a humorous approach, creating a comedic photograph, appropriately captioned to amuse the recipient.

The same printer who mass-produced your headshots can create a mini version printed vertically on postcard-sized paper with your name on it. Picture postcards are a wonderful, cost-effective tool for marketing yourself as a commercial actor.

How Much Will It Cost and How Long Will It Take?

Photographers: These vary in price depending on what part of the country they work in, their level of experience, and the amount of prestige they have built up in their market. Rates can range from $200 and up in regional areas to $350 and up in larger markets. As with anything else, higher price does not necessarily guarantee higher quality.

Stylists: Expect to spend approximately $125 to $175 for a makeup person/hairstylist. The same person should be able to do both.

Proofing: These costs are generally included in the photographer's shooting fee. Your photographer may show proofs on a monitor during or just after the session. Some photographers burn and ship the proofs on a CD. Some display proofs online.

Enlargements: If not included in the shooting fee, 8×10 enlargements can run on average $25-$35 and up for paper prints; $15 and up for digital enlargements.

Retouching: Some photographers include one or more enlargements—with or without basic retouching—in the session fee. Basic retouching generally includes minimizing or removing minor distractions like stray hairs or laugh lines, teeth whitening, eye sharpening, crow's feet, blemishes, etc. If retouching is billed separately, budget approximately $25 to $35 and up for a basic retouch (more for complex jobs).

Printers: Lithos can run from roughly $65 (and up) for 50 8×10 color copies (printed on one side of the paper) to roughly $100 (and up) for 500 8×10 color copies (one side). Mass-produced photographs run approximately $20-$40 for roughly 10 8×10 color prints (per image) to roughly $135-$160 for 200 8×10 color prints (per image). NOTE: Many labs charge a set up fee of approximately $10-$30 (per image). Picture postcards (4×6s) run approximately $65 for 100 copies. Expect to pay an additional $25–$35 design fee at some printing houses.

All things considered, expect to spend approximately $600 to $1000 by the time you've gotten through the process of shooting, enlarging, retouching, and printing your photos.

TIME FRAME

There are many variables to consider here. The amount of time it takes to get through the process may change due to individual schedules or unforeseen problems (like power outages, damaged or lost image files, etc.). Basically, these are the time frames you may reasonably expect:

- *Researching photographers* (including calls, interviews, portfolio review, and making appointment): Approximate time frame, two to three weeks.

- *Getting proofs back from the shoot*: Approximately two to seven days. Many photographers may have images available to view immediately after capture, at the end of the session, or within a few hours or days (if posting proofs online, for example, or if burning/shipping proofs to a CD).

- *Getting input on proofs, making your selections, and getting order to photographer*: One to two weeks.

- *Getting enlargements (if applicable) back from the photographer*: Approximately two days to one week, depending on if the photographer prints the enlargements herself or is sending the work out to a professional lab. Many photographers simply burn the images to a CD (or emails them to the actor). The actor is then free to choose a lab to make enlargements, to choose a printer for mass reproductions, to email or post images online, etc.

- *Retouching*: If done by the photographer, allow approximately one day to one week. Add a few days to a week or more if using a professional retoucher (turnover times can vary, based on the artist's backlog of work).

- *Getting mass reproductions of your headshots*: Turnover time for ordering large quantities of (lab printed) headshots on photographic paper is roughly two to three business days. If hiring a printer who specializes in producing mass reproductions of talent headshots and/or picture postcards, budget in an average of three to five business days.

Total amount of time to get through the process, from researching photographers to getting mass reproductions: Approximately six to ten weeks. *Ten weeks!* You can see why it is important to get moving right away. Use the tip sheets that follow to help yourself move smoothly through each step as you create the most important part of your marketing package. Your ability to get through the step of getting your pictures done could very well be the first indication of whether you have the fortitude to continue in this business.

CHAPTER SUMMARY

"TO DO" LIST:

- Research photographers
- Call for appointments
- Choose photographer
- Make appointment for photo session
- Prepare for shoot
- Order enlargements (digital and/or paper prints)
- Arrange for retouching (if needed)
- Order mass reproductions from printer

Congratulations! You've just completed one of the most important tasks in compiling your presentation package. You have your commercial headshot. You're ready to move on to the next step.

2.

Résumés and Cover Letters

What Goes on a Résumé and in What Order?

Do include:

- *Your name* (centered at the top of the page).

- *Union affiliation* (if applicable), or note that you are "SAG-AFTRA eligible" if that's the case. If you are Fi-Core (Financial Core), it would be your decision to include that information or not. Fi-Core is a SAG-AFTRA member who has declared this status— making them eligible to work either union or non-union jobs in a union state.

- *Agency representation* (if applicable). In regional areas, your agent generally will provide you with stickers or labels to put on your résumé to show that they represent you.

- *Statistics*. Statistics (stats) include your name, union affiliation and agent (if applicable), height, weight, eye and hair color, and a contact number.[1]

- A *cell phone number* as a contact. If you have an agent, the agent's name and number should appear as the main contact.

- Your website address or any YouTube references.

---

[1] NOTE: If you have an agent, include the agent's contact information. If you have no agent, include a cell phone number where you can be reached. Do not list personal contact information, such as home phone or address.

- *Experience* (credits in theater, film/TV, commercials, etc.).
- *Training* (classes, workshops, college degrees, etc.).
- *Special skills* (dialects, American Sign Language, skydiving, horse-back riding—anything you do *well*). These can be arranged in alphabetical order.

  Don't include:

- *Your social security number, your address, or your personal phone number* (for security reasons).
- *Your age or an "age range."* Let casting directors look at your photo and decide for themselves if you are what they are looking for. If you are under 18 years old, you should include your date of birth.

Presenting the Information on Your Résumé

How you list industry-related experience on your résumé depends on which market you will be working in. In Los Angeles, film and television credits are usually listed first (fig. 9). In New York, theater credits are mentioned first. If you live in smaller, regional areas, start with your strongest credits. When in doubt, list theater credits first. Theater provides a strong foundation for actors and is the purest form of acting experience.

If you're just starting out, you'll probably be relying primarily on your look, training credits, and special skills to open doors for you. After you have a well-developed résumé, your experience (credits) will be your best PR tool. Don't worry if, at first, you don't seem to have much to put on your résumé; there are ways to present your humble beginnings (without lying) that will give your presentation a professional appearance while you are building your credits.

In a beginner's résumé, for instance, present community theater experience. Mention the name of the production, the role you played, and the theater or theater group. Figs. 10 and 11 demonstrate how a regional beginner's résumé can be cleaned up to look more professional without exaggerating or fabricating credits.

When listing *commercial* experience on a résumé geared toward the Los Angeles, New York, or Chicago market, it's best to simply put "List Upon Request" next to that category. Listing a commercial could imply

Wylie Small

SAG/AFTRA/EQUITY
www.WylieSmall.com

The
Culbertson
Group   323.650.9454

FILM

Gerald	Lead	Dir. Marc Clebanoff, Odyssey Motion Pictures
The L.A. Riot Spectacular	Supporting	Dir. Marc Klasfeld, Visionbox Pictures
Only Hope	Lead	Dir. Joseph Francis, Prometheus Pic.
Movin' To Montana	Lead	Dir. Rodolfo Riva Palacio, Independent
Deep End of the Ocean	Supporting	Dir. Ulu Grosbard, Mandalay/Universal
Naked Gun 33 1/3	Supporting	Dir. Peter Segal, Paramount
Nobody's Fool	Supporting	Dir. Evelyn Purcell, Island Pic.

TELEVISION

Harry's Law	Co-Star	Dir. Mike Listo, NBC
The Event	Co-Star	Dir. Michael Watkins, NBC
The Darkness Descending	Series Regular	Dir. Marc Clebanoff, KoldCast.TV
Cold Case	Co-Star	Dir. Gwyneth Horder-Payton, CBS
Brothers & Sisters	Co-Star	Dir. Gloria Muzio, ABC
According To Jim	Co-Star	Dir. Steve Zuckerman, ABC
Night Stalker	Co-Star	Dir. Rob Bowman, ABC
24	Co-Star	Dir. Kevin Hooks, 20th Century Fox
Gilmore Girls	Guest Star	Dir. Lee Shallat Chemel, Warner Bros.
Nip/Tuck	Guest Star	Dir. Elodie Keene, Warner Bros.
The Drew Carey Show	Co- Star	Dir. Gerry Cohen, Warner Bros.
Ally McBeal	Co-Star	Dir. Peter MacNicol, 20th Century Fox
The Practice	Guest Star	Dir. Alex Graves, 20th Century Fox
7th Heaven	Guest Star	Dir. Les Sheldon, Warner Bros.
The Bold and The Beautiful	Recurring	Dir. Bradley Bell, CBS
Beyond Belief	Guest Star	Dir. Jack Angelo, Fox Network
Babylon 5	Guest Star	Dir. Kevin Cremin, TNT
Total Security	Guest Star	Dir. Mike Fresco, ABC

THEATRE (Selected Credits only, comprehensive list upon request)

RAP*	Lead	Dir. Rodney Nugent, Zephyr Theater
Openings	Lead	Dir. Jolene Adams, Actor's Art Theatre
Welcome to Andromeda	Lead	Dir. Jolene Adams, Actor's Art Theatre
Two Rooms	Lead	Dir. Sarah Knight, The Actors Lab
In Search of Lost Wings	Lead	Dir. Patrick Kerr, Meisner Center
The Walking Wounded*	Lead	Dir. & Writer Lynn Mamet, Meisner Center
Dark Of The Woods*	Lead	Dir. Alan Vint, Meisner Center
The Beard	Lead	Group Repertory Theater
The Job	Lead	Dir.& Writer Lynn Mamet, Meisner Center
The Great Nebula In Orion	Lead	Dir. Marc Durso, Meisner Center

COMMERCIALS (List upon request)

TRAINING
Actor's Studio, American Academy of Dramatic Arts (Graduate), Meisner-Teacher: Martin Barter (Graduate, 2yr. Intensive Program), John Ruskin's Master Class – **Guest teacher: Anthony Hopkins,** Margie Haber – Advanced Intensive, Cold Reading- Brian Reise, Improv – Second City and Harvey Lembeck's Comedy Improv

SPECIAL SKILLS
Precision driving experience, former registered lifeguard, skiing (down hill and cross country), general contracting experience, Blue screen experience, Dancing (Ballroom, Tango, Swing, Disco) and Dialects (Cockney, British, Southern, Irish)

THEATRE AFFILIATIONS
Founding Member of the Sanford Meisner Center and a Lifetime Member of The Actor's Studio
(* Drama-Logue Award, LA Weekly Pick, LA Weekly Recommended)

FIG. 9: Professional résumé (Wylie Small).

John Jennens
419-535-7722

Height: 6'2"   Weight: 190 lbs.
Eyes: Brown   Hair: Brown
Suit: 44L   Shirt: 16 ½ / 34-35
Pants: 34/36   Shoe: 10 ½

TV COMMERCIALS/INDUSTRIAL FILMS
List available upon request

TRAINING
Acting: Manchester College, North Manchester, Indiana

Commercial: Bowling Green State University, TV Commercial course
          - Terry Berland – TV Commercial Workshop

EDUCATION
Bachelor of Arts, Communication-Radio/TV/Film
Bowling Green State University, Bowling Green, Ohio

THEATER
High School and College

SPECIAL SKILLS & INTERESTS
Motorcycling, Automobile (standard and automatic), Truck Driver, Auto
Restoration, Bicycling, Carpentry, Construction, Piano, Harpsichord, Trombone,
Voice, Volleyball, Basketball, Hockey, Ice Skating, Tennis, Swimming, Radio &
TV Announcing, Voice Overs.

CURRENT OCCUPATION
Video Production

PREVIOUS EMPLOYMENT
WKBN TV (CBS), Youngstown, Ohio – Sports reporter and Anchor
WVBKC AM, Chardon, Ohio – News reporter and News Director

Fig. 10: Undeveloped résumé
(John Jennens).

JOHN JENNENS
(419) 535-9722

Height: 6'2"   Weight: 190lbs.
Eyes: Brown   Hair: Brown
Suit: 44L   Shirt: 16 ½ / 34-35
Pants: 34/36   Shoe: 10 ½

THEATER
"The Thirteen Clocks"   The Prince
"The Imaginary Invalid"   Father
"Night of January 16th"   Defense Attorney Stevens
"Cheaper By The Dozen"   Frank
"The Valiant"   James Dyke

TELEVISION-RADIO
WKBN – TV (CBS), Youngstown, Ohio – Sports reporter and Anchor
WBKC – AM, Chardon, Ohio – News reporter and News anchor

TV COMMERCIALS/INDUSTRIAL FILMS
List available upon request

TRAINING
Acting: Manchester College, North University, TV Commercial course
Commercial: Bowling Green State University, TV Commercial course
            Terry Berland, Los Angeles – TV Commercial workshop

EDUCATION
Bachelor of Arts, Communication – Radio/TV/Film
Bowling Green State University, Bowling Green, Ohio

SPECIAL SKILLS
Video Production (Videography, Editing), Voice Overs, Motorcycling,
Automobile (standard and automatic), Truck Driver, Auto Restoration, Bicycling,
Carpentry, Construction, Piano, Harpsichord, Trombone, Voice, Volleyball,
Bowling, Baseball, Basketball, Hockey, Ice Skating, Tennis, Swimming.

Fig. 11: John Jennens' developed fledgling résumé.

that you have a conflict, which would eliminate you from any related casting opportunities. If you are pursuing work in a region where there are non-union commercial opportunities (or if you don't plan to pursue these opportunities), it is the trend to list commercials you have already done to show that you have experience, or to list ad agencies and production companies you have worked with.

Be sure to include TV credits, including:

- *Series Regular:* A series regular is one of the main characters that the series revolves around.

- *Guest-Star or Co-Star:* Co-Star is a small part that is more than five lines. Usually a one-scene Guest-Star is a large part with a lot of dialogue. It is the billing right under the Series Regular. The billing of Co-Star or Guest-Star is determined by the show itself.

- *Recurring Role:* Can be used in any category where you are reappearing on the show.

- *Under Five:* A part where you are speaking under five lines.

After you've outlined your experience in the industry, it's time to list any industry-related *training* you've had. Begin with classes you've taken—scene study, improvisation, or cold-reading, for instance—and workshops. Specifically list the training and the name of the person you trained with. If you are working in a small regional area and the person you trained with is a well-known coach from a large market, include the market the coach comes from. If you have a degree in theater arts, put it in your résumé (M.F.A. in Acting, Yale School of Drama, for example). Certainly include any voice and dance training.

In the beginning of your career, casting directors will be considering the extent and focus of your training as well as where and with whom you trained. Especially at the early stages of your career, it's important to demonstrate your devotion to the craft by developing the training portion of your résumé. Take ongoing classes, take part in community theater, and take every opportunity to audition (there's no better experience than on-the-job training). Before you know it, your fledgling résumé will become a focused, professional promotional tool.

Last on your résumé is a section listing *special skills*. Any special talents you have that might be useful in the business would be listed here. Start with your strongest special skill first. List special skills like mime, dialects, or musical instruments you play well. Athletic abilities are extremely important, such as skydiving, horseback riding, tennis, volleyball, and skiing. Be specific when mentioning special skills. For example, don't list vague categories such as "martial arts." Instead, specify "Karate (black belt)."

If you drive a car (automatic and/or stick-shift), motorcycle, and/or truck (pickup to eighteen-wheeler), mention it. Almost anything else you do well—like electronics, photography, American Sign Language, foreign languages, and CPR, for example—can be noted in the special skills section of your résumé. If you enjoy working with animals and/or children and babies, this is a great place to mention it.

List your special skills alphabetically. When a casting director is looking for a special skill it's much quicker for them to identify the skill, rather than muddle through a list.

NOTE: If you say you can do something on your résumé, you had better be able to do it—and do it *well*. Limit the list to activities you can perform at an advanced or professional level.

Printing Your Résumé

In a large market such as LA, agents look through hundreds of head-shots and casting directors look at literally thousands of headshots and résumés weekly. The last thing they want to do is spend a lot of time looking through a poorly organized list of credentials. It is in your best interest to see to it that your résumé is attractively laid out, is easy to read, and draws immediate attention to your strengths as a talent.

Use the sample résumés in this chapter to help you lay out your own material. You can use your home computer or have your résumés professionally typeset. Keep in mind the following dos and don'ts when setting up your résumé:

Take care to line everything up neatly on the page.

Try using all caps to help distinguish headings from the rest of the material. Use bold typeface for headings. It is easy to read 12-point type. Try a slightly larger type for headings (14-16-point), with 24-point type for your name. Experiment a bit before committing to print.

Attach your résumés to your headshots in all four corners with a stapler (or an adhesive that won't damage or show through on the picture or the résumé). Make sure the paper is trimmed to the exact size of your 8×10 headshots. Attach your résumés to your headshots as you need them (a small quantity at a time). *Never* give an agent or casting director a headshot and résumé unattached. Doing so looks lazy and unorganized. The résumé can easily get separated from the photograph, in which case you are left with no way to be identified or contacted.

You may use your home computer to print your résumé on the back of your headshots, but don't print up too many at once. You will be updating your résumé constantly. And you will want to hand in the most current version of your résumé every time you audition.

Don't clutter your résumé with full sentences and non-industry information. Think in terms of an outline of your experiences and abilities.

Use a letter-quality or laser printer to make copies of your résumé as you need them. If you make Xerox copies of your résumé, make sure the machine delivers good, clean copies (no streaks or spots, please). Clean the glass before each use and take care to line up the paper in the machine properly.

If you have your résumés professionally typeset, the printer will give you a range of prices based on the number of copies you order. When ordering, keep in mind that you will be updating your résumé often. Try to negotiate a quantity that includes occasional updates as needed. Don't forget to ask the printer to print your résumés on 8×10 (not 8½×11) paper. When using a computer, you will have to trim the résumés to fit your headshots yourself, using a paper cutter—not scissors—for a clean, professional look.

Updating Résumés

Your résumé should be updated regularly to include new credits, training, and special skills. Using your home computer, simply insert the new information and delete less-impressive credits, reformatting as necessary. If your résumé was professionally typeset, your printer will help you reformat your material.

Consider leaving a bit of white space (unused area) on your résumé in each category. That way, you could easily insert new information by neatly hand-printing a line or two until you create a new document. Be sure to use a black pen to match the type.

NOTE: When creating their original résumés, some actors leave a section at the bottom of the page to add updates. This allows them to continue (temporarily) using the résumés they have on hand.

What Is a Cover Letter and What Is Its Purpose?

A cover letter is a letter of introduction (fig. 12). Sent along with a headshot and résumé, a cover letter is a polite way to introduce yourself and to ask for what you want. If, for instance, you are looking for representation, you would send your headshot out to agents, requesting an appointment. Keep your cover letter brief and to the point. Using a contact name as a referral (mentioning the name of a colleague or mutual acquaintance) can be helpful in catching the attention of agents and casting persons. They will naturally gravitate toward someone who has been referred by a person they are familiar with and trust.

Some sample statements you might make in your cover letter include:

- I've just graduated from . . .
- I've taken a commercial workshop from . . .
- I'm ready for work.
- I'm in such-and-such play.
- I'm looking forward to meeting you.
- I'd like an appointment.

Once you have created a good cover letter, you're ready to start sending out your headshots and résumés.

Targeting Your Headshot/Résumé Mailings to the Right People

The first group of people you'll want to target your mailings to is agents and/or managers.

Look on the SAG-AFTRA website (http://www.sagaftra.org) for franchised agents. Also utilize the Association of Talent Agents (http://

(date)

Alisa Harris
324 East Beaumont
New York, NY 10036
(212) 555-1234

Betsy Berg
Betsy Berg Talent Agency
5 East 60th Street
New York, NY 10036

Dear Betsy,

I recently graduated from Yale School of Drama. Comedy is my strong point. I am a member of Gotham Improv Theater Group. Terry Berland saw me perform in a recent showcase and suggested I get in touch with you.

I am looking for representation and would love to make an appointment to meet you. Thank-you for your time and consideration.

Looking forward to hearing back from you.

Alisa Harris

Alisa Harris

FIG. 12: Sample cover letter.

www.agentassociation.com) website, which lists reputable agents around the country.

Be aware that in small regional areas that are "right-to-work"[2] states, most—if not all—agencies will not be SAG-AFTRA franchised. Be sure to do some research to make sure they are legitimate businesses (see Chapter 8, What You Need to Know about Agents, Managers, and Unions).

Casting directors can be found online and in directories for both major and secondary markets.[3] For example, the *Ross Reports* in New York and Los Angeles lists casting directors. Other resources are the *Biz Directory* in the Dallas/Austin area and *Performink* in Chicago.

There are Internet sites in every part of the country where actors can resource information. Be wary of sites that are based on gossip. The way to find out about legitimate-information sites is to connect with actors in your area. Participate in community theater, contact local agencies, and check out the drama section of your neighborhood bookstore. Consider attending talent seminars, workshops, and/or conventions in your area. Be sure to check out the credentials of the casting directors or agents advertised as attending the event. All casting directors can be found on the Internet.

Once you have prepared your promotional tools, compile a list of the people you want to direct your mailings to. First, check their website to see if they mention how they prefer to receive submissions. Call the agent or casting director offices and ask if they would rather receive submissions via email or snail mail. Send a single headshot, résumé, and cover letter in an 8½×11 envelope to each person on your list. Keep track of whom you send mailings to, when you sent them, and any responses you get.

Follow Up on Your Mailings

Usually, agents will call you if they are interested in meeting you. If you have not heard anything approximately two weeks after you do a

---

[2] In a right-to-work state, companies cannot refuse to hire someone because he does not belong to the union or does not want to join the union.

[3] For more on secondary markets, refer to Chapter 14, Working in Regional Markets.

mailing, follow up with a phone call to make sure the person received your package.

Most likely, you will be talking to an assistant. Ask for an appointment. If the answer is no, thank them for their time, hang up, and make the next call. If the answer is that the agent is too busy to give appointments at this time, the best way to follow up is by sending your picture postcard mentioning any updates regarding your acting career. If the answer is yes, thank the assistant or agent for her time, get your appointment time and date, tell them you are looking forward to meeting them, hang up, and make your next call to try to secure another appointment with another agent. Usually your appointment time will be a week or two away. Just because you get an appointment for a meeting does not mean the agency will necessarily represent you. Setting up several appointments could shorten the process of finding representation.

In larger union markets, if you are non-union, find out which agencies have non-union departments and target those agencies. It could take several months for an agent who is interested in you to call you in for an interview. You'll be making a lot of calls and sending a lot of emails for appointments in this industry, so it's important to have on hand the proper tools to (a) keep in touch with the industry, and (b) keep track of your activities, appointments, earnings, and expenses.

The next chapter will help you get yourself organized, motivated, and focused.

CHAPTER SUMMARY

Prepare an attractive, easy-to-read, one-page résumé of personal/ professional information, including:

- *Name*
- *Union affiliation* (if applicable)
- *Agency representation* (if applicable)
- *Phone number where you can be reached* (cell phone or agent)
- *Statistics* (height, weight, hair and eye coloring)
- *Any videos of yourself*, including those posted on websites and YouTube

- *Experience* (credits in theater, film/TV, commercials, etc.)
- *Training* (classes, workshops, college degrees, etc.)
- *Special skills* (dialects, sign language, skydiving, etc.)
- Get your résumé printed. Remember to print small quantities at a time, upgrading information as needed. Have your résumé printed on paper the exact size of your professional headshot, or trim it.
- Attach your résumés to your headshots in all four corners (using staples or glue).
- Create a cover letter to accompany your headshot/résumé submissions. Try to include the following:
  - *The name of a colleague or mutual acquaintance* (if possible)
  - *A class or workshop you've taken* (or degree recently earned)
  - *A production you're currently in* (or have recently completed)
- Compile a list of people (agents, managers, casting people, etc.) you want to target your headshot/résumé mailings at. Keep records of whom you mailed to, the date of each submission, and any follow-up notes. Have your photos, résumé, demo reels, and follow-up materials online to send out swiftly, as needed.

Follow up on each submission (to make sure your headshot arrived and to request an appointment).

Have picture postcards on hand for any kind of follow-up communication to agents, managers, casting people, or producers.

3.

Other Tools You'll Want to Consider

Now it's time to consider a variety of tools that actors use to stay on top of opportunities in the industry. Agents and casting directors are not willing to chase you down to give you a job. It is your responsibility to make yourself accessible to them at all times, or they will simply contact someone else. Being unavailable to receive calls, texts, and messages can result in lost wages, lost contracts, and lost opportunities.

Equipment for Keeping in Touch

SMARTPHONES

A (smart) phone is your number one tool. You want to be able to be reached immediately by phone, text, or email. Your agent may be contacting you regarding an audition taking place within the hour, a booking, or a change in appointment time. How long do you think an agent will wait before deciding it's easier to simply get in touch with someone else? Whenever possible, make a point of being available to respond to important information.

A smartphone enables you to quickly video yourself if needed, send voice-over auditions, receive breakdowns, and download any scripts or videos attached. The sooner you can view incoming messages—and ask any questions you may have—the better.

or your phone is (and should be) turned off when auditioning. Get in the habit of turning it back on when you leave the audition. You want to be available if that casting director is calling you for more info, or wants you to come back for whatever reason.

Other Tools You'll Want to Consider

RECORD-KEEPING SUPPLIES

Since making commercials is a business, it is important to keep accurate records. Keeping track of expenses, income, appointments, and audition information is crucial to your success as an actor. You'll also need to write thank-you notes and keep a journal of your goals and networking efforts (see Chapter 6, Networking, Marketing, and Goal-Setting). The minimum requirements for keeping track of all of these things include:

- *Daily planner/appointment book or digital device* that allows you to keep track of auditions, callbacks, jobs, and other appointments. A section for notes, important calls, and new contacts is helpful.

- *Record-keeping materials*—including a journal for keeping track of income and business expenses for tax purposes and a travel log to record mileage and other travel-related expenses.

- *Networking/goal-setting journal*. Whether you prefer to write in a notebook, use a computer word-processing program, or journal via a personal or professional blog, it is important to outline, then flesh out, your daily, weekly, monthly, yearly, and long-term (five to ten years or more) goals, as well as whom you need to network with in order to accomplish them.

- *Thank-you notes*. Ready-to-go note cards can be found online as well as at most office-supply, department, and drug stores. Custom note cards can be ordered online and off. A quick Internet search for note card printers should provide you with a variety of printing houses who would welcome your business. You can also use your picture postcards as thank-you notes. This can be another way to keep your face in front of people in the business while expressing appreciation for industry-related opportunities and kindnesses.

4.

Training

How Classes in Commercial Technique, Improvisation, Scene Study, and Cold Reading Prepare You to Do Commercials

Commercials have one thing in common with all other acting media: you (the performer) have to come off as real, authentic, and connected. The only difference in commercials is that the work is done in a shorter time and in a smaller space. Many of the elements are similar to a short acting scene. That is, with very few words you have to be very specific. Studying improvisation, cold-reading, and scenes and monologues provide a solid foundation for—and add ease and excellence to—acting in commercials.

Classes in *commercial technique* teach you how to act out a situation in a fifteen-, thirty-, or sixty-second format. They should do the following:

- Teach you how to analyze a script.
- Teach you to make the most of the physical space you're given to work with.
- Show you how to reveal your personality.
- Eliminate self-consciousness in front of the camera.

The result of your commercial training should enable you to step up on the mark that you are given to work on, and in that small amount of space, immediately give dimension to your performance and the space.

In *improvisation classes*, you are given the framework of a scene, scenario, or sketch—the gist of an idea. You make up your own lines, create your own relationships, and bring out your own personality. Improv classes help you:

- Learn to loosen up, become less inhibited.
- Learn to think fast (and in this business, this is a definite plus).
- Exercise the creative muscles in your brain. Improv training will help you learn to take direction and make decisions quickly and seamlessly.

In *scene/monologue study*, you spend weeks or months working on the same material. Each time you approach it, you bring new levels to your performance. You learn to do in-depth research, script analysis, and background and relationship histories, which are really the core of an actor's work—creating "real" relationships.

An actor can be brilliant in an acting class yet not be able to audition well at all. The greater your knowledge of acting, the easier it is to do television commercials, because a TV commercial is actually a mini short-scene.

Cold-reading classes teach you how to audition with little or no preparation. Cold reading teaches actors to assess the material quickly, pick out the clues given in the text, and then let their individual personalities come through in a committed manner. Every commercial audition is essentially a cold reading. Most of the time you do not receive any material (script) ahead of time. You arrive at your audition, pick up the script, and prepare right then and there.

Finding a Good Coach

In larger markets like Los Angeles, New York, and Chicago, it is fairly easy to find a good coach. In smaller, regional areas, it can be tough. Word of mouth is always a great way to find out whom the better actors are training with. Ask for referrals from local agents, managers, casting people, and other actors. Armed with a list of referrals, an online search should yield a wealth of information about each coach.

If possible, audit the classes you're considering to see if you like the way the coach relates to the class and if you would fit in. Do not be surprised if many coaches feel that auditors are a disturbance. Especially in the more dramatic scene-study classes, where the work is deep and layered, auditing may be considered a breach of privacy. In larger markets, where the names and reputations of prominent coaches are well known, it is easy to check the credibility of any coach or class. And you should do so.

Try to train with the best coaches you can afford, and know that if you come from a smaller market, you may need to go to a larger market periodically to get professional training.

Good actors never stop training. Expect to invest a considerable amount of time and money in ongoing classes and workshops. You must also be willing to honestly assess your strengths and weaknesses as an actor if you are to succeed in your career.

It is important to find coaches you really "click" with. Each coach has her own teaching and communication style. Sometimes you may have to try two or three (or more) coaches before you find one who teaches in a manner that facilitates the way you process and apply the information being offered. It doesn't mean that any of the others were bad coaches. Success in classes and workshops has a lot to do with how you process and utilize information—and how willing you are to do so. When you are ready to receive the information and find a coach you can really relate to, you'll get much more from your classes.

Cost of Training

How much should you expect to pay for classes? This varies, depending on the location and size of the class and the credentials of the teacher. In major markets for an ongoing theatrical class with a top-notch, well-known coach, expect to pay approximately $300 for a five-hour class once a week for four consecutive weeks. These programs vary from four to twelve weekly classes to a two-year program. Private coaching can run you anywhere from $75 to $300 per hour.

A commercial class, once a week for six weeks, for three hours each week, can run you $350–$400. A two-to-three-day on-camera work-shop with a well-known teacher may run $200–$475. If you are in a regional area, well-known coaches may be willing to come to your area to give a workshop. Keep an eye out for opportunities to train with these coaches. A few well-directed calls to several schools and coaches should give you a nice range to consider. Again, study with the best coaches you can afford.

FINAL NOTE: Be wary of schools that want to sell you a package where photographers are included. You should make your own decision as to which photographer you want to use (see Chapter 1 on photographers and Chapter 5 on scams).

How Often You Should Train

In this industry, training is a way of life. Any time they're not actually working, successful actors are working out in class. To do well in any career, you must take the relevant courses and then take refresher courses to stay current and to fine-tune your professional skills.

Newcomers to the business will spend the bulk of their time in class. You can expect to spend several years developing basic auditioning and performing techniques until you are consistently able to book work in the industry.

At some point, bookings will begin to take priority, with study taking place in between jobs. Just know that in some form or another, be it on-the-job training or formal classes, sharpening your skills must become a way of life if you are to become successful and stay on top in this business.

Creativity is an ongoing process. The university level is just a taste of what performing is about. After that, if you have decided you want a career in acting, you will want to go to a market like Chicago, Los Angeles, or New York and get into a school where you can really develop. Class is the place where one gets nourished and grounded— the place where creativity soars.

Joseph Pearlman, one of Hollywood's top acting teachers and private coach to celebrities like Zooey Deschanel, guides us through some styles of training:

> Your college or conservatory acting classes can give you a well-rounded acting foundation balanced with voice and speech training, movement classes, theater history, and theater technique. But when you get out in the real world of auditioning and working on the set, other venues or styles of acting have to be considered.

Since acting is a perishable skill, it's vital for the actor to always hone their craft. There's often a considerable gap between skills developed in a conservatory program and the real world demands of an industry that is ever changing. The goal of any worthwhile training is to give the actor tools to enter every scene emotionally full. While conservatory training offers a variety of techniques and methods to reach that fullness, it doesn't prepare the actor to create a winning and memorable audition when you have seconds to arrive at a full emotional preparation after slating for the camera.

Additionally, the experience of walking into a major film or TV audition can be quite intense. Similar skills are required when walking on set. There's literally no time for "acting technique" when you have seconds to prepare. As a private coach, I help actors activate that emotion in a flash—as if on the tips of their fingers—ready to go seconds after their slate or call of "Action" on the set. A top-tier private acting coach and acting class should address all of the following:

Audition Preparation and Technique: To prepare an actor/actress to make strong and specific choices for a winning and memorable audition.

Cold-Reading Technique: How to make all necessary choices when a casting director has given you new sides to prepare in a short period of time—typically 10-20 minutes.

Improvisation and Sketch Comedy Training: Studying improvisation is essential to a well-rounded actor's instrument. It trains the actor to put the text into their own words; this develops a stronger physical and emotional connection to the material. Improvisation is a tool that should be utilized across all styles of acting training. There are a variety of great sketch comedy training schools around the country.

Scene Study: A top-notch scene study class should teach the actor/actress practicable skills to clearly and specifically analyze a scene from the moment you receive the text to the performance. Specific and fun choices must be made. In a proper scene study class, the actor must choose, at the onset, what style of scene he or she is working on—a scene for film, TV, theater, audition, cold-read, etc. Most scene-study classes around town offer the opportunity to work on a scene within the safe bubble of a classroom, for the purpose of pleasing the teacher. Avoid those types of classes.

Some Thoughts on Responsible Training: Acting training is similar to the training an elite Olympic athlete must endure prior to competing in the actual game-day event. When a scene is properly analyzed and specific choices have been made, the actor must then let go of the technique and training; they must learn to actually throw it away. It's like a flutist who no longer thinks about where she places her fingers on the holes of her instrument. She becomes one with the piece. Likewise, the training is absorbed into the actor's muscle-memory.

The difference between "good" and "great" is the actor's ability to bring his/her unique personality to the piece. If the preparation was specific enough, the scene will unfold beautifully, moment-by-moment, until the last syllable. You can never act your technique. It only serves to strengthen and elevate the performance.

Finding a good acting coach involves looking for someone who is current—someone who does not try to make actors into something they are not. The coach should use each person's uniqueness and raw ability to help develop them into a marketable commodity.

Sharon Chatten, acting teacher and private coach to many celebrities, reflects on authenticity:

> Most beginning actors think if they learn how to "say the words right," they will get acting work. It is not about "inflection," it is about living the part. An actor, for many roles (barring character work), must know how to bring their unique self to the text. The actor must first learn to bring his/her authenticity to the script, allowing himself to be in the moment, and to involve himself truthfully within the given scenario. It is important for an actor to be able to live in their own skin; accessing their own way of speaking, physical expression (without extraneous tension), personality, intelligence, sense of humor, and emotional response to the given dialogue.
>
> Very often, I hear directors complain that a particular actor "sounds like an actor," and not a real person. Often these actors have to be told from the director to "Stop acting. Just talk to me." To be truthful as an actor, you need to be able to live the role and the experiences given in the text. This requires technique and study, and the willingness to get to your own truths as a person. Relaxation and privacy are key, and a good class will provide an arena for these things. Privacy is creating the "fourth wall," where you truly feel there

is no audience, camera, or director there at all; that you are living the situation with the other character or characters in the story and you are not "performing" for anyone.

As an actor continues to study and grow, he can then of course approach the roles that are different from himself. But this character work must be carefully crafted to be done well. Most casting directors for film and television bring in actors who seem very close to the type of role they are trying out for. But there are exceptions to this, and a great actor can be called in for a role that is NOT their type and craft it brilliantly!

When you first come to a larger market (no matter how much work you were doing in your smaller, regional area), know that you are coming in at square one. You will have to swallow your ego and be willing to learn how things are done in the larger market. Your goal at first is simply to learn what it takes to do well in the new market.

Know that you may have to get new headshots and/or rework your résumé. You may have to fine-tune your cover-letter writing skills. It may take a while to acclimate. Use that time in class, learning and/or fine-tuning your craft with the best coaches you can afford. Concentrate on learning to audition effectively—and to create and/or take advantage of opportunities to perform.

It's important to start networking and taking advantage of the vast opportunities that come with being in a major city. Go to union functions, attend readings and lectures, and don't be afraid to ask questions. Find out who the agents, casting directors, and directors are.

A *caveat*: Exercise caution when meeting people. Make sure they are who they say they are. A quick Internet search will answer your questions (see Chapter 5 for more information about identifying and reporting scams).

People who take their careers seriously work continuously to fine-tune their skills, whether they are doctors, lawyers, teachers, or performers. Those in the top of their fields engage in ongoing study and take courses. It's a way of life. Top athletes spend countless hours in the gym, working out regularly so that they maintain a high level of fitness and performance. Likewise, actors must flex their creative muscles regularly to stay on top of their game. And the place actors go to work out is in class.

Each acting venue—commercial, comedy, improve, voice-over, and dramatic acting—all have a different acting technique. In your dramatic acting classes, you will learn the strong basic foundation with consistent working-out for more depth. Then there are choices of variations to be on top of your game.

5.

Scams

Unfortunately, there is a rather unsavory element invading the industry—one that feeds on the hopes and dreams of unsuspecting thespians—promising fame and fortune, separating you from your money, and then delivering little or nothing. These charlatans of show business are called scam artists. They're slick. They're smooth. And they're ruthless in the pursuit of a quick buck.

Why Scam Artists Are So Successful

Frankly, scam artists are very good at what they do. They often make an impressive presentation, citing the names of well-known agents, managers, production companies, and stars, all of whom they claim are their close industry contacts. Scam artists prey primarily on young aspiring actors and parents who, in their excitement and enthusiasm at the prospect of getting involved in the business, forget to take the necessary steps to ensure that the people they are dealing with are who they *say* they are and can do what they say they can do.

People who normally exhibit amazing common sense have been known to throw caution to the winds when it comes to making decisions concerning their (or their child's) potential career in show business. As scam artists become more creative and elusive, aspiring talent and their parents must become more scrupulous in discovering which industry-related activities are legitimate and which are not.

How to See a Scam Coming a Mile Away

By applying some common-sense rules, you should be able to avoid being taken by a scam artist. Before getting involved with anyone who claims to be able to help you build your career, consider the following:

■ You should never have to pay someone up front to get work in the industry. Think about it: If you were going to get a job at Burger King, you would never consider paying them for the privilege of working for them. You would never consider paying up front for an employment agency to get work for you. They would get a commission or fee *after* getting you a job. It's the same with agents and managers in the business. They make money when *you* make money, by taking a percentage of your income. Agents that are members of the ATA (Association of Talent Agents) take 10 percent as commission for getting you the job.

Do some research. Is the agency *really* obtaining work for its talent? Or is it a front for the website or book its owners are publishing? Look online. Check the Better Business Bureau, local production companies, or other actors in your region to see if the agency is legitimate.

■ If anyone tells you that, for a certain amount of money, they will get you an audition, guarantee you work, or "make you a star," turn tail and run. There are no guarantees in this business. As in other industries, talent people must invest a considerable amount of time and effort before they can hope for ongoing success. Anyone who tells you otherwise is full of beans.

■ There is no reason you should have to disrobe to interview or audition for a job. Both the unions and the networks in commercials that audition and air in the United States prohibit nudity. For auditions, you could be asked to wear a two-piece swimsuit (females) or a bathing suit (males). Other common requests would be for you to wear a halter-top or an outfit that shows off your figure. When the commercial is filmed, there are ways to close in with the camera to imply nudity. This might be done in a shower or bathtub shot in an ad for a soap product, for example.

■ In major markets, steer clear of interviews and auditions to be held in personal hotel rooms at unseemly hours. Never put yourself in a position where you could be taken advantage of. Newspapers and magazines are full of frightening stories about young, inexperienced people meeting so-called agents, managers, casting people, or photographers who turn out to be kidnappers, child-molesters, rapists, and murderers. In some cases, failing to use common sense can result in personal disaster.

Even in a legitimate work situation, sexual harassment can be a problem. For example, one young model/actress was hired to do a print advertisement in which only her head and shoulders would show. During the photo session, the photographer asked her several times to open her blouse. This young lady handled herself appropriately, refusing to open her top (why would that be necessary in an ad showing only her face?) and reporting the incident immediately to her agent. The agent then called the client, who fired the photographer.

Individuals who harass and defraud talent can leave a bad taste in the mouths of those who have been taken. Such behavior demeans the efforts of legitimate industry professionals and reflects poorly on what is otherwise a terrific working environment. As aspiring talent become more scam-conscious—making wiser, sensible choices—the negative publicity surrounding the industry will begin to dissipate. Use your head when deciding whom to work with, whom to trust. The payoff will be a career unmarred by frauds and tragedies.

Remember: If it seems too good to be true, it probably is.

Common Industry Scams

Here is a list of things to avoid:

- Ads seeking talent of all kinds, no experience necessary. You go to these interviews and *voila!* You are the most amazing talent and/or look these people have ever seen. *You* are going to be a star!

Chances are, these folks are going to do one of the following:

  - Ask you to pay to be interviewed by them for the opportunity of being represented by them *or* ask you to pay for the privilege of being seen by them.
  - Ask you to pay to be on a special website that goes out to all the agents, managers, and casting houses (no one hires from these websites).

- Say how much work they could get you if only you would pay them to supply the required pictures of you—no matter how wonderful your existing pictures are, they will not be suitable for whatever they are doing—and they just happen to have a photographer with them to take those pictures.
- Tell you they think you're just wonderful, but you need a little coaching—and they just happen to have a seminar that will teach you everything you need to know.

■ "One-time" opportunities where you are told, "It's now or never. Only so many people will be accepted (you lucky dog). But you have to act fast." Time to go. Leave the room. *NOW!*

■ Agents or managers who offer to represent you as a talent without even having *seen* you. All you have to do is send in a small fee . . . This should send up an immediate red flag. Reputable talent agents simply don't sign up actors without having them come in for a formal interview to see if they have the right look, talent, and experience to be marketable to their clients. (And remember, you never should be required to pay fees up front.) You can check an agent out online with the Association of Talent Agents ("Since 1937—The Voice of Unified Talent and Literary Agencies").

■ Ads for a talent agency looking to sign people. They then ask you for money to sign you as a talent.

■ Impressive websites for acting schools and when you arrive, the school has misrepresented itself. Call other people in the industry and check around before you sign up with a school. Look for any bad press on the Internet.

■ Websites that claim you can be cast from your picture appearing on the site.

■ Photographers who come into town (often on the pretense of being a "big name" in some major market) and book sessions based on the premise that they are scouting for some big agency or are otherwise able to guarantee a connection resulting in paid work. Again, there are no guarantees. Although there are good test photographers who are brought into smaller, regional areas to photograph talent (by reputable local agencies and schools), they do not promise you work—they are simply there to help you develop your portfolio (models) or to take talent headshots.

Be suspicious of so-called famous magazine photographers. Chances are, if they really shoot covers and tears[1] for major magazines, they wouldn't have the time or interest to come to a regional area to test models and shoot headshots.

In a common scam, a photographer comes into smaller, regional areas with slick ads and a lot of hype about whom he knows and what he's done. The local talent lines up and signs up for a series of pictures, paying (of course) in full, in advance. If all goes well, the actors have a lot of fun and can't *wait* to see the results. They're happy. The photographer's happy. And why shouldn't he be? He's just made several thousand dollars, he's on his way out of town, and he's not coming back. The pictures? Well, if there ever was a memory card in that camera, it was put there for show.

Make sure you know whom you're working with if you use an out-of-town photographer. If someone says she shoots or scouts for a well-known agency or magazine, get specific information (name of agency or publication and a contact who can vouch for him or her). Get in touch with the company and ask if that photographer is representing them on the particular named project.

- A "major production house" coming to your town, auditioning talent for parts in a feature film. You're fabulous, an amazing talent—but not a member of the union. This creates a problem, but if you give them a few hundred to several hundred dollars, they will cut through the red tape, get you into the union, and you're ready for work. No. *No. NO!* There are very specific conditions for joining the unions. A simple call to the local SAG-AFTRA office (look up the number on the Internet) will tell you how to qualify to become a member of the union. They can also tell you if that film is registered as a union production.

- A casting director who claims he or she is casting for a recognizable TV show or network, such as Disney or Nickelodeon. Call the TV show and find out if this is true.

---

[1] Tears (tearsheets) are pages from commercial print advertisements, editorials (fashion pages or covers), and catalogs that models tear out to place in their modeling book (portfolio).

Reporting and Investigating Scams

If you suspect that a person or group in the industry is misrepresenting themselves, don't hesitate to make some phone calls to check out their claims. Start with the Better Business Bureau to see if there are any complaints. Ask your local Chamber of Commerce if the suspicious person or group is registered with them.

Generally, anyone involved in businesses that exchange goods or services for money must have a business license. Such a person should be able to produce a copy of that license, and you should be able to verify its validity with the government agency that issued it. (Look at the license itself to find out whom to contact.)

Scam artists are usually eager to get rid of someone who is too smart to be taken, focusing instead on those more likely to fall victim to their deceptive games. Those who are on the up-and-up will not object to you checking out their credentials, their contacts, and their prior business activities. So unless you know you are dealing with a well-known, reputable person or company, check things out before jumping into anything that seems even remotely suspicious. Search the Internet for any negative news.

If, in spite of everything, you find you've been "had" by a con artist, don't be embarrassed to admit it. Call the Better Business Bureau and the press about what happened. Doing so protects others from being scammed and will help make sure the offenders either make restitution or are prosecuted for their crimes.

If you are scammed, try to learn from the experience. Become a wiser, more conscientious consumer so that no one can take advantage of you again.

6.

Networking, Marketing, and Goal-Setting

Who you know, how well you stay focused on your goals, and whether or not you follow through have a tremendous effect on your career and its progression. It's important to surround yourself with a strong network of industry friends. You must also learn to set clear, attainable goals and take consistent, continuous steps to turn your dreams into reality.

Networking

It is no secret that successful people tend to surround themselves with a select group of industry friends and colleagues. Networking with the right people can move your career along at an accelerated rate. Who are the "right" people?

Fellow Performers

Associate with fellow performers who are motivated and active in the pursuit of their goals and who have a positive, outgoing nature. Hanging out with unmotivated people with negative attitudes will drain you emotionally and creatively.

Make it a point to spend time with people who are excited about their lives, who take advantage of the opportunities available in the industry, and who know how to make the best of a situation, no matter how crazy things get. Remember, the people you surround yourself with are a mirror of yourself and the way you relate to the world around you. Like attracts like. Take care to spend your time only with people who support you and whose efforts you admire.

Organizations

In larger markets such as New York and Los Angeles, there are organizations of supportive networking groups you can join. For instance, in Los Angeles there is a group started by Veterans for Veterans. In major markets and regional markets, there are smaller groups of actors who get together to support, encourage, and share ideas. These groups come and go. You can find out about them through word of mouth or on the Internet. There are also systems set up that are accepted by the industry that enable you to target and meet the people you want to meet. A little research and common sense will lead you to legitimate industry resources and protect you from con artists and scams (refer to Chapter 5, Scams).

There are also people and organizations in larger markets who specialize in goal-setting and marketing for actors. Remember, acting is a business. To be successful one must have a plan and carry it out in incremental steps. Sometimes things "go by plan" and other times hurdles get in your way and cause you to change course a bit to get to where you want to go. Many businesspeople leave their profession at some point in their lives to pursue their passion of acting. These businesspeople do very well in moving forward in their acting career by implementing their organizational business skills from their previous career.

Industry Professionals

Make yourself visible to the movers and shakers of the industry— agents, managers, casting directors, directors, producers, etc. Attend workshops and conventions where there are opportunities to meet and talk with people who may be in a position to help you build your career. Read trade publications in your area for a list of classes and other networking opportunities. Follow industry people on Facebook and Twitter. Subscribe to industry blogs and websites.

Market yourself through your own website or blog, and social networking sites like Twitter and Facebook. Send your picture postcards to casting directors. Be on the lookout for casting directors with online presences on social networking sites, websites, and blogs.

Make it a point to get to know everyone worth knowing in your market. Always have copies of your headshot/résumé with you as—well as online—so you can send it out at a moment's notice. Have business cards available with your photo and contact info on them (including cell number and your website address). Be courteous to and appreciative of every contact. Even though the person you just met may not be able to make a direct impact on your career, he or she may be able to steer you toward someone who can. That includes everyone from assistants and receptionists to casting directors. They are most likely in a position to help you move ahead.

Show sincere appreciation for anyone who does something nice for you. Send thank-you notes to the agent who gave you an appointment, the casting person who called you in, the receptionist who was so helpful at the audition, or the coach who took a special interest in your career. It not only brightens that person's day but also can help advance your career. Everyone wants to feel appreciated. Unfortunately (or fortunately for you), many people fail to properly thank those who have gone to bat for them.

You'll never succeed if you spend your time at home on the sofa dreaming about your first Academy Award. Get out there and meet people, whenever the opportunity arises.

Networking Websites

Keep an eye out for networking websites in your area. Watch out for scams (see Chapter 5 for more information on industry scams).

Mentors

Nothing helps young, aspiring talent catapult to success (talent and training aside) more than having a strong, successful mentor. A good mentor believes in you, sometimes (at first) more than you believe in yourself.

Mentors serve as role models, teachers, confidants, and friends. They shoulder the tears when you take a fall and give you a swift kick in the pants if you start to slack off. Having a mentor who is well known and respected can not only raise your self-esteem considerably, but also elevate your standing in the industry. People can't help but notice that this influential person has faith in your ability to do well in the industry. You'll find that with the right mentor, doors previously closed to you suddenly begin to open.

How do you *find* a mentor? Generally, a mentor finds you. He or she may notice how hard you've been working, how much promise you seem to have. Mentors are often at a point in their lives when they have had a certain degree of success and now want to give something back. And, lucky you, they decide to take you under their wing and guide your career. That is one way it happens.

Another option is for *you* to spend some time deciding whom you would like to be your mentor. Look for someone you admire who has the personal and professional traits you desire and who, over time, seems interested in helping you develop your career.

Often, talent managers take on the role of mentor, grooming an actor into a well-rounded, marketable commodity. You may have a mentor who focuses primarily on one or two aspects of your career. A mentor may come into your life suddenly, bestowing his or her special gifts (lessons) upon you, and then move on to someone else who needs help more. Some mentors become lifelong comrades. In either case, if you're lucky enough to find a mentor, count your blessings and take care to make the most of the opportunities your "guardian angel" has to offer you.

Goal-Setting

There is no question of the direct correlation between success and the simple act of setting one's goals down on paper. Goal-setting helps you to stay focused as you work on the day-to-day activities necessary to do well in the industry. Remember:

If you are failing to plan, you are planning to fail. There are numerous books and CDs on the subject of goal-setting, all of which cite the following tips for setting solid, achievable goals:

■ Make a habit of regularly writing down your goals.

Studies show that the simple act of writing down your goals sets the wheels of success in motion. The process puts your dreams in clear focus so that you can prioritize them and begin taking action to bring each goal to fruition.

■ Break your goals down into the following categories:

• *Yearly goals.* Write a broad overview of the things you would like to accomplish over the next year.
• *Monthly goals.* At the beginning of each month, prioritize those things you want to get done over the next thirty or thirty-one days. Be specific as you break down your yearly goals over the next twelve months.
• *Weekly goals.* Begin each week by writing down your goals for the next seven days. Be realistic about what you can accomplish in this amount of time and make sure that you spend time working toward the accomplishment of your most important achievements. (It's easy to get wrapped up in the day-to-day stuff, neglecting the tasks that would really make a difference in your career.)
• *Daily goals.* Little by little, you've been breaking your most important goals into smaller and smaller pieces (yearly, monthly, and weekly). Now divide your goals into even smaller "bites," planning something to do each and every day to move your career forward. As you complete each step on your daily "to do" list, you'll begin to notice that you are making strides in the major, annual goals you set for yourself.

Deciding what *specifically* you want, then consistently taking *action* to do the things that make you more marketable, will provide the strong foundation necessary to create an ongoing experience of achievement.

As you write out your goals, it's important to know that you can't have it all, certainly not all at once. It's very hard to succeed if you are scattered, pursuing too many major goals at one time. For instance, it would be very hard to become a doctor and an actor at the same time. Becoming a doctor involves many years of study and practice. Becoming an actor requires equal dedication in time and effort to stand a chance of succeeding. Over time, you could certainly become both a doctor and an actor (the late Graham Chapman of Monty Python fame did just that), but it would be very difficult to pursue both careers at the same time.

You must prioritize your list of goals and be reasonable about what can be accomplished in a given block of time. Go over your list and as you attempt to decide which goals you are going to pursue (at this time), ask yourself:

Do I *really* want to accomplish this goal? Am I willing to make this goal a priority in my life, working every day in some way to make this dream a reality? Am I willing to pay the price of achieving my goal—to devote the time and effort necessary to make things happen? What am I willing to sacrifice in the pursuit of this goal (TV time, nights out socializing)?

Why do I want to achieve this goal? Be honest with yourself. Make sure the goal you set is chosen for the right reasons, that you are doing this for yourself, that it's something you *need* to do—not because someone else wants it for you. You will have to work very hard to achieve your goals. Do some soul-searching to make sure that what you are trying for is something you really want.

What are all the wonderful things that will happen if I am able to achieve my goal? For instance, "If I lose weight, all my favorite clothes will fit, I'll look better on camera, etc." Visualizing all the fabulous results of achieving your goals will inspire you to follow through.

What are the not-so-wonderful things that will happen if I *don't* achieve my goal? Spend some time contemplating the results of *not* taking consistent action to see your plans through to completion.

"I didn't follow through on a connection I made at the casting. As a result, the part went to someone else." "I never did sign up for that cold-reading class. As a result, I was visibly inexperienced at the audition." Just thinking about what you felt like when you didn't achieve a goal, then comparing that to the way you felt when you did, should motivate you to take action today to complete one of the vital tasks you've listed on your goal sheet.

> *When you get right down to the root of the meaning of the word* succeed, *you find it simply means to follow through.*—F. W. Nichols

As you work your way through your list of goals, you may over time find that certain goals no longer seem important to you. Your priorities can (and do) change. Be flexible when this happens. Review your goal sheet periodically and update it as needed.

Also pay attention to which efforts are producing positive results for you—and which ones aren't. Revise your strategy when necessary. Keep doing whatever is working; stop doing whatever isn't. Be willing to try new things (no guts, no glory), and be willing to make mistakes along the way. Realize that behind every setback is the opportunity to learn and grow.

Be willing to do whatever it takes to accomplish your goals (providing it is neither illegal nor immoral). Take classes, get out and meet people, work on your public image, eliminate the "negatives" from your life. Make time to plan out your life—and make no excuses. There is always time to do the things that are really important to you.

If you're not doing something on a regular basis to make your dream a reality, it could be that you don't *really* want this goal at all. Only you can decide how badly you want to change your present circumstances. A bit of soul-searching as you review your progress should provide you with the answers you need. Remember:

> *If you do not take the time to write down specific goals and consistently*
> *act on them, you will wind up working for someone else who did.*

There are no shortcuts to greatness. Greatness comes with consistent effort and begins with the little things you do each day as you build your career. Stay focused and determined to succeed, and before you know it, your wildest dreams will begin to become reality.

CHAPTER SUMMARY: SUPER SUCCESS STRATEGIES FOR CONSISTENT GOAL ATTAINMENT

- Make note of your goals and refer to them regularly. Doing so keeps your goals in clear focus. Studies show that people who write their goals out on paper tend to achieve much more than those who do not.

- Be specific about what you want to achieve. For instance, "I want to be called in for more auditions a year by casting directors, so I will have the chance to make more money," then determine the amount of auditions you want to be called in on.

- The more specific and detailed your plan of action, the better the chance you will reach your goal when you plan to reach it. For instance, if you are currently being sent out on five auditions a year, an attainable goal could be, "Next year I want to be sent out on twenty auditions a year from the starting date of this exercise."

Once you've decided how many auditions you want and the time frame you want to do it in, be very specific about what you're going to do in the next year that will generate more interest in you. Make a list of things to do that will help you achieve your goal to the level you've aspired to. For instance "I want to build up my résumé with classes to reflect my comic ability. I want to take an improv class, a comedy class, and I want to do more comedic theater pieces." Make a list of things to do that will help you achieve your goal: "I am going to look up and contact three acting classes today. I am going to look for theater audition opportunities in the trades." Refer to the list at least once daily (preferably first thing in the morning and again in the evening), and try to do something every day that will bring you closer to reaching your goal.

Review and revise your goals regularly, as needed. Keep your goals in plain sight and review them often to see what's working, what's not, and whether or not the goal needs to be revised before it is truly attainable. Maybe your goal was not realistic. Maybe you need more time to attain it. Sometimes the desire for the goal diminishes and another goal takes priority. Goal-setting should be an ongoing process.

Associate with achievers. Watch the company you keep. Surround yourself with supportive, positive people. Find people who are doing what you would like to be doing, who inspire you to achieve and maintain a level of excellence. Avoid those who find a million excuses for not achieving their goals. If you are surrounded by people who don't support your desire for growth, find a new group of friends and colleagues who do. Your success depends upon it.

- Take consistent action in attaining your goals. *NO MORE EXCUSES!* Whatever you want to do, get off your butt and get to it. No matter where you are now—no matter what your financial state, your educational level, or where you live—start with whatever resources are available to you and *get going.* There will never be a "perfect" time or a "perfect" set of circumstances. The best time to begin is now. Even a small effort, when consistently applied, will create phenomenal change. In fact, the simple decision to write and act on clear, precise goals produces a certain positive momentum. All things are possible. You *can* create the kind of life you want if you invest regularly in these simple, highly effective goal-setting techniques.

I know of no more encouraging fact than the unquestionable ability of man
to elevate his life by conscious endeavor —Henry David Thoreau

Goal-Planning Sheet

TO-DO LIST	NOTES
	NEW CONTACTS
IMPORTANT CALLS	**THANK-YOU NOTES**

FIG. 13: Sample goal-setting sheet.

SECTION 2

TAKING YOUR ACT ON THE ROAD

7.

The Key Players in the Industry

Now it's time to meet some of the key movers and shakers in the commercial industry. They are instrumental in the advancement of your career, so it's important to know who these people are and how they fit into your life as a performer. Each acting venue has a system in place consisting of people involved in the process from breakdown to audition to booking. Each venue also has a different typical rhythm and timing. Following are the people involved in the commercial venue.

Agents

The agent is the person who represents you, who secures auditions for you. He or she accepts bookings for you, negotiates money and employment terms, receives the payments you get from the booking, and distributes the money (minus his or her commission) to you. The agent protects you according to the guidelines of the unions.

If you have any questions or complaints, your agent is the one to straighten them out for you. Some problems or issues that could potentially arise include:

- While on a shoot, the contract you are signing states that the commercial is running (airing) in a different way from what you were told when you booked it.

- You were booked as an extra and you are now recognized in the commercial. You feel you should be upgraded to a principal.

- You are no longer under contract for a commercial and a friend of yours calls and says that the commercial is running again.

It's your agent's responsibility to keep records of your bookings and product conflicts (products you are under contract for). However, ultimately you are your own business manager and must keep your own records.

Managers

It is the manager's job to help you shape your overall career. You might, for instance, be doing a lot of commercials, and then decide it's time to move more into film. Your manager should be able to tell you if your timing is right and, if it is, introduce you to film opportunities and film agent representation.

With your manager's help, all aspects of your career (theater, film, commercials, etc.) should be considered and a plan of action put into effect. Your manager is someone else on your side, taking your hand and offering personalized attention and guidance as you develop your career. Managers have fewer clients than agents, so they can take time to develop talent. If you have an agent, technically the agent would secure the booking and negotiate the monies, after discussing the details with your manger.

Casting Directors

The casting director is the one who calls the actor in to audition, either directly or through an agent. He or she is responsible for the initial selection of actors from all available talent. The casting director also directs the actor during the filmed audition, and then presents this audition to the creative team.

A casting director may be the first person of importance to see your work. If he believes in you and likes your work, he will call you in on any audition he feels you are right for, even if you don't have an agent. In this case, the casting director could be instrumental in introducing you to an agent. Although you can obtain auditions directly from the casting director, ultimately, you have more exposure to auditions when you have agency representation. Many casting directors will communicate character descriptions to agents, referred to as "breakdowns," which results in expanded opportunities to audition for actors who have agents. A casting director gets no payment or commissions from an actor.

Producers

The producer is the person who puts together all the elements of the commercial's production, and is one of the members of the creative team who have a say in who gets booked for the job.

Directors

The director is the one who actually directs the spot. Often, the director's opinion as to which talent will work best for the spot holds great weight. (For more on producers and directors, see Chapter 11, The Selection Process).

8.

What You Need to Know about Agents, Managers, and Unions

All About Agents

Agents are always looking for talented individuals who have the potential to book jobs and make money for them. As a talent, you are most marketable when you are properly trained and prepared to go out on auditions. Being prepared means having your marketing tools in order, especially your professional headshot and résumé.

You must supply your agent with digital photographs and together decide which photographs will best represent you for online submissions. Have a supply of hard copies on hand to bring to auditions. If your agent wants hard copies, of course supply them with the amount they want. Most submissions are done online, and therefore agents typically will not keep a supply of your hard copies.

The agent acts as a go-between with the casting directors, producers, and ad agencies. Although you should be proactive with networking and finding out about auditions, the main job of your agent is receiving breakdowns of auditions, submitting your name and photo, taking care of avails, first refusals, and bookings and making sure the actor gets paid the appropriate amount of money (refer to Chapter 12 for more on "avails," "first refusals," and "bookings"). This keeps the talent from being put in the middle of the uncomfortable position of bickering about money when a problematic situation occurs. The agent can step in and be the bad guy, always looking out for the talent's best interests.

Reputable agents in states other than "right-to-work" states belong to the ATA (Association of Talent Agencies). These agents follow union guidelines. The talent agency is bonded so that it is able to handle the talent's money. The actor is thereby protected by the rules and ethics set down by the union.

What You Need to Know about Agents

Most actors in most regions are registered with and may be sent out by more than one agent within a given market. In Chicago, this is called *multi-listing*. In New York and other areas, it's called *freelancing*. The other way of being represented is to sign an exclusive agreement, meaning that a single agent represents you for each acting venue. Los Angeles is a *signed* town. An actor there is represented exclusively by one agent for commercial and one agent—which could be different from the commercial agent—for film and television. You could also have different agents exclusively for voice-over, sports, dance, and industrials.

HOW TO FIND A GOOD AGENT

There are several methods by which talented people find good, reputable agency representation. The major union markets are New York, Los Angeles, and Chicago. Each market has directories of talent agents published by knowledgeable people in the industry. Ask other actors about agents they have dealt with. Look on the ATA website for listings of licensed agencies in or near your area, or call the Better Business Bureau and make sure an agency you're considering has a business license. Call theaters, acting schools, and other actors to see what they know about the agency.

Do You Want a Manager?

With a manager, you have another person working on your behalf, and this can be beneficial. A manager is often more willing to work with newcomers in the industry, taking a more personal interest in developing budding careers. Agents need people who are ready to work. They are generally too busy booking people for jobs to spend time developing talent. A manager, on the other hand, might advise newcomers on all aspects of their career. A good manager acts as a business consultant, a middleman between agents and talent, a mentor, and a confidant.

If you are working in secondary markets such as Florida, Atlanta, or Texas and are looking to make the move to New York or Los Angeles, it might be a good time to consider finding a good manager. A good manager would be one who has agent contacts to introduce you to and get you signed with in New York or Los Angeles. Be sure your manager is well connected, which would mean more potential opportunities for you. Competition is fierce in this industry, so the more people you can get behind you, the better.

The New York and Los Angeles markets are more manager-oriented because the industry is much larger there, which makes it easier to get lost in the shuffle than in smaller areas. A good manager in the major markets can be a real asset.

The downside of having a manager is that you have to pay them 15 percent when you get booked in addition to the agency commission. So experiment a little when you first start out. Go out there without a manager and see how it goes. If you are not getting the results you want after a while, try getting a manager and see if things improve. What you can't do is use a manager to connect with agents, to get your career going, and then leave the manager once things start clicking for you. In the beginning a manager puts a lot of time and effort into you without any compensation. Although it may not appear that the manager is still working hard for you after you've established a connection with your agent(s), know that your manager is working for you behind the scenes.

If working with a manager means you are working more, then the extra commission is well worth paying.

Conducting a Dynamite Agent Interview

So, you've done your homework, you've researched the available agents in your area, you've done your mailings, and you've followed up with a call to each a week later. Congratulations! You've gotten your first request to come in for an interview. Go to your interview clean and casual, looking like yourself. Dress to suite your type (see Chapter 1 for a list of looks and types booked for commercials).

Questions to Ask before Taking On an Agent or Manager

When meeting with agents and managers, keep in mind that ultimately you are interviewing them as much as they are interviewing you. Make sure you are comfortable with the person you are dealing with and that you are satisfied with their answers to the following questions:

- How many people do you represent? How many in my age range, type, and gender?
- What can I expect from you as an agent/manager?
- What do you expect from me?

Once the agent/manager is interested, ask:

- What kind of contract (if any) would I be signing?
- Which photographs would you like?
- How—and how often—would you like me to keep in touch?

You should discuss with an agent (and especially a manager) what, at this point, you want out of your career. He should be aligned and attuned to you and your needs. If the agent or manager doesn't have the same aspirations for you that you have for yourself, he should tell you what direction he sees for you. If you do not like what he suggests, he is not the right person to represent you.

You may have one meeting with the agent who has shown initial interest in you, and a second meeting with all other agents in the office. They then decide if it would be mutually beneficial for them to represent you.

Here are a few tips from industry pros on attitude and presentation at that all-important meeting.

LAURA FOGELMAN, AGENT, LOS ANGELES: "You have about five minutes to win people over and knock them out during the interview. You have to be positive, upbeat, and keep the conversation going. If you are boring, you are dead in the water. That's it. I have people who come in to my office and sit in a chair, wait for me to ask questions, and give me one-word answers. It takes two people to have a conversation. One-word answers give me nowhere to go. Find things to talk about. It's easier for us if someone comes in and is very conversational and chatty. It makes us want to talk more.

"Also, actors have to look interesting when they walk in the door. They have to dress the part. I don't mean upscale. They just have to have themselves put together. They should have a sense of style. The girl should be unique and interesting, in a way that makes people want to look at her. I have seen girls come in in coveralls and look fabulous because they have a whole 'look' down pat. Have a sense of style and look confident when you walk in the room."

SARAH CARPENTER, AGENT, ATLANTA: "Confidence is very important. As well as knowing your brand and who you are as an actor. You should be able to come into my office and tell me all about you, your strengths and weakness and your goals in the first ten minutes. I also expect potential clients to do their research before coming to meet with me. They should know all about our agency and the market, what's being shot here and which projects they are right for."

TRACI DANIELLI, AGENT, FLORIDA: "I expect talent to show up and be on time. Also, it's important for actors to just be themselves. Don't try to be something you are not. Don't try to impress me by throwing around important names or bragging about the work you've done. Don't be negative or make excuses. I have heard every excuse in the book. I know it's hard, but don't be nervous. Just relax and be yourself."

ROBERT SCHROEDER, AGENT, CHICAGO: "I like actors but I like people even more! I am always looking to meet talent that have something new to say. I want to sit down and speak to a person, not an actor. I can read your résumé to find out what you have done. Speak to me about what you want to do or what you like to do on the weekend. Things you are interested in outside of acting. Don't worry about what we are looking for. Be comfortable with who you are. Let us know what you have to offer. You are the person who can play you best."

NANCY JOHNSON, AGENT, TEXAS: "Attitude and presentation at the 'all-important meeting.' You must have a PhD:

P = Purpose (not ego). Presentation. Positive mental attitude.

H = Hopeful, happy, honorable, and hustle!

D = Dedication, determination, durability.

"Going to an acting interview is different from going to a job interview. You should look comfortable and casual. You should wear clothes that reflect your personality and look. If you are a funky-type person, you would dress funky. If you are a conservative, you would dress conservatively. If you are an upscale-type person, you would dress upscale."

Keeping in Touch with Your Agent

Once you have found an agent, ask him how often and when you should be in touch. Some agents want you to call in every so often. Others prefer you not call them unless you have some specific business to discuss. Calls or emails every five minutes to see if they have anything for you is generally regarded as a nuisance and will frustrate your agent.

Your agent's function is to communicate all day with casting directors to secure appointments for you with production companies and ad agencies, negotiating contracts, and straightening out any problems or issues that come up. Consider a typical day in the life of an agent. The agent is communicating with the casting director, preparing a breakdown consisting of either lists of actors or photo submissions, getting appointment times from casting directors, giving appointment times out to actors, getting confirmations from actors, and giving confirmations or cancellations back to casting directors. The agent also receives or puts out call times for callbacks and bookings.

Understanding what agents do can help you realize that, although it is important to stay in touch with them, you must do so in a manner that is productive for both you and your agent. Find out how your agent would like you to keep in touch. Different agents have different policies. Some have "open door policies," which means you are welcome to drop in anytime; others prefer emails or phone calls. Be aware that your agent's job is to arrange auditions and bookings for talent. If you are constantly demanding an agent's time, you are disrupting his or her job.

Don't automatically assume that your agent is not working hard for you just because you are not auditioning. If you really feel you are being forgotten by your agent, contact the agent to arrange a discussion about this, assess their answer, and either stay or move on. You should not stay with an agent you are not happy with, and there is no reason why agents would want to keep any actors on their rosters who do not want to be with them. If you are auditioning and not booking, of course that is not your agent's fault. The agent can only get you the audition.

Handling Contracts and Agreements

ATA agents use a standard contract to sign their talent, guided by union rules. Always read it over and don't be afraid to discuss changes you desire. The answer will be yes or no. You sign a one-year contract, which is renewable for three years after the first year. Non-ATA agency contracts should be gone over carefully before signing. Be sure to ask questions about any points that seem vague or unreasonable.

The two main points to check for in a non-ATA contract are commission and the "out clause." Beware if the commission is more than 20 percent. The standard commission dealing with non-union talent is 10 to 20 percent. Pay particular attention to the out clause, which indicates the conditions for getting out of the contract. The contract should indicate either how many auditions the agent needs to send you out on or how many bookings you need to secure within a specified amount of time for the contract to remain binding.

If the out clause is not satisfactory to you, have a lawyer examine the contract before you sign it. After you and your lawyer discuss areas that should be amended, take the document back to the agent, who may or may not be willing to renegotiate the terms of the agreement. Just know that, ultimately, only you can decide whether signing the final version of the document is in your best interests. Many commercial agents do not have you sign a contract because they are not interested in keeping you if you don't want them. Payments for any bookings that are secured while with the agent will be sent to them and in turn, they then pay the actor's commissions. In essence if you leave, the agent has not lost any money due to them.

Why Actors Might Want to Drop Their Agents

The number one reason actors want to drop their agents is that they are not being sent out on enough auditions. They think if they were with someone else, they would have more opportunities. Sometimes, it's simply a case of the grass-is-always-greener mentality.

The people who jump around tend to be the ones who are having a difficult time booking jobs. The agent could very well be submitting the actor for auditions, but the casting director or whoever decides who gets to audition is not choosing that actor. Here is where your picture is very important. You might not be getting chosen because your picture is not capturing the eye of the casting director. If you suspect that you are losing opportunities because your headshot isn't strong enough, ask your agent if she thinks you need a new one. Many times, just changing up the picture for whatever reason, seems to stimulate interest and activity.

If you're getting called for auditions but not getting called back and/or booked, it could be that your auditioning skills are not honed well enough to have the competitive edge. If you have hit a dry spell, use the down time to study your craft; ask your agent for referrals to good coaches in or near your area.

An actor may choose to leave his agent if he disagrees with the agent as to what types of castings he is being sent out for. Most people want to leave their agency because they are not getting enough work. Actors must remember that "getting work" is not what an agent does. An agent's job is to get actors auditions and interviews. The actor must then "win" the job.

If you are not happy with your agent, arrange a meeting to discuss the issues. If you cannot come to a satisfactory conclusion, it may be time for you to leave. Remember, however, that the agent still gets residual payment for any jobs secured for you while you were represented by them. Other than that, most agents agree that if you are not happy with them, it is better for all concerned for you to move on.

Why an Agent Might Want to Drop an Actor

The number one reason agents want to drop an actor is repeated unprofessional conduct. For example, if you do not show up on time, do not show up at all, book out[1] too much, try to bypass the agency by giving your phone number to a producer or ad agency, or are difficult to work with.

You must trust the agent you are working with and be able to take constructive criticism. Agents generally do not drop actors because they are not booking. They expect it could take a year or more to book something. As long as you are selected to come in and audition, you are enthusiastically auditioning, your craft is honed, and you have a positive attitude, your agent will stick with you.

The Unions and Their Jurisdictions

The unions—SAG-AFTRA (Screen Actors Guild–American Federation of Television and Radio Artists)—represent and govern the industry in film, television, commercials, industrials, voice-over, animation, daytime dramas, web series (webinars), and any "new media."

WHY JOIN THE UNION?

In regions where the work is split fairly equally between union and non- union work, and in right-to-work states, actors will be faced with the choice of either joining the union or not. If you have the choice, it may be wise for an actor to choose not to join for the first couple of years. After you build up a lot of credits and are booking frequently, you may reconsider joining the union.

In areas such as Los Angeles and New York, where there are more opportunities for union television and film work, you'll probably want to join the union to attract those opportunities. If a SAG-AFTRA film or commercial is shot in a state that is not a right-to-work state and wants to hire someone who is not a member of the union, the casting director has to obtain a Taft-Hartley waiver for that actor. This waiver allows the production to use you without the production being fined. In essence the Taft-Hartley waiver letter has to meet union approval

---

[1] When talent "book out," they give the agent or manager dates when they are not available for work.

which substantiates that fact that you are devoting your profession to acting. Your résumé must get union approval that considers such things as past experience in theater, television, film, and professional acting training.

Film and television will be much more attracted to you having already done your due diligence and proven yourself with the outcome of being a member of the union.

Benefits of joining the union include:

- *Protection.* Union contracts establish minimum (scale) payments for talent performing in all industry-related media under their jurisdiction. They also make sure that performers on union jobs are employed under reasonable working conditions. The unions determine work standards and establish guidelines for children on the set.

- *Health insurance, pension coverage, and cost-of-living adjustments* (COLAs).

HOW TO JOIN THE UNION

There are several ways to join SAG-AFTRA. The most common:

- Getting a job on a union project. After you do one union job, you become "Taft-Hartleyed," meaning you can do as many union jobs as you want for the next thirty days, after which you must join the union and pay your dues before you can do another union job. If you don't, the ad agency who employed you will be fined.

- Getting hired as an extra on three union jobs. Check with your local SAG-AFTRA office. Rules and regulations regarding extra work vary from state to state.

- Booked on a web series (webisode). Check the SAG-AFTRA website for updates on the ever-changing updating of rules.

In a right-to-work state, companies cannot refuse to hire actors because they do not belong to the union or because they do not *want* to join the union. The biggest misconception union actors have about working in a right-to-work state is that they can do both union and non-union work. Union actors who work on non-union projects are violating Rule One of the agreement they signed when they joined the union. Check online for union specifics if you are working in a right-to-work state.

FI-CORE (FINANCIAL CORE) UNION STATUS

Once you join the union, you can declare a status called Fi-Core. It means you are still a member of the union, but have given up certain union rights for the ability to do both union and non-union work. If you truly believe in the union because of the protections it affords you—the ability to gain health insurance and eventual pension payments—you should think hard about the decision to declare Fi-Core status, since good union actors putting themselves in the position of working non-union only weakens the union.

Actors usually declare financial core if they are suffering financial hardship and feel the need to do both union and non-union work. Obviously the union discourages this status and does not usually include this option on their website. Call your SAG-AFTRA chapter and speak to a representative who can explain the details of your loss of rights by doing so.

Interviews with an Agent and a Talent Manager

Now that you have become familiar with the roles of agents, managers, and unions in the business of making commercials, you may want to read the following interviews, which explore the nuts and bolts of these jobs. Carol Ingber, New York agent, and Al Onorato, who works as a talent manager in Los Angeles, offer these insights.

CAROL INGBER, AGENT:

What does it mean for an actor to sign with an agent? What is freelancing?

To sign with an agent means the talent signs either an agency general services agreement or whatever particular contract the agency uses for exclusive representation of talent for a time period of up to eighteen months. This means the actor cannot go out on commercial auditions for any other agency. After the initial contract expires, the actor has the option to renew with a one-, two-, or three-year contract.

The reason people feel they need to be signed is so that they have a business relationship with someone who will groom and take care of them. My first responsibility as an agent is to my signed clients—if a casting director calls and gives me a time slot for an actor, I'm going to give that time to one of my signed clients first.

Freelancing means an actor can work with multiple agents. In New York, actors can freelance—in Los Angeles, however, actors must sign exclusive contracts with one agent for each venue: commercial, film and television (known as theatrical), voice-over, sports, and hosting.

What do you look for when deciding whether or not to represent an actor?

I look for someone who has a good attitude, who treats people with respect regardless of their position in the business. (In an industry where today's assistant can become tomorrow's agent, it pays to be respectful to anyone you work with in the industry.) Also, if one of my assistants says to me, "I just got off the phone with so-and-so who sent in a picture—she really sounds nice on the phone," I'll make a point of remembering that person.

I treat talent in a professional manner and I expect the same in return. I'm not interested in people who either show up late or not at all. If I leave a message for an actor, I expect a return telephone call in a timely fashion and not one twenty-four hours later. I also expect actors to tell me when they're going out of town or "booking out." It's important for an agent and talent to work together as a team—a true fifty-fifty partnership.

If you sign a talent who doesn't book right away, how long will you continue to represent him?

When I believe in someone, I'll continue to work with that person for as long as it takes. I have a client who has been with me six years and she just booked her first network spot. I also have had clients who booked immediately—either way, if I believe in that person I am loyal to that person.

There is a statistical rule as to how many auditions it takes to book a job. This is because of the competition factor—there are fewer auditions to go out on and more people in the talent pool.

What is the actor's job in developing his career?

To be professional, take classes, be an observer of life—this is the actor's part in the teamwork with the agency. When talent are not up to par, they have to listen to their agent. If their agent says they have to do something, they must do it!

What do you look for in a headshot/résumé?

I like to see that an actor has done some theater, TV, or film work. I look for a picture that sort of hits me or I may be attracted to something in the cover letter. It's hard to define specifically what makes me want to call someone in, but something in the presentation grabs my attention and makes me want to meet the person.

Any thoughts about what should be in the cover letter?

Don't write a two-page letter, every agent knows why you're writing us. Make it short and sweet—I get more than thirty pictures a day and I want to be able to read the note fast.

Do you expect actors to have a demo?

No—I don't look at them or listen to them. I would rather get an idea of the actor's potential from observing the person in front of me.

What do you look for in a general interview?

Actors come across best when they are just being themselves. If I ask an actor where he comes from, make the response short, sweet, and honest. Let the agent guide you—there are certain things we need to get out of that first meeting. What you think is important may not be—say what you need to say and allow your personality to come out. Don't respond to the agent's questions with one-word answers, but don't go on for a long time, either. Try not to come across as desperate or overanxious.

Are there pet peeves actors should avoid?

Actors who don't want to accept early audition calls are high on my "peeve" list. I have to be in my office at 9:30 A.M., even after going out to the theater and returning at 1:00 A.M. If I have a client in the show, we may go out afterwards, yet I still have to be in the office on time. If I am not, you, as an actor, will have a problem with that. So, if I can be in my office early in the A.M., you can do it too.

Actors with bad attitudes don't go over very well with agents. You see this in actors who don't return phone calls, don't tell their agent when they'll be out of town, and blow off auditions. Some actors treat commercials lightly—as a secondary interest—yet commercials can be a powerful venue for actors to showcase their talent. I have seen a lot of clients who have gone on to TV and film because they were noticed in a commercial. Actors have been written up in newspapers and magazines because of a sensational commercial they've appeared in—commercials can definitely lead to better things.

Will you work with someone who isn't in the union yet?

Of course. It's very exciting when an actor gets his first booking and is waivered into the union—commercials are the way for many people to gain union status. I am interested in talented people with an acting background, which includes people who have studied in small colleges in the Midwest as well as students from Yale or Juilliard.

How much can someone earn from a single commercial?

An actor can make anywhere from scale to $100,000 or more from one commercial. I have a client who has made six figures from a spot that has been running for six years. In fact, I have known many actors who have appeared in commercials that have run for years and have easily made six figures.

What is the most important piece of advice you can give to actors?

Believe in who and what you are. Hang in there and don't give up. Always be honest with the people you are working with.

AL ONORATO, MANAGER:

What is the difference between an agent and a manager?

The basic difference is that SAG-franchised agents are licensed and managers are not.

Agents are interested in finding jobs for their clients. Managers are interested in shaping their client's careers for the long term. Also, agents generally handle a lot of people, while a manager has to be selective. For instance, an agent may handle a hundred people. A manager would have perhaps twenty-five.

A manager puts a lot of time and effort into nurturing and building the career, whereas an agent doesn't have time for that kind of personal attention. If, for example, someone is going to an audition, a manager would work with that person on the material, doing as much preparation and getting as much information on the audition as possible and following up on the results. It is also up to the manager to try to get feedback as to how an audition or a meeting went and how the talent is doing in one-on-one situations.

How does someone find a good manager?

Get out and talk to people. It's like finding a doctor, a minister, or a dentist. Many times, you just have to go on instinct. Ask managers for their ideas on building a career. Ask what types of people they handle. You might inquire about other people in the business they network with. The word *clout* comes in here: If they need to get someone on the phone—be it the casting director, the head of a studio, or a network executive—can they do it?

Is there a point when doing commercials might be a detriment to someone's career? When should someone stop doing them?

If you're in television and you want to make a move into the movie industry, it can be a detriment to be too well known as a television personality. It's the same principle with commercials.

If you're building a career, you want to be seen enough to make people want to see more of you, but avoid being overexposed in one medium. Visibility is very important in the beginning; then you want to stop doing things so that people will want to see more of you.

9.

The Auditioning Process

Getting Auditions

FINDING OUT ABOUT CALLS

In the primary markets (New York, Los Angeles, and Chicago) as well as in the secondary markets (i.e., Dallas, New Orleans, Austin, Boston, Miami/Orlando, and Atlanta), the best way to find out about auditions is through an agent. Agents are aware of most of the calls and will set up appointments for their clients.

You will quickly become aware of the casting directors. And as much as you want to get to know the casting director, the casting director will want to know what talent is around and available. No matter what market you are in, you should be promoting yourself by sending your headshots and résumés to agents and casting directors. In smaller, regional markets, consider sending your promotional materials to local production companies. However, if there are agents in your area, agency representation should be your ultimate goal.

INTERNET SUBMISSIONS

The two main breakdown services that casting directors and agents use to communicate with each other are called Breakdown Services and Casting Network. These two services originate out of Los Angeles and have reached out successfully nationwide as a legitimate organized systems for putting out breakdowns and receiving submissions. If a particular small regional area advocates a local breakdown service, it is easy to check out the service via an Internet search. Some of the smaller local breakdown services will tend to come and go.

Be cautious when dealing with companies that claim to be Internet casting services. You could get caught up in a scam where you are asked to pay money to have your photo(s) appear on a website that casting directors supposedly cast from. Call your local casting office and ask if it uses a breakdown service and, if so, which one. Give the office the name of the breakdown service that is soliciting your business and ask what it knows of the service.

The legitimate breakdown services offer a minute-to-minute means of photo submissions by agents to casting directors over the Internet. There is a section on each of these services' websites that is set up to accept open submissions by actors with no agency representation for projects posted by casting directors. These projects are usually for nonunion projects or for talent searches for very specific special skills.

Casting directors tend to have Facebook and Twitter business pages where they post opportunities. The smallness of a regional area can act to your advantage, as it is easy to find out who is legitimate and who is not.

Trade magazines such as *Backstage* (which you can purchase at newsstands and bookstores, or subscribe to for hard copy delivery or online access) also provide information on auditions. Most of the auditions listed are "open calls," also known as "cattle calls." This means the auditions are open to the public. You will probably have to wait in long lines to audition for what are often nonpaying jobs in low-budget films, student films, and theater. The end result could be that you get some great film on yourself and some valuable on-the-set experience. Work in such jobs can also be a wonderful way to start relationships with up-and-coming filmmakers.

HOW AN ACTOR IS SELECTED TO AUDITION

The typical casting-call scenario begins with a casting director getting a call from a director or producer. The art director, producer, writer, and director present the casting director with a *storyboard*, a frame-by-frame pictorial layout of how the commercial is to be shot (fig. 14). The character breakdown is then put out by means of whatever breakdown system the casting director has in place. In addition, the casting director always has his or her own ideas of who would be good for the character breakdown from past experience with actors or after seeing an actor in previous performances.

The commercial process has now started and it moves along at lightning speed. If the casting director is using an online breakdown service, submissions start coming in instantaneously. Since Los Angeles is the largest market, the number of agents and managers who respond to a breakdown is approximately 712. New York is a smaller market and the number of agents and managers who represent talent is approximately 80; Chicago will have a response of approximately 25 agents.

If you are in a regional market, you can look online to find talent agents in your area and that will be the number of agent/manager responses a call can expect in that market.

In Los Angeles a breakdown typically receives as 1,200–1,500 submissions per character. Every ethnicity is typically considered for all characters. It is easy for a breakdown with six characters to have as many as 4,000–5,000 submissions. Throughout the country, breakdowns go out via Internet submission services, phone calls, and emails to agents. The Internet is widely used, even in circumstances where a casting director asks agents to send talent photos and résumés of actors the casting director does not know.

As you can see, Los Angeles has many opportunities, but the competition is fierce. (More on this in Chapter 14, Working in Regional Areas).

After the audition selections are given to the agents—whether that is through an Internet service, phone calls, or emails—if an agent feels strongly about an actor who was not chosen to audition, the agent may go to bat for the actor (pitch the actor) and try to convince the casting director to call that person in. While you might have all the right elements defined in the character breakdown, it's possible that you won't be selected because the casting director already has enough people for the role.

OPEN ON A COCO'S CHEF AND A COCO'S MANAGER SEATED AT A CUTTING BOARD TABLE. MANAGER HAS AN ADDING MACHINE. CHEF HAS A PILE OF FRESH VEGETABLES.

MANAGER: Mr. generous Coco's Chef here has created something new for dinner.

CHEF NODS SMUGLY.

Calls it his Three Course Dinner.

CUT TO ECU SLOW TRACKING SHOT OF ENTREES

He gives you a choice of six of our most popular entrees. ...

TRACK TO FULL SCREEN ECU OF TERIYAKI CHICKEN.

like Teriyaki Chicken

SETTLE ON FRESH RED SNAPPER.

or fresh Red Snapper...

FIG. 14: Sample storyboard.

FOLLOWED BY SOUPS AND SALAD,

plus hot soup or salad, ...

THEN A COUPLE OF APPETIZERS

and your choice of four delicious appetizers ...

AND A FEW DESSERTS.

or six tempting desserts.

CUT BACK TO MEN. AS MANAGER TALKS,
CHEF PUSHES ONE TOMATO FORWARD.

Then he says to sell it all for just $7.99,
to which I say...

HE THEN CHOPS IT IN TWO, FORCEFULLY,
WITH A LARGE CLEAVER AND LOOKS
MEANINGFULLY AT MANAGER.

SFX: Chunck!!!

Good idea. Very good idea.

CUT TO FULL PRODUCT SET-UP.

SUPER: $7.99. COCO'S.

AVO: Coco's Three Course Dinners, Just $7.99.

MANAGER: (VO) Very, very good idea.

WHAT TO DO WHEN YOU GET THE CALL

Once the casting director has decided whom to call in for the audition, she notifies the agents. The agents then let the talent know they have the audition, and provide all the pertinent information. The breakdown services allow the agents to email the talent their audition details. The service also enables the agent to enter notes and confirmations into the system, communicating directly to the casting director.

If your audition is not coming to you via email or text for you to keep for your records, always be ready at a moment's notice to take notes. This is a very fast-paced business. It is a mark against you if you are not prepared to move smoothly and quickly as agents run off the important facts about the audition. Nothing annoys people in this business more than having to repeat themselves (or wait) because you weren't prepared to take their call. And if an agent forgets to tell you something, be sure to ask.

You should be given the following information about the audition:

- The date of the audition.
- The time of the audition.
- The date of the shoot. Never audition if you are not going to be available for the shoot. It is a horrendous waste of everyone's time.
- The product the commercial is advertising.
- Any conflicts. You must be free of contractual ties to commercials for competing products.

  In a union commercial, you cannot be under contract to two competing products (such as Tide and Wisk detergents). An advertiser would never want the same person on the air selling a competing product. Never assume you know what all the conflicts are. There can be surprises. For instance, you might not realize that a detergent has a whitener in it, creating a conflict not only with other detergents but with other products containing whiteners.

  When you accept a job you will enter into a contract in which the conflicts are unwritten, yet you are legally responsible to be free of them.

- If there is any food involved. If so, ask if you will be required to eat the food. Never attend a food-related audition (when eating is involved) if you cannot eat the food. If, for instance, you are a vegetarian and the commercial involves eating a pepperoni pizza at the shoot, you will not be able to pick the pepperoni off.

■ How the commercial is going to run. Terms like *network, regional, spot, test, dealer, seasonal, cable,* and *Internet* give you some indication of how much play the commercial will receive (see Chapter 13, How Much Can I Make?).

■ What to wear. If an agent doesn't know, consider the product being advertised and who you are in the spot, then dress for that part.

The Day of the Audition

WHAT TO WEAR

Dressing for the part improves your chances of getting the job. Most of the time you are given instructions as to what to wear as part of the breakdown. If you're supposed to be at a party, dress up a bit. If you're supposed to be cleaning a bathroom, dress more casually. If you are told you are a doctor, a paramedic, or a construction worker, dress for the part.

The breakdown might not give you detailed wardrobe preferences. It might just indicate that you should wear casual, clean, and comfortable clothes. Jeans are okay, but stay away from all-white clothing. White causes the camera lens to close down, making you dark and hard to see.

Don't wear all black either. Black is a serious, dramatic color, contrasting with the happy, playful energy of most commercials. If, however, black is called for by the character (such as a poet at a reading, or a guest at a cocktail party), *do* wear black. Otherwise, wear colors that enhance your skin tones, making you look fresh and healthy.

Men, regarding necklaces—stay consistent to the character. Gold necklaces can be interpreted as slick. This would be inconsistent with a character such as a warm dad, guy-next-door, or anyone portraying vulnerability. If you wear an earring, wear it if you feel the character you are auditioning for would actually wear one—for example, if the character is a musician, a slacker, or someone with an edgy "street" attitude.

WHAT TO EXPECT WHEN YOU GET THERE

Be on time or, even better, be ten to fifteen minutes early. This will give you time to find which room your audition is in, relax, warm up your voice, and look over your script (if applicable). Come in with a positive attitude, knowing good commercial technique. Have your headshot/résumé with you in case you are asked for it. The casting director will not always collect it, but always have it with you. Please note: Do not submit a photograph without a résumé properly attached to it (stapled or glued in all four corners and cut to fit your 8×10 picture).

Résumés are important for several reasons. Something on your résumé might catch the casting director's eye and possibly generate a conversation between the two of you. Or, there might be a special skill on your résumé that will interest the casting director for another project he or she is working on.

Many commercial directors also direct film and television. They could look at your résumé and feel you are also right for some other type of project they are directing.

To submit a photo without a résumé shows no respect for yourself as an actor and no respect for the casting director as someone interested in talent.

In the audition's reception area, there will be a SAG-AFTRA Exhibit E sign-in sheet (for union jobs) to fill out, a non-union sign-in sheet that will ask for your agent's phone number and/or your cell phone number, and there might be a size card or sheet that you are required to fill out as well. Whenever casting directors ask for your cell phone number, give them that information. (See fig. 15 for a sample of a size card and fig. 16 for the SAG-AFTRA Commercial Audition Report sign-in sheet.) The size cards might be referred to during the initial casting process and are definitely referred to at a callback.

Always make sure your cell phone number is included on the size card. You want the casting director to be able to reach you directly, if need be. But always keep your safety in mind. Just because you are asked for information doesn't mean you have to give it. You do not want to risk identity theft or other related issues as a result of giving out your Social Security number unnecessarily. Your Social Security

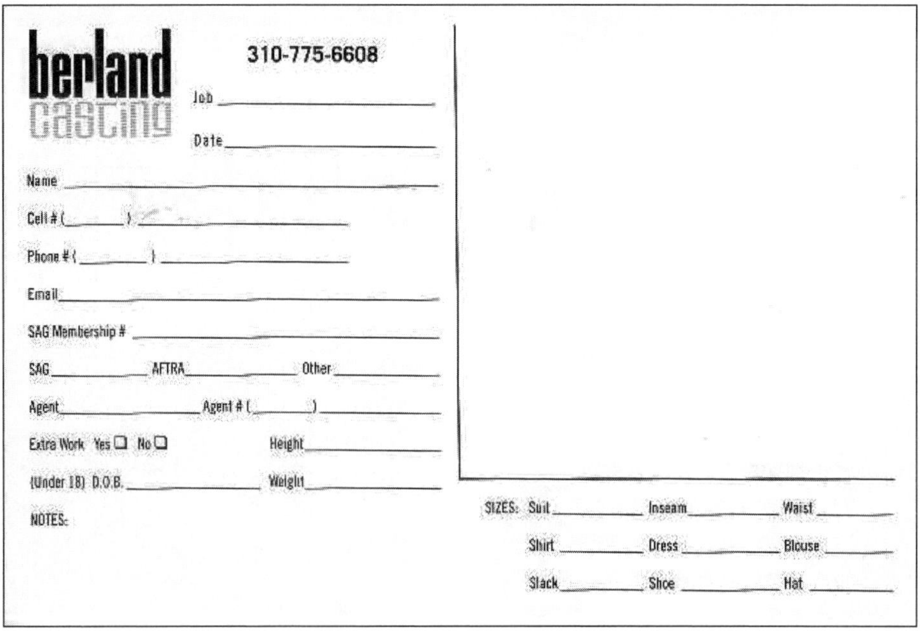

berland casting

310-775-6608

Job _____

Date _____

Name _____

Cell # (_____) _____

Phone # (_____) _____

Email _____

SAG Membership # _____

SAG _____ AFTRA _____ Other _____

Agent _____ Agent # (_____) _____

Extra Work Yes ☐ No ☐   Height _____

(Under 18) D.O.B. _____   Weight _____

NOTES:

SIZES: Suit _____ Inseam _____ Waist _____

Shirt _____ Dress _____ Blouse _____

Slack _____ Shoe _____ Hat _____

FIG. 15: Sample size card.

number is private, *not* public information. The only time you need to give your Social Security number or home address is for final contract and/or payment after you have actually booked the job.

NOTE: After the job is cast, the size cards are thrown into a garbage pail. It has been reported to SAG-AFTRA that garbage disposals have been picked through and the size cards taken by unsavory characters, who then become a nuisance (to say the least) to the actors listed on the cards.

• • •

When you get to the reception room, you may not want to sign in right away. Wait until you have had a chance to freshen up a bit, relax, and look over the script.

EXHIBIT E
SAG/AFTRA
COMMERCIAL AUDITION REPORT   PAGE _____ OF _____

TO BE COMPLETED BY CASTING DIRECTOR

(X) WHERE APPLICABLE ON CAMERA □	PRINCIPAL PERFORMER □ OFF CAMERA □	EXTRA PERFORMER □ TELEVISION □ RADIO □	AUDITION DATE

INTENDED USE

UNION: SAG □   AFTRA □

Person to whom correspondence concerning this form shall be sent: (Name & Phone Number)

CASTING REPRESENTATIVE NAME	COMMERCIAL TITLE - NAME & NUMBER	ADVERTISER NAME
PRODUCT JOB NUMBER	ADVERTISING AGENCY AND CITY	PRODUCTION COMPANY

INSTRUCTIONS: Circle the name of principal performer if known.

* SPANISH LANGUAGE TRANSLATION SERVICES

TO BE COMPLETED BY PERFORMERS

NAME (PRINT)	SOCIAL SECURITY OR MEMBERSHIP NUMBER	AGENT (PRINT)	ACTUAL CALL	TIME IN	TIME OUT	INITIAL	CIRCLE INTERVIEW NUMBER	SEX (X) M F	AGE (X) +40 -40	ETHNICITY (X) AP B C LHNA	PWD (X)
							1st 2nd 3rd 4th				
							1st 2nd 3rd 4th				
							1st 2nd 3rd 4th				
							1st 2nd 3rd 4th				
							1st 2nd 3rd 4th				
							1st 2nd 3rd 4th				
							1st 2nd 3rd 4th				
							1st 2nd 3rd 4th				
							1st 2nd 3rd 4th				
							1st 2nd 3rd 4th				
							1st 2nd 3rd 4th				
							1st 2nd 3rd 4th				
							1st 2nd 3rd 4th				

The recorded audition material will not be used as a client demo, an audience reaction commercial, for copy testing or as a scratch track without payment of the minimum compensation provided for in the Commercials Contract and shall be used solely to determine the suitability of the performer for a specific commercial. AUTHORIZED

The only reason for requesting information on ethnicity, sex, age, and disability is for the talent unions to monitor applicant flow. The furnishing of such information in on a VOLUNTARY basis. The Authorized Representative's signature on this form shall not constitute a verification

Asian/Pacific — AP   Latino/Hispanic — L
Black — B   Native American — NA
Caucasian — C   Performer with Disability — PWD

FIG. 16: Sample sign-in sheet.

Expect the waiting room (fig. 19) to be full of people who are your type. Expect to see a script and/or a storyboard. Dialogue often will appear on the right, and any direction on the left. Read all posted materials, which might include audition direction, callback dates, and shoot dates. Sit down and wait to be called in. Use this time to go over the script and perhaps get familiar with the other actors. You'll tend to see the same people at many auditions, so becoming friendly may be useful.

WHAT TO DO AFTER YOU ARE CALLED INTO THE AUDITION ROOM

In a typical audition room setup (fig. 20), expect to see a camera, a television monitor (which is positioned so the screen is not visible to you), lights, and a cue card. Generally at a first-call audition, the casting director and/or session director would be the only person(s) in the room with you, but many times you may not even meet the casting director. If he or she is not in the room with you, the casting director may watch the audition telecast into his/her office, or watch a recording of it later after the auditions are over.

Read over the cue card first. Get used to the handwriting and the sentence structure, which may be different from your printed script. Keep track of any words that have been changed or added.

THE ACTUAL AUDITION

When you enter the audition room, the person running the session (a casting director or a session director) should give you basic or specific direction regarding the attitude and "read" expected for the particular situation. He may ask you to rehearse once. This way, the session director can give you any adjustments, notes, or "tweaks" he feels are necessary. Then your audition will be recorded. You may hear the following words and phrases during the process:

■ *Take your mark* (fig. 21). There is a mark on the floor; standing on the mark will place you in the proper light and at the correct distance from the camera.

■ *Roll camera.* This means the camera is on and recording your audition.

■ *Slate your name.* Say your name—with personality.

FIG. 17: At a casting facility that has many audition rooms, find your room listed according to product and casting director.

FIG. 18: Find instructions, storyboard, script, sign-in sheet, and size card.

FIG. 19: Waiting room.

FIG. 20: Session director, casting director, cue card.

FIG. 21: Inside studio. On your mark.

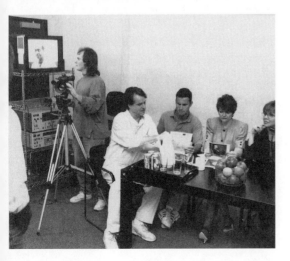

FIG. 22: Callbacks with clients.

- *Profiles, please.* Turn slowly, showing one profile of your face, and then turn your body and face to show the other profile. Remain smiling, showing personality.
- *Action.* This means it's time to say your lines.
- *Cut.* The camera is no longer recording.

You may be recorded once or twice. Do not try to determine whether or not the director liked you based on the number of recordings that were made. The creative team has predetermined how many takes are necessary. The next time you'll hear about the job is when (or if) you get a *callback*. Getting a callback means that you are asked back to read again for (usually) the director and producer from the production company, as well as for the producer, art director, and writer representing the ad agency (fig. 22).

WHEN YOU CAN EXPECT TO BE INFORMED IF YOU GOT THE JOB

Usually, you will know within a few days to a week after the first casting session if you got a callback. Generally, the auditions are completed within four to five days, with callbacks taking place the following week, but this varies considerably.

During this time the actor is put on an "avail" or "first refusal" for the shoot dates. By accepting this "avail," you agree to "hold" open the time to be available for the shoot days, if you are booked.

Two to three days after the callbacks is a preproduction meeting at which the choice of talent is shown to the client for approval. The shoot is generally scheduled approximately three days to a week later. But nothing in this business is carved in stone—you could conceivably get a call to shoot the next day.

When the casting director gets the final okay for the booking from the producer, she then calls the agent (or the talent directly if the talent auditioned without an agent) and books the talent. Since the talent already has cleared the time by agreeing to an avail or first refusal, there should be no question as to the talent being available for the booking.

Seven Elements that Give You the Competitive Edge

Now that you know how the auditioning process works, consider these seven ways to make sure you come out on top:

- KNOW COMMERCIAL TECHNIQUE. Know how to analyze the script quickly and make you and the situation you create in the audition seem one hundred percent real and honest. (Chapter 10 sets out specific techniques for auditioning.)

- MAINTAIN A POSITIVE ATTITUDE. It's not always easy to keep a positive attitude when you walk into a waiting room full of people who look a lot like you and who may have more professional experience.

  Feel the positive force behind you. The casting director wants you to do a good job. (Casting directors are only as good as the talent they bring in.) The agent who represents you believes in you and also wants you to do a good job. (The only way agents make money is from earning commissions from your bookings.).

  Just by getting the audition, you've already passed a screening process. You've been given this opportunity over many, many other people.

  So stay positive throughout the audition, even when the unexpected happens.

- ALWAYS EXPECT THE UNEXPECTED. Things do not always go as planned in this business. Being able to go with the flow is a crucial trait successful actors cultivate. For instance, you may worry when you see the crowded reception area. Chances are the casting director has set up the audition to run smoothly (not to be overcrowded), but some unplanned event has caused a backup. For example, the casting director may have been asked to bring people in four at a time, and then on the day of the audition, the creative team decides to see people two at a time. This will cause a backup. Or, the first group of actors to be auditioned is late, causing a backup.

  Sometimes a backup is unavoidable. The casting director may get a call from the ad agency or production company informing them that the script has changed, or there may be technical difficulties. It is important not to let such happenings affect your attitude. At any audition, you should always seem pleased to be there, from the moment you walk into the room until after you have left the site.

Also, if you sense any negative vibrations in the audition room, focus on the fact that you are not the cause. It could be that the art director and the producer disagree about something creative, or they just got word from their location scout that they lost their favorite location for the shoot, or any number of concerns. Don't assume that it has anything to do with you.

You may find it difficult to keep a positive attitude when you find out how quickly the auditioning process goes. You wish you had more time. Realize that what is asked of you in the auditioning room is all that is needed of you. Don't make yourself crazy trying to analyze your performance after you leave the audition. Just give it your best, then go on to the next thing.

- ALWAYS EXPECT TO BE PUT AT A DISADVANTAGE. Be prepared for such things as the session being canceled. Maybe the character you came in for has been changed. The cue card may be difficult to read. Props that could make it easier for you to audition may not be supplied to you. Do your best to take each thing as it comes without getting visibly discouraged or frustrated. It's all part of being professional in this industry.

- BE FLEXIBLE. Be open to change and direction. For example, you've figured out how you're going to do your copy. You get into the room and the casting director gives you an entirely different set of directions. You must be flexible and say, "Okay."

  If you aren't flexible, when things change, you'll become frustrated and will not be able to give a good audition. Avoid showing frustration and *never* show anger. Do not present yourself in a negative light.

- CONVEY THE FEELING THAT YOU ARE INTELLIGENT. Being knowledgeable about the business and knowing commercial technique lets the creative team know that you are an intelligent professional and serious about your career.

- GIVE THE FEELING THAT YOU HAVE AN UNENDING WELL OF CREATIVITY. Leave the creative team with the impression that you have much more to give, even after the camera has stopped rolling.

10.

The Technique

Getting Started

ENTERING THE AUDITION ROOM

It is important to realize that you are essentially auditioning from the moment you enter the room. Since commercials are basically playful and upbeat, you should walk into the audition room with a positive, happy energy, feeling very pleased. You must be comfortable enough to smile confidently.

Film or television auditions usually last about ten or fifteen minutes: You come into the audition room, chat with the casting director, then get into the mood and read one to four pages of copy. In commercial auditions, the pace is much faster. Your audition will last only about five minutes, its length depending on whether there is copy and how much copy is involved. There is no time to waste.

Be ready to audition as soon as you enter the doorway. Put your personal things down and out of the way. If you are wearing a sweater or jacket that you know you want to take off for your audition, take it off before you get in the room. Avoid making such adjustments once you enter the room. You say your hellos (no handshakes) and walk to your mark ready and eager to receive your direction. You must be comfortable enough to smile confidently.

If you are auditioning with other people, you want to appear comfortable with them right off the bat. Doing so will create a favorable impression with the person directing you, setting the mood for a positive auditioning experience. You also should appear excited and delighted to be there—and why wouldn't you be? This is the moment you've been waiting for, the chance to audition for a commercial spot!

To win at the commercial game, you have to *be* the character one hundred percent. You want to feel as though you are experiencing (or re-experiencing) the situation and avoid appearing "removed." You *must* look completely involved and connected to each commercial scenario. In order to achieve this, the first thing you must be familiar with is the space you are given to work with.

COMMERCIAL SPACE

You have a certain amount of space to work with in front of the camera. It is very different from space used in film, theater, and television. It *certainly* is smaller than the space available to you in the other mediums. But there is a way to expand the space, make it feel bigger to work and play in and look bigger to the creatives watching your audition.

The commercial space is like a sandbox. Its parameters seem small, but you can really have fun in it: You can bring a friend into it. You can make sandcastles and mud pies. You can throw sand out of the sandbox or up into the air. You can run into the corners, dig holes and tunnels, and jump up and down in your sandbox. All of a sudden, what you thought was a relatively small space doesn't seem so small. There isn't much room to walk around, but there is plenty of space to play and to release and reveal your personality.

The following exercises will help you see how you can expand the space you are given and give your performance more dimensions. Tape your practice sessions with a video camera and review them afterward.

Exercises

EXERCISE 1

Pretend you are reaching for something on a table. Try doing it two ways: First, stand firmly in place, extend your arm, and pick something up from the table. This shows one dimension.

Now, reach for something on the table by putting one leg in front of the other and tilting forward. This gives the feeling that you have just walked over from somewhere else and have not quite finished getting to where you are going. You are still "in frame" (visible on the monitor) and have given the space more dimension by this forward movement.

While you are giving your small space more dimensions, you are building in time (beats) for yourself—giving yourself opportunities to express your personality. This is important because what the client is buying is your personality.

There's only one way to give yourself time, and that is to be familiar with the space. Giving the space different dimensions helps you gain the edge needed to win in commercials.

EXERCISE 2

While on camera, try looking over to your side. As you'll see when you look at the recording, you have given the viewer the impression that you are looking over at something. You have now expanded the space to another dimension simply by looking slightly off camera.

Now, record yourself looking off camera and laughing at what you see. Look back at the recording and see how your mind conjures up images of what might be going on. Record yourself looking off to the side and appearing curious about what you see. Play this back and see how the viewer might be affected by your performance.

To effectively expand the space, you must really "see" what you are imagining. To do this, you must go into great detail as you imagine each scenario.

BODY LANGUAGE

Try leaning forward and saying something to the camera. See how leaning in implies closeness, creating a sense of intimacy with the viewer. The slightest body tilt can change a relationship on camera.

EXERCISE 3

Work with a friend. Stand next to each other with your bodies facing forward toward the camera. Look at the camera, then look at each other. Now, look back into the camera. Because your bodies face the camera, your primary relationship is with the viewer.

Turn your bodies in slightly toward each other and look at each other. Your primary relationship is now with each other. Keep your bodies turned in slightly toward each other and turn your faces to the camera. Now, the viewer is your secondary relationship. Turn your bodies straight toward the camera again.

Once again, your primary relationship is with the viewer and your secondary relationship is with each other.

It's important to know how your body position can affect your relationship to the camera (the viewer) because you can use your position to enhance your performance. With this knowledge, you have control. You can make certain choices.

Now, stand together and nudge each other with your elbows. Something else happened to the relationship—a sense of mischief or fun, perhaps. The slightest movement can mean something different. In some ways, commercial space is microscopic and unforgiving. Everything you do in this space is important to the message you are conveying.

In the Audition Room

TAKING YOUR MARK

There will be a mark (usually a piece of tape) on the floor for you to stand on (fig. 21). This mark will place you in the position for the best lighting and camera focus during the audition. Positioning yourself on it is called *taking your mark*. Ultimately, you will learn to take your mark, then immediately create a specific sense of place and dimension to your personality. The previous exercises will enable you to do that.

WORKING WITH CUE CARDS

A *cue card* is the script written out in large print on a large sheet of paper (fig. 20). The cue card should be placed so that it is easy to read while looking into the lens of the camera. This makes it easier for your eyes to sweep across the cue card while looking into the camera. In any unionized state, a cue card is required by SAG-AFTRA.

Usually care is taken to place the cue card in a position to make it easiest for the actor to see and make eye contact with the camera. Sometimes, however, a cue card is placed in a position that puts you at a disadvantage during the audition. If, for instance, someone places the cue card underneath the camera lens, you will have to look down at the card, then up at the camera, then down again at the card, etc. Reading a card that is placed next to the camera lens is much easier. The slight back-and-forth motion of your eyes as you read the cue card and look back to the eye of the camera is acceptable and expected.

If the cue card is placed much too far away from the camera lens and you see it can be easily moved (if it's on an easel, for example), you may ask for it to be moved. Be aware, however, that your request may or may not be received favorably, especially if the casting director is pressed for time.

The cue card stand would really have to be very far away from the camera to ask this. It is not your job to go in and arrange the room to suit your needs. An example of an instance when you might understandably ask for the cue card to be moved closer is if you wear glasses, but forgot them. We are all human and sometimes forget to bring everything we need with us, but try never to forget something as important as your glasses, especially when going to an audition.

Think of the cue card as your friend. You can emote expression toward the cue card as opposed to searching in your memory bank and your eyes looking blank.

As soon as you enter the audition room, look over the cue card. Make sure you can read the handwriting. Look for any changes in the script. A word may have been changed. Being comfortable with the cue card will make it easier to move your eyes smoothly from the cue card to the eye of the camera. Try to look at the camera as much as possible.

Here's what you can do to practice:

EXERCISE 4

On a large piece of paper (from a 24×18-inch artist's pad, for instance), write down copy taken from a magazine ad. On a separate piece of paper, draw a circle approximately the size of a camera lens and place it next to the copy. Position both sheets of paper at eye level on a wall in front of you. This will simulate cue card copy and the lens of the camera. Practice moving your eyes from the copy to the lens (eye of the camera).

MEMORIZING COPY

If you are auditioning in New York, Chicago, or Los Angeles (where cue cards must be provided under SAG-AFTRA rule), it is best not to waste energy trying to memorize your script. If you memorize the script and words are changed on the cue card, it could throw you off.

Another problem can surface if you haven't completely memorized the material; Your eyes can go blank as you try to remember the words. The cue card is there so you don't have to be concerned with remembering the script. Your energy can best be put to use preparing your character, analyzing the script, and making your performance as real as possible.

RELATING TO THE CAMERA

A big difference between auditioning for commercials and auditioning for television and film is that for commercials you want to look into the eye of the camera as much as possible, but in on-camera auditions for television and film, you should not look into the camera at all.

When auditioning for commercials, think of a laser beam running from your eye to the center of the camera lens, into the back of the television monitor, and out through the monitor to the person viewing the audition. The way for you to relate to the camera is to look directly into the "eye" or center of the lens. Relate to the camera the way you would to a long-cherished friend you are extremely familiar with, hang out with, have no secrets from, and have had a lot of laughs and escapades with.

You want to come across as open, friendly, and approachable. It's easier to avoid being intimidated by the camera if you pretend it's someone or something you feel warm, friendly, and familiar with. The camera will no longer be a cold, intimidating piece of plastic and metal if it's your very best pal, or your favorite aunt. Make the camera someone you can be vulnerable with, someone you can let your personality out to.

Unless otherwise indicated, talk to the camera as if you are talking to one person. Keep in mind that if you have a background in theater and stage, you may tend to be too "big," projecting your character and lines the way you would on stage when you are performing for a theater full of people. In commercials, you need to have a one-to-one relationship with the camera, as you do when you are talking with someone who is right next to you.

HOW YOU ARE "FRAMED" (HOW YOU LOOK IN THE CAMERA)

For auditions, assume that you are framed from the mid-chest up or waist up. Never ask, "How am I framed?" You do not have to be concerned with the technical aspects of the audition. You should be acting from head to toe, no matter how you are framed.

If, for instance, you are supposed to appear tired, not only should your face look fatigued, your body language should say, "I'm tired," as well. Your responsibility is to act properly within the context of your mark.

Generally, the person directing you will be standing somewhere near the camera. The monitor will be facing him. He can either look and talk directly to you, or he can look at the monitor while talking to you. The director usually looks at the monitor because things look different on the monitor than they do to the naked eye. Viewing the monitor is the same as viewing the playback auditions.

Before the camera starts rolling, if the director speaks to you and relates to you while looking at the monitor, the way to relate to (or look back at) him is to look directly into the eye of the camera. If, however, the director looks at you while speaking to you, look at him when you speak to him. But as soon as the camera starts rolling, relate directly to the camera's eye.

When the camera is rolling and someone interviews you from off-camera, ask the director if you should respond by looking directly into the camera or off camera. Usually, the answer will be into the camera. It's okay to ask, just to be sure.

In two-person auditions, the person running the camera wants to frame the shot so that both actor's faces can be seen clearly with the shoulder and chest areas visible. The chest area indicates the energy of the whole body. In commercials, body language is important. The following exercise will help prepare you for two-person auditions.

EXERCISE 5

Stand about four feet from a friend. Notice that on the monitor you appear to be much farther apart. You appear unfriendly. Now stand close together, facing the camera with your arms slightly brushing. Generally, this position might feel a bit too close for comfort (perhaps even a bit intrusive). On the monitor, however, you look comfortably close and friendly.

Usually you will get a chance to rehearse before the camera starts rolling. Rehearse (out loud) the way you plan to do the commercial for the camera. That way, the person directing you can give you any adjustments or notes (changes in the way the material is to be presented).

As an actor, it is important that you be open and willing to take direction. Do not comment on or critique any direction you may be given. Be accommodating when you are given adjustments, maintaining your positive attitude the entire time you are in the audition room. Be careful that your nerves are not interfering with your listening abilities. You should be like a piece of putty, molding yourself to the director's instructions. After you do what is asked of you, you may suggest doing it again, incorporating an idea you have.

In some cases, you might not get a rehearsal because something totally spontaneous is desired. If this happens, just try to relax and give it your best shot.

SLATING YOUR NAME

The first thing you'll be asked to do after the camera begins rolling is to *slate* your name. This means you say your full name. During the slate, you should smile and look very pleased to be there. Your personality should already be radiating energy, flowing up through your body and out to the viewer.

When you slate, look right into the eye of the camera and speak clearly with an upbeat, positive attitude. After you say your name, maintain your smiling, happy persona for a solid beat (a moment) while continuing eye contact with the lens. Staying with the camera a beat or so after slating gives you a moment to collect your thoughts before you begin to deliver the script. It also gives the viewer a chance to hear and register your name and face.

Good Slate: A good slate involves keeping solid eye contact with the camera before, during, and after the slate. It means maintaining a consistent, upbeat attitude. Basically, what you're saying as you slate is, "I'm really pleased to be here."

Bad Slate: One way to get a bad slate is to let your eye dart over to the side. This makes you look nervous, not confident. The same is true if you allow your eyes to look down toward the floor and back up. This looks as if you are insecure and don't know how to use the camera.

If you are slating with another person, the second person should wait a full beat before saying his or her name. In a two-person shot, sometimes the person directing you might point to you when it's your turn to slate. Sometimes, on a tighter shot, you'll notice that the camera will be on the first person slating, then move over to the second person.

Here's what you can do to improve your slating technique:

EXERCISE 6

Practice slating in front of the camera. While you are saying your name, dart your eyes off to the side (off camera).

As you play back the tape, notice how distrusting you look when you do this. If you were to say hello to a friend, then dart your eyes away, it would appear to your friend that you were hiding something or that you were distracted. This is exactly what happens if you dart your eyes off to the side while slating.

TRUTH IN THE EYES

The eyes are very important in this medium. They can make you come across as truthful and trustworthy—a must in commercials. To do this, create active, detailed visuals that give the effect that you are actually seeing something.

EXERCISE 7

Practice looking blankly into the camera, then create a visual, a mental image, that represents something delicious to look at. See every detail of the visual you choose. When playing the tape back, notice the difference in your eyes when you give yourself an effective visual. Truth in the eyes can give you the competitive edge, making the difference between booking and not booking the job.

VISUALIZING AND REACTING

Your reactions allow you to show specific, individual attitudes and personality. You want to create opportunities to show attitudes in your audition. One way is by reacting to something after you look at it.

Remember to *look . . . see . . . react . . .* whenever you are given the opportunity to visualize something. It is not enough just to *look*. Actually *see* what you are looking at. You do this by using the sensory and visual exercises presented in this section.

Then it's time to *react*.

EXERCISE 8

Imagine you're looking at a dog licking a baby's face. See the baby in vivid detail. See him laughing. See what he looks like, what he is wearing, etc. See him sitting on the carpet. Notice the color of the carpet. See the puppy in complete detail. Finally, see the puppy licking the baby's face. React. Chances are, after giving yourself visuals like these, you will be smiling and reacting with certain facial expressions. These reactions let special traits—your unique personality—come out.

Don't be afraid to take the time to really *look* at the visuals you've created. Some people don't take enough time to really *indulge* in that beat. You must allow yourself to get into the moment and really experience it. You want to expand the space you are given. Give it dimension and apply your personality.

It is very important to create visuals for yourself. No matter how much direction you receive from the script or the director, you must keep giving more and more information to yourself. *Sensory practice* involves pulling from memory the visuals and feelings you need to project in order to do an effective job with the script.

Sense memory exercises involve recalling sensations of touching, feeling, and smelling that are stored in the memory. When you recall them, you are recreating an actual experience of these sensations, rather than coming from a purely made-up reaction.

EXERCISE 9

Close your eyes. "See" a glass of water on the table. Sit in front of the glass of water. Create a situation in your mind that will make you feel very thirsty. Maybe you've just finished jogging in hot weather. You can't wait to quench your thirst with a cool, refreshing drink of water. Now, open your eyes and "see" the water. Reach for it, drink it, and allow yourself to indulge in the feeling of satisfaction. Look, see, react.

Develop your ability to use visuals and sensory work (drawing on all five senses to realistically recreate an experience) to fine-tune your auditioning skills. Strive to get to a point where you feel you're actually there: jogging in the heat, seeing the puppy and the baby—whatever the scenario.

Everything must seem honest. If you mime reaching for a glass, your hand should look as if you are picking up the glass. Your arm should show intention, moving toward the glass like you intend to pick it up. If you are picking up a piece of pizza, your hand should look like you are actually picking up and holding the pizza. You might even use the other hand to hold up the end of the slice to prevent imaginary cheese from sliding off.

When picking up something small, like a tiny piece of chocolate, your hand and fingers should be positioned as they would be if you were really doing it. Practice on-camera reaching for many different objects, from very small items to larger, bulkier things.

EXERCISE 10

- *Think about sucking a lemon. Close your eyes. See the lemon being cut. Bring it to your mouth and suck on it. Feel your mouth start watering and puckering up from the tart sensation of the lemon juice hitting your taste buds.*

- *Open up a can of cat food. Really smell the odor of the cat food.*

- *Reach for a little piece of candy. Watch how your hand holds it. Think about the way the candy will taste when it gets to your mouth. Put the candy into your mouth and savor the rich, delicious flavor.*

- *The winning lottery numbers were just posted. Pick up your lottery ticket. Begin rubbing off the numbers, one by one. Feel the excitement build as you realize that each of your numbers matches one of the winning digits. React to the realization that you have just become a lottery millionaire!*

  Another way to do this exercise is to build up to the moment when there's only one number left (you have all the others). You rub off the last one (the excitement builds), then react to the disappointment of discovering that you did not win after all.

Analyzing the Script

Now that you are familiar with the camera and you have your sense memories warmed up, it's time to learn how to analyze a script (fig. 23). You need to make particular choices, have particular intentions, and stay with your intentions. You need to come from someplace and end up someplace, so you are not performing in a void.

Every script, every improv, every situation in a commercial audition is an opportunity to *express your personality*. Do not think of yourself as selling anything. Your job is to let out your personality within a small working space and in a very short amount of time (fifteen, thirty, or sixty seconds). First, you must understand how the agency uses the script to sell a product.

An ad agency uses you as a vehicle to help sell their product. You should use the script or improv as a vehicle for you to let out or apply your personality to the situation. Ask yourself, "Where are the opportunities within the script to show the agency's creative team various aspects of my personality?"

The three main tools used to sell a product are frustration, put-down, and humor. Generally, an outline of a commercial's "story" that uses frustration and put-down will go like this:

- *Some form of frustration and a problem to be solved are introduced.* Since commercials are generally lighthearted, any frustration shown has humor in it. By adding humor to the situation, you become likable and approachable and the viewer will smile at you.

- *You are finished with the product or situation that is not working anymore.* You are ready to leave/switch.

- *There is a transition in the script at this point.*

- *You discover a new product.* Life becomes grand and your outlook is much brighter.

- *There is a statement about your discovery* and how it has changed your situation.

- *A put-down or jab is made toward the other competitive product.*

- *Your satisfaction with the product is restated.*

- *A final comment (called a "button line") ties up the story.* This final statement provides an excellent opportunity for you to release your personality.

My vacation had a very dull beginning./Don't get me wrong,/
Florida's wonderful./But I came down on the airline with no
movies./2 ½ hours of looking out the window –/very boring./
I'm going back on National Airlines./The only airline with
movies in every cabin of every wide-bodied plane./Why be
bored on an airline with no movies/when you can say,
"National Airlines, take me. I'm yours."

FIG. 23: Breaking down the script.

Fig. 23 shows an example of a very basic commercial script. Use
the following steps to analyze this script.

■ *Read the script over* to get familiar with the material.

■ *Identify what the script is selling.* In this case, the "product" is National
   Airlines. It is important to know that you are not expected to "sell"
   the product. The commercial script is designed to do the selling. All
   you have to do is let out your personality.

The *sell line* is the first line that mentions the product name.
Underline this sentence—in this case, "I'm going back on National
Airlines." This does not mean you are expected to hit it hard or to sell
hard. Underlining the sell line just lets you see where the sell comes in.

Notice also the frustration that comes just before the sell. It builds
so that when you introduce the discovery of the product, there is a
sense of relief from your frustration. This sets up the sell. The delivery
of the sell is relatively simple. You simply become delighted and
brighter or have a feeling of conviction because you have discovered
this wonderful product.

■ *Find any specific "sell" information.* Don't fall into the trap. You will notice
   that there is not a lot of sell information in this script. The applicable
   line in this case is, "The only airline with movies in every section of
   every wide-body plane." The sell information usually comes right after
   the introduction of the product. Put a box around this area so you can
   see it clearly. The trap is to lose your personality and start sounding like
   a spokesperson. Stay in your personality while saying the lines.

■ *Find any put-down lines.* In this script, "Why be bored on an airline with no movies" is a direct put-down to those other inferior airlines. Sarcasm would be a good attitude to apply here.

■ *Divide the script into "beats," or moments of emotional or attitude change.* Label each beat or attitude change with a slash mark (/).

Commercial copy is just like any short scene in a film. In a very short amount of time you need to present yourself very specifically. This includes conveying the feeling of being very connected to the material (the "Who am I?" and "Where am I?").

You are not given much information; you need to be somewhat of a sleuth and find it yourself. An actor would never consider himself as having given a good performance in a film—even if he only had to deliver four lines—without having presented himself as a specific character with a feeling of connection to the entire scene.

The secret of delivering commercial copy *well* is to be knowledgeable that a commercial is a scene that requires the basic elements of acting.

As mentioned earlier, in an on-camera commercial audition you will want to look directly into the camera. Treat the camera as though it is the person you are talking to, or a third person. Television and film auditions are very different. You do not look directly into the camera. You treat the camera as though it is nonexistent.

Auditioning for commercials is also very different than the actual shoot. When the commercial is actually shot, you will not be looking directly into the camera.

In your audition you will want to show a lot of emotional changes within the context of the script. Think in terms of creating a woven piece of material. Each change of emotion or attitude represents weaving a different color into the material. In this case, the more colors, the prettier the end result. Although you want to make strong choices, it's more effective to make changes with smooth transitions.

In a commercial script you can pretty much find a slight emotional change wherever there is a comma, a period, or any other punctuation (and sometimes somewhere in between). The arrows in fig. 23 indicate emotional changes. Down arrows indicate frustration. Up arrows indicate feeling bright. Forward arrows are a cue to the actor to speak with more conviction. Double underlined words are to be "punched up" (with more personality).

Markings such as these are individual. Develop your own system of markings so that a script has meaning for you.

- *Divide the script into a beginning, a middle, and an end.* Doing so helps you realize that a basic script is not very long. Take it one step at a time. You'll notice that, in fig. 23, the beginning has only three beats, the middle has five, and the end only two. Tackle each section in the same way you would undertake skiing down a large mountain. Instead of looking at the enormity of the task of getting to the bottom, break the mountain up into smaller sections, then traverse one section at a time. Before long, you find that you have accomplished your goal with relative ease.

- *Decide where you are physically.* Then use active visuals, not passive ones. For example, an active visual would be running on a beach and feeling exhilarated. Just sitting on the beach and feeling nothing is passive. You want your audition to feel real—to be multidimensional. If you don't specifically come from someplace and go someplace, you are in a void.

In this case you could choose the airline terminal. See what it looks like in great detail and hear its sounds.

- *Define your attitudes,* using very strong visuals. Create a very real situation for yourself. You should appear as if you are either experiencing what is happening or are re-experiencing the situation. Make particular choices. Have specific intentions, and stay with your intentions.

- *Establish relationships.* Know who (or what) you have a relationship with in the script. Give them (or it) a detailed history. Remember to stay playful (unless the script clearly calls for something different).

In this script, relationships are with (a) National Airlines, (b) the people you were with when you were in Florida, and (c) the person you are telling your experience to.

It is best to choose one particular person to speak to—someone you are extremely familiar with and with whom you can be loose and playful.

If an idea comes to you that is not consistent with your personality, don't stop yourself. Use it. Be open to discovering and exposing the many layers of your personality.

The following are examples of active visuals that will help you prepare for attitude changes. The script has been broken down into beats.

My vacation had a very dull beginning/

This opening expresses a sense of frustration. Think about how you will create that sense of frustration within yourself. And even though you are frustrated, you must also give the viewer the sense that you are likable and playful.

For instance, think about the way you would feel if you planned a vacation in Florida and it didn't go the way you had envisioned. You were going to surf in crystal-blue waters. You could actually *see* yourself riding the crest of the waves with the sun reflecting off your fabulously tanned body. This was your dream vacation and you couldn't wait to go, but when you actually got there, it *rained*. You found yourself in your hotel room with nothing to do. What a bummer.

Visualize the entire scenario. *Be* there. Coming from this visual, you can really say the line with frustration. You can *feel* the frustration.

Don't get me wrong/

Make your attitude a little brighter. You are coming out of frustration, and relating directly to the viewer.

Florida's wonderful/

Your attitude is even brighter now. Visualize what you like about Florida—the huge waves and the beautiful, clear water.

But I came down on the airline with no movies/

You're going back into a sense of frustration. Think of it raining. Sitting in the hotel. You are stuck inside. You have one week of vacation and it's *raining*.

2½ hours of looking out the window/

Now you're going deeper into frustration. Think of yourself sitting in the hotel room. Think of all the things that are going wrong. As you say the line, look three-quarters away from the camera as if you are looking out a window. *Look, see, react.* Then turn back to the camera and react with humorous boredom and frustration:

Very boring/

Your frustration is deepening. Your whole vacation is ruined. It's so bad that it's funny. You're setting up the typical sell–frustration right before the discovery of the product that will make everything right again.

You are now going into the transition of the script. You are finished with the things that don't work and you have made your decision to change to something that does work. You have definitely changed course.

I'm going back on National Airlines/

This is your sell. This is brighter. You have your solution. You've made a discovery. Keep in mind that brighter doesn't mean louder or even big and happy. To hit hard on the sell line is old-fashioned. You can be empathetic, knowing, or enlightened.

To prepare your attitude, you might imagine that you are trying to book a flight to sunny Florida. You call one airline and get a recording—you can't get a human being to come to the phone. You call a different airline and are cut off in the middle of the call. A third attempt to yet another airline finds you put on hold indefinitely. Finally, you call National Airlines and a customer-service representative picks up the phone and helps you right away. Life becomes so much easier.

The only airline with movies in every cabin of every wide-bodied plane/

This statement reinforces the prior statement.

Why be bored on an airline with no movies when you can say . . . /

Here is the put-down. You are being condescending to the other airlines.

National Airlines, take me. I'm yours! (end)

This is the button line. You can make it coy, big, embarrassed, shy—whatever you want.

After you finish your last word, look into the "eye" of the camera for a solid moment, with a final expression. This is usually a subtle expression seen in your eyes. This is called a "button."

The following techniques can be applied to almost any script you're working through:

■ Find humor.

■ Use active visuals.

- Experience and re-experience the situation.
- Find visual references—*look, see, react.*
- Deliver the script as though you are talking to your best friend.

Don't beat yourself up if you didn't get every word right during the audition. Although you should try to get the words right, that's not what the audition is all about. You can make a mistake and still book the job. It will be obvious to the people selecting you that you are good, but your tongue got tied. You will probably be asked to do it again. If you keep messing up again and again, however, you probably won't get booked.

Leaving the Audition Room

Be sure to leave the audition room the same way you walked in—looking confident, positive, and happy to have been asked to audition. Thank everyone for bringing you in and don't criticize yourself. You have performed; you let it out, now let it go. You've given a good audition. Now it's time to find out how the selection process works.

11.

The Selection Process

The Creative Team

It's time to meet a commercial's creative team and find out what part they play in the selection of talent. It takes at least eight people to decide who gets the job. Here's who they are:

The *producer* is responsible for putting together and keeping together all the elements that make up the production of a commercial. These elements include budgeting, selecting the director, coordinating the decisions of all the people involved, and making sure the production is on schedule, including the editing of the final spot.

The producer has a say as to who will be booked. If a producer knows your work and requests that the casting director include you in the audition, the casting director will definitely do so. It is a big plus when a producer is familiar with your work.

The *art director* is the person who visually conceives the spot and makes it come alive through drawings and visuals. In short, he or she is responsible for the way the commercial will look. The art director works very closely with (or is part of the team with) the writer.

The *writer* puts the message of the commercial into words. The writer and art director have to be in total alignment about the message they want to get across.

The *creative supervisor* oversees the activities of the art director, writer, and producer.

The *creative director* is responsible for the work of all creatives in the advertising agency, and thus sets the tone for the entire agency. (An agency's tone might be "on the cutting edge," "hip," "conservative," etc.)

The *director*, of course, directs the spot. The director is hired for his creative input—his ability to enhance the spot. Many times, at the end of the creative selection process the director ultimately decides who will be presented to the client.

The *account executives* from the advertising agency serve as the liaisons between the client and the agency. It is their ongoing responsibility to talk directly to the client. Their assessment that the client will probably "buy" the actor at the preproduction meeting is essential.

The *clients* are the executives who represent the product being advertised, be it Pepsi, Apple computers, or Discover Card. All selections of talent are presented to them at a preproduction meeting and they have final approval. The account executives are sometimes called "the suits.")

How the Talent Are Selected

The creative team collectively decides who would be best for the job, and the client makes the final decision (fig. 24). The casting director has very little to do with the actual selection process after the auditions are completed, although she might be asked to comment on a specific talent's acting ability and performance ability.

Realize that the creative team is trying to be just that—creative—and turn out a nice piece of film. At the same time, they need to sell the product, meet legal specifications, and anticipate the client's tastes— knowing that, ultimately, it's the client they have to please. The client has to approve the final look and production of the spot as well as the actor(s).

Always keep in mind that the decision-making process is very subjective. The writer, for instance, might think that your type of face is not the type that would be cleaning floors in the kitchen—that you look more upscale and would more likely be dressed up at a cocktail party.

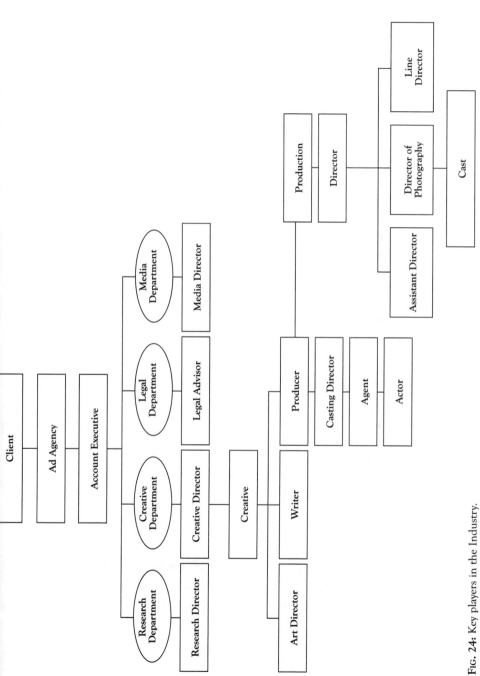

Fig. 24: Key players in the Industry.

The producer, however, might feel that your face *doesn't* look upscale. Or perhaps the producer may not want you simply because you look like his ex-wife. It happens.

The one thing you have control over is your ability to audition well, and this is the factor that will give you the competitive edge in the long run. All you can do as an actor is give a good audition. Once you've done that, it comes down to a "look" and people's subjective opinions.

Many times, the way you are asked to audition has very little to do with how the final spot is actually done. You may be asked to do a broader range of emotions at the audition than when the spot is shot. The team needs to know that you are capable of handling whatever they throw at you. The day of the shoot is very demanding, so the creative team shies away from booking actors who are fairly one-dimensional. Thus it pays to expand your technique to show many dimensions.

Who Sees the Auditions during the Selection Process

After the audition, one copy of the audition is viewed by the creative team. A copy is sent to the director to view. This happens very quickly. At the end of the audition day, the audition session is sent via the Internet to all the people who have a voice in the selections. Once the selection process occurs, certain actors are then called back for another audition.

The selection lists of the agency and director are generally compatible. Both lists of talent are called back. If the two lists are significantly different, the agency will realize that the director is envisioning the commercial in a way that is not consistent with theirs and will call the director to discuss his choices.

If the director is seeing the spot in a different way than the agency envisioned, the callback is a good time to see what is working and what is not.

The Callbacks

All callback choices are auditioned again. The director is there to direct the actors. The writer, art director, and producer are also there to experience the actors' performances. They want to see how well each actor takes direction, to envision how each actor fits into the original ad concept, and to see what each actor brings to the concept. Final choices are made. Following is an example:

The commercial involves a family consisting of a mom, a dad, and two teenaged daughters. Instant photos of each actor are laid out on a table as a quick visual reference. The two daughters tentatively chosen are blond cheerleader types. Next to those two choices are two alternate teenaged daughters. One is blond; the other is brunette and "edgier" than the blondes. The art director says, "Look what happens if we replace one blond teenager with the brunette." Because of the differences created by the alternate daughter, the family dynamics have changed. The team decides this combination of teenaged daughters is more interesting, so the brunette gets booked instead of the second blonde.

The decision was not based on the actress's performance. All performances were good. The final selection came down to a viewpoint concerning the *feeling* the creative team wanted to project with the look of the family. With all performances being good, the final decision can also come down to an actor's essence. The actor can be too funny, not funny enough, too urban, too suburban, etc.

The creative team picks their first choices and backups, and then an edited version of the selected callbacks are sent back to the ad agency right away (via the Internet) by the creative supervisor, creative director, and the account executive for approval before presenting to the client.

Presenting the Callbacks to the Client

Finally, the commercial's preproduction meeting takes place, with as many as twenty-two people present. Every aspect of the production day is discussed, including the final selections of talent. The creative team presents their first choice of actors to the client, showing the callback on a monitor. With luck, the client nods his approval and the producer calls the casting director, giving the okay to book the talent. All personalities involved in the selection process are satisfied. Whew! What a feat.

Time between the Final Selection of Talent and the Shoot

Casting is the last element to fill before the shoot. Usually, casting begins the week before the actual shoot date. Callbacks could be two days after the first call, and the shoot three days after the callbacks. However, there are no rules. Many times the shoot will be the day after the callback. If there are multiple spots with many characters to cast, the time between the first call and the callback could be a week or two.

Understanding the History of a Commercial

As an actor, you must realize that each commercial has a "history" that the creatives help to develop. The history might consist of where the family in the commercial comes from, as well as their interests, relationships, and economic state. The type of furniture the family would own (including the type of fabric on their sofa) is indicated, along with the type of clothing each family member would wear, and how they relate to one another.

It is amazing how effective commercials can be, especially since they are only fifteen seconds to one minute long. In that short span of time, a commercial can create a myriad of emotions—sadness, envy, joy, humor, and curiosity.

In many ways, the commercial is the ultimate form of storytelling. In just thirty seconds we meet characters, identify with their struggle, then watch them change and grow in a narrative complete with introduction, climax, and resolution. Moreover, the advertiser accomplishes the task of showing us that, like the characters in the story, we too can solve our dilemmas, look smarter, be healthier, and otherwise have an easier life by purchasing the advertised product.

Now that you are familiar with the people who create, direct, and produce commercials and have an understanding of how talent is selected, it's time to give you a more extensive look at what to expect concerning callbacks, bookings, and commercial shoots.

12.

The Callback, the Booking, the Shoot

The Callback

Congratulations! You have given an impressive audition and the creative team has called you back to have another look.

Callbacks may involve as many as ten to twenty actors per character. The good news is there are more opportunities to get called back. The bad news is, there is more competition.

Keep a positive attitude. Keep feeling special. You *did* get called back. Always keep in mind the positive energy force behind you. Everyone wants you to do a good job. Certainly, the casting director who called you in—and your agent—want you to do well at the callback. And the creative team viewing the session wants lots of good choices to consider.

Now the selection process begins again, and the same subjectiveness applies as in the auditions.

INFORMATION YOU SHOULD BE GIVEN WHEN YOU GET THE CALLBACK

When you get the email, text, or phone call to notify you of a callback, you should receive the following information. If you don't, *ask*.

- WHEN AND WHERE THE AUDITION IS BEING HELD: If you do not know how to get there, go to your computer and log on to the MapQuest website (www.mapquest.com). You don't want to be late. It's a good idea to get the phone number of the place you're going to, so if you *do* get lost, you can call to get instructions.

■ THE SHOOT DATES: You might be put on *avail* (availability) or *first refusal* for the shoot dates, travel days, and weather days. An avail or first refusal is a handshake agreement made among the actor, the agent, and the casting director by which the actor guarantees that the client will have first option on his time on the specific dates set aside for the commercial shoot. This way, when the creative team sells the actor to the client at the preproduction meeting, and the client says yes, the casting director can book the actor with every confidence that the actor will be available and will accept the booking.

If another client wants to book the actor for the time of the avail or first refusal, the actor's agent has to go to the casting director who has the actor on avail or first refusal. That casting director then has to go to the client, giving him first choice of either booking or releasing the actor. If the client releases the actor, the actor is then free to accept the other booking. (This is referred to as a *book or release* situation.)

■ WHAT TO WEAR TO THE CALLBACKS: You do not have to wear the same clothes you wore when you first auditioned, even if the wardrobe description is the same as for the first call. If, for instance, the first call was casual and so is the second, you would still wear casual clothes, but you could wear a different outfit. Of course, if you are asked to wear the same thing you wore for the first audition, do so. Many actors like to wear the same thing for added recognition in relationship to their first audition. Some talent feel if the outfit worked the first time, why mess with it, keep it the same.

Sometimes, however, the situation changes. For example, the creatives might have chosen you for a different character from the one you first auditioned for. You could be asked to dress differently.

■ HOW THE SPOT RUNS (IS AIRED[1]): You should have been told at the original audition how the spot was running. At this point, the information should be reiterated. You might hear terms such as *national, network, spot, dealer, cable, seasonal, regional, New Media,* and *Internet* (see Chapter 13, How Much Can I Make?).

■ TYPE OF CONTRACT: You might also hear the term *standard*. This means the contract remains as written with nothing crossed off

---

[1] The places it runs are referred to as markets.

the back. On the back of your contract (in small print), there is a section that gives the client the right of use for theatrical (in movie theaters), foreign, new media, Internet, and cable at scale payment. This is a very acceptable practice and should not create a problem for the actor.

■ MONEYS AND PAYMENTS INVOLVED: If there are moneys involved other than scale (basic union usages), this is a good time to confirm the amount to avoid possible misunderstandings at the time of booking or at the shoot, when you are signing your contract.

There could be, for example, situations in which monies are guaranteed per *cycle* for the actor. A cycle is thirteen weeks. This means that the actor would receive an agreed upon amount of money (guaranteed) every thirteen weeks. (For more on talent payment, see Chapter 13, How Much Can I Make?)

■ CONFLICTS: The actor cannot be under contract for a conflicting product.

WHO WILL BE AT THE CALLBACK

Part or all of the creative team will be at the callback to direct and observe the actor. Among the people who might be present are the *producer* from the ad agency, the *writer*, the *art director*, the *director from the production company*, and the *production company producer*.

It is common to have at least five people watching you audition at the callback. The person who will actually be directing the shoot (the director) will most likely direct during the callback. This gives him the opportunity to see how flexible you are and to see if you and he can get along well. It also gives the director a chance to see how his concept of the direction will work. It's unlikely that he'll go heavily into this at the callback, but he will get a sense of what is (or is not) working.

Many times, the director will pick something unique to your personality from your performance and build on that with you. Something special in your audition that sparks interest from the director could be the deciding factor in whether or not you get booked.

HOW YOU SHOULD CONDUCT YOURSELF AT THE CALLBACK

It is important to be on time for the callback. Your appointment was scheduled specifically for the director to have a certain amount of time to work with you (and another person if you are paired up with someone for the audition).

Have your picture and résumé with you, in case it is asked for. You will be escorted into the room by the casting director or the session runner and be shown your mark, where you will stand. Do not approach the creatives in the room. Do not shake each person's hand and introduce yourself. Go to your mark, say hello if the creatives are paying attention to you, smile, be open, and wait for your direction.

Many times the creative team pays no attention to you until they are ready to watch your audition. The director will most likely have the casting director direct you and, after your first performance, will then get involved in communicating with you. Even though the very people you are trying to impress are now in the room with you, don't try hard to establish a relationship with them. Know that the best you can do is be open and friendly, listen, take direction, and be flexible. Give a good audition, say your goodbyes (don't go up to anyone and shake their hands), then leave the room with a positive attitude.

WHAT THE CREATIVES ARE LOOKING FOR

What is the purpose of a callback? It's another chance for the creatives to see how actors perform. Naturally, something in your performance may be slightly different from your first one. Callbacks give the creative team time to work with actors to see how flexible they are and how broad a range they have. They can see if there is something special and very personal the actor brings to the performance, and they can watch the actor apply new ideas that the team may have come up with since the first call. If there are two or more actors in the commercial, the creatives can observe the chemistry (or lack thereof) between the actors.

The team determines how much they like the actor personally. Would they feel comfortable working with the actor all day? Is the actor cooperative? Do the actor's eyes have life and sparkle? Does the actor seem intelligent? Does he seem to understand the script? Does she appear natural and genuine?

Don't put pressure on yourself to do anything particularly different. Remember, if you understand the script and the circumstances of the spot you're appearing in, and know your technique, your focus will be on being the character in the scene. As with real life, something a little different might happen—perhaps a slightly different inflection in the voice, a slightly different attitude, or a slightly different movement. You are not expected to act exactly the same as on your first audition. So just be yourself and *do* be spontaneous at the callback.

If the situation calls for two or more people to work together, you might be mixed and matched. You may be called into the audition room with one person, and then asked to wait and come back in the room with another person. Take notice of how your energies and chemistry change with different people.

Sometimes what you are doing will work better with one person than the other. This is normal and expected. If you are called in with someone you do not work well with, it doesn't create the best possible experience. But it also does not mean you won't get booked. If you are doing well but the other person is not good for the spot, the creatives can see it.

No matter what occurs, keep doing your best at the audition. Don't play into the negative energies (or the bad choices) of the other person. Work with the person as much as possible without bringing yourself down. In fact, within the scenario, try to bring the other person's performance up to par.

The Booking

HOW MUCH TIME ELAPSES BETWEEN THE CALLBACK AND THE SHOOT

It can take anywhere from one day to two weeks from the callback to the booking, depending on many, many variables. In a standard situation, the creative team at the callback will make their selections, and then present you at a preproduction meeting approximately one to three days later. Final approval is left to the client (the executives who represent the product). The ad-agency producer then quickly calls the casting director and informs him of who should be booked. The casting director immediately calls the agent and books the talent. No time is wasted; the sooner the casting director gets the actor off of avail or first refusal and booked, less are the chances of losing the actor to another booking.

INFORMATION YOU SHOULD BE GIVEN WHEN YOU ARE BOOKED

The actual booking call consists of giving the actor the shooting's time, date, wardrobe fitting (if applicable), and the location he should report to. An actor can be called by wardrobe before he is booked, but cannot be called in for the actual fitting until after he is officially booked. The terms of agreement (run and usage) and conflicts (if there are any) should be gone over too.

WARDROBE

After the official booking call, the wardrobe person (or stylist) will contact the actor and set up an appointment for the actor to be wardrobed. The stylist already has the actor's sizes from the size card filled out at the audition. Several different outfits will be tried on the actor at the fitting. The fitting usually takes an hour. According to the SAG-AFTRA contract, the actor is paid for a wardrobe fitting. If you are asked to bring and wear your own clothing to a shoot, you are compensated for doing so. If you are booked for a non-union commercial, you could very well not be paid for a wardrobe fitting, or you could likely be asked to bring your own clothing to the shoot. Remember, your rights to payment for services are protected more under the SAG-AFTRA contract.

The Shoot

WHAT IS EXPECTED FROM ACTORS ON THE SET

An actor must have an understanding of the script. She must appear genuine and natural. Sometimes an actor is chosen because she interpreted the script better than anyone else.

When you arrive on the set, you might find that you have been made the core of the scene and the cast will have been built around you. Sometimes the way two actors work together makes things happen. The creative team will have the actors spend a lot of time together on the day of the shoot before they actually start filming, to see what might happen between them. They might then use this relationship for the commercial.

Actors must be cooperative, be prepared to listen, and take direction well. You should come to the shoot with a sense of involvement and energy.

An actor should be aware of the totality of the spot, not just what her little piece involves. You need to know what you are trying to convey and whom the client is selling to. Actors should have their lines memorized beforehand. It's up to the agency producer to get the material to the actors ahead of time so they can memorize it. The script might be given to you at the wardrobe call.

Flexibility is important. Actors must be prepared to make adjustments in their interpretation of the script. In situations where the actor was hired because of his creativity, there will be times when unique spins on the situation will be welcomed.

The two main ingredients in a successful spot are the finest director and the best talent. The spot is nothing if you have a great director and poor talent (or vice versa).

WHAT GOES INTO THE PREPARATION FOR A COMMERCIAL SHOOT

The creative team does a lot of preparation before the shoot. The ad agency draws up storyboards, which the director interprets. Next, a shooting board is drawn up. This is a tightly scripted, tightly drawn board laying out all the shots for the commercial. This is done after considering the input of the clients, the agencies, the account executives, and the director.

The creative team, with the director, blocks out the shots precisely. There are hours and hours of meetings regarding locations, props, and how to shoot the commercial to best capture its theme. Nothing is left to chance. The team also discusses the types of plates, food, clothing, and other props they are going to use.

WHAT IS THE USUAL LOCATION OF THE SHOOT

Actors can be called *anywhere* to shoot. Travel arrangements will be made with their agents. Be on time. If, for instance, you will be traveling by van with the production company and the departing time is 7:30, don't get there at 7:35. Time is crucial on a commercial shoot.

There are times you will have to travel to a shoot out of town. Travel arrangements to fly to a location are made between you and the producer. Under the SAG-AFTRA union contract, you will be compensated for airfare and travel to and from the airport by the production company. If your job is non-union, specific arrangements will have to be made to cover travel to the shoot, parking, etc., at the time of the booking.

WHAT HAPPENS THE DAY OF THE SHOOT

On the day of the shoot, dozens of people are present: the director, producer, copywriter, art director, film/shooting crew, makeup person, stylist, script supervisor (who is responsible for accuracy in keeping with the scripted words), and the clients. Expect to see up to six of the client's people on the site, including marketing managers or product managers.

Remember, the client is an ally; all of his needs should be met. Video monitors are set up off to the side so that everyone can watch the monitor instead of standing around and watching the actor. This helps sharpen the team's eye for what is seen on the TV screen. On a soundstage, headsets are used by everyone watching the monitor to listen to the lines, when it is not possible to hear the actors directly.

WHAT HAPPENS WHEN THE ACTORS FIRST GET ON THE SET

The producer usually introduces himself to the actors first. The agency producer or the second AD (assistant director) will give the SAG-AFTRA contract to the talent at the beginning of the day. This will confirm the start of a particular job. Then, an instant photo is taken of the actors in their wardrobes so the team can refer to it at a later time.

WHAT IS EXPECTED OF ACTORS IN TERMS OF THE CONTRACT

The contract is given to the actors to be signed. They should be aware of the provisions beforehand, including how the commercial is sup-posed to run. All this information has been given to their agent.

Occasionally, the contract could look different from what the casting director discussed with the agent. In this case, the first thing an actor should remember is to maintain a professional demeanor, and then call the agent and explain the situation. The contract differences are then worked out by the agent (sometimes the casting director) and the producer. If you have been booked directly–without an agent–make sure to read over your contract and discuss any differences. It is your right to try to have the production stick to their original agreement.

All initial contract information should be exchanged by email so you have a record to refer back to.

AT WHAT POINT THE PRODUCT IS INTRODUCED TO THE ACTORS

The actors should be familiar with the product being used so that when it is put into their hands, it is not foreign to them. They should be asked at wardrobe whether they have worked with the product—for example, a particular type of razor. If not, they are given the product to become familiar with before the day of the shoot.

A technical advisor will be on the set. If the product is gum, the actor will learn how to load[2] and chew gum; if it's a soft-drink spot, she'll learn how to swallow and use the product in the correct way.

THINGS ACTORS SHOULD AVOID WHILE ON THE SET

When there is down time, actors should observe what is going on, staying within the confines of the set and developing some camaraderie. The worst thing that can happen is for an actor not to be accessible because he is on the phone, texting, emailing, or out eating somewhere. Actors should let the assistant director and the agency producer know where they are at all times. If a shot comes up and an actor is not around, it creates a problem. Also, no family members, pals, or kids should visit the set. In short, the actor should always be there and committed.

The talent should adhere to the provisions of any NDAs (Non-disclosure Agreements) that they have signed. Even if a non-disclosure is not signed, the talent should be cognizant of the fact that the spot they are shooting is a concept that should not be revealed to the competitors or the public until it is released on air (starts running). Absolutely no tweeting about what is going on onset, no emailing about the spot, no taking photos with your smartphone, and no posting about it on Facebook or any other social media until the commercial starts running.

Actors should be polite and courteous, and relaxed and comfortable with everyone on the set. Everyone is counting on them to come through. They are the center of attention for the day, and they have to be comfortable with that.

---

[2] A technical way to put gum into the mouth for a commercial.

Finally, actors should not ask for things on the set. Do not ask, for instance, if you can have the clothing you wore on the shoot. If someone offers to give something to you, that is different.

HOW LONG A COMMERCIAL TAKES TO SHOOT

There is no standard time; a shoot can run eight to sixteen hours a day. How the commercial is being shot is a primary consideration. Factors such as location shooting and special needs (like a sunrise or sunset) all affect a shoot's time. Consideration must also be taken for children (see Chapter 17, Kids in the Business).

There is a union rule requiring a twelve-hour turnaround for the crew. This means that twelve hours must elapse from the time you wrap (end) until you can start again. This may result in a later call for the next day's shoot.

Usually, on a stage, you might have a crew call at 6:30 A.M. with the actors arriving at 7:30 to be put into wardrobe. The shoot might start at 8:30 or 9:00, once lighting is set. A shoot is over when it's over.

If the shoot goes beyond twelve hours, people begin to get tired and wear down. Sometimes, the shoot is scheduled to go into another day, but that is not always possible. The agency producer has the responsibility of keeping things going.

There is always a lot of waiting around on the sets. Different camera setups and shots are required, which result in a lot of down time for actors. A standard shoot day is eight hours. Being budget conscious, it is preferable for a shoot to end before having to pay any overtime. If you are doing a non-union commercial, a typical shoot day is usually ten hours. It is not unheard-of for an agreement to ask for a twelve-hour day.

IS THE COMMERCIAL SHOT IN SEGMENTS?

An actor may shoot the spot from beginning to end in its entirety, or the commercial may be shot in segments. For example, all the *master shots* (wide shots that show the entire scene) may require the same kind of lighting, in which case they'll be shot at the same time. Then the director might jump to a shot that would appear third or fourth in the commercial. All the close-up shots might be done at the same time because afterwards all lighting and lenses must be changed. It's pretty rare for a commercial to be shot from the beginning straight through to the end.

HOW MANY TAKES CAN AN ACTOR EXPECT?

Ad-agency creatives want several different interpretations of the commercial script because they have a lot of people to satisfy. A shoot may involve anywhere from a couple of takes to twenty or thirty. A good actor can endure many takes of specific direction. At some point, though, he hits his performance peak, and then it goes in a different direction.

WHO DIRECTS THE ACTORS? DO THE ACTORS HAVE ANY INPUT?

The director has primary contact with the actors on the set. The director is the sole focal point—the sole voice that actors should be hearing. If someone on the set wants to request something from an actor, the request should go to the director.

Whether or not actors can give suggestions to the director during the shoot involves a lot of tact. There is protocol on the set. Actors should let the director direct, *and then* they may be allowed to offer other interpretations.

Actors should *not* tell the director that they don't like something or don't want to do it. An actor could possibly say, "How about this?" or "Can I try something?" Remember, the actor is hired for his uniqueness. Therefore, his interpretation might very well be welcome, especially in comedy.

13.

How Much Can I Make?

The commercial industry is one of the most lucrative in the entertainment business. Performers from all over the country have financed college educations, upgraded lifestyles, and catapulted themselves into other areas of the business as a result of working in commercials.

A long-running national commercial can net an actor over $200,000. Even a small regional spot pays hundreds of dollars for a single day's work. An actor was in a network commercial for Wrigley's that ran for three years, and he made $90,000. That's for a single day's work. This sort of thing can happen. More often than not, each commercial spot will bring in considerably less. On the other hand, the commercial could be shot, you get your shoot-day payment, and the commercial may not run at all.

Payment for commercial work is determined by factors such as:

- How often the commercial runs
- Whether it runs locally, regionally, nationally, and/or on the Internet
- Whether it is a union or non-union commercial

The non-union agreements can buy you out in perpetuity or for a specified limited amount of time. When you sign an agreement for a non-union commercial, you should be informed as to the time you are agreeing to allow your image to appear in the commercial being used. Of course anything running on the Internet is in perpetuity, by nature.

If you are doing non-union work, you get "bought out," which means you get paid a certain fixed amount of money, and the client owns the spot and can play it as much as they want. You don't get residuals (payments made to the talent every time the spot runs) in such cases. Obviously, the potential earnings from this kind of commercial are limited to the buyout amount. Non-union buyouts can range from $75 to $100,000. The amount of the payment should be posted on any breakdowns you audition for. In addition, always look at paperwork that you will sign, which you should receive before shooting the commercial. Don't shoot the commercial before looking over all the paperwork.

Information to Look For in Paperwork Concerning Non-Union Payments:

- Number of shoot days
- Number of hours for the shoot (usually ten hours)
- Wardrobe fittings
- Where the commercial is running
- How long the usage will be (how long the client has the right to use it)
- How many spots there will be (sometimes additional spots are cut from the original)

Usage rights could include TV, industrial, website, new media, Internet, and print.

With union commercials, however, there are payment rules and regulations that protect the talent—with elaborate systems checked by tracking methods that make sure everything is handled correctly. The following is a look at how performers are paid for work on television and radio commercials.

Television

SESSION

When a commercial is shot, its performers are paid a session fee as compensation for an eight-hour day of work. The session fee also provides the advertiser with the right to use that commercial for thirteen weeks and prevents the actor from doing spots for competitive products for the length of the twenty-one-month contract, unless formally released before the contract expires. To maintain the rights to use the commercial and to "hold" the actor, the actor is paid an additional holding fee every thirteen weeks (see Holding Fees/Exclusivity below).

Following are payments one can receive for working on a commercial under a SAG-AFTRA contract. You can check their current rates on the SAG-AFTRA website: http://www.sagaftra.org.

- A session fee for an on-camera performer for an eight-hour day
- A session fee for off-camera TV performance (a voice-over)

Performers receive a session fee for each commercial produced or each day of work, whichever is greater. For example, if five commercials are recorded in a two-hour session, five session fees must be paid. Session fees are usually fully creditable against reuse fees. Reuse fees are paid every time a commercial airs or is used again after its initial run. "Special provisions" cover any agreement details that do not appear in the standard contract. These include money above scale and special travel arrangements.

Extras are paid a single fee, or *buyout*, entitling the advertiser to the use of an extra's performance in a commercial throughout its broadcast life. In other words, extras do not receive residuals.

- A session fee for an extra performer is based on an eight-hour day.
- The current hand-model buyout fee is also based on an eight-hour day.

OVERTIME

SCALE SESSION FEES (regular union session fees) cover one eight-hour day. If the performer is required to work for longer than eight hours, overtime is paid as follows:

- The ninth and tenth hours are each paid at 150 percent of the scale session fee for one hour (the hourly rate is equal to one-eighth of the eight-hour day session fee). This overtime rate is called "time and a half."
- The eleventh hour and beyond are paid at 200 percent of the scale session fee for one hour. This rate is called "double-time."
- An additional 10 percent must be added to the above hourly rates for performances that take place between 8:00 P.M. and 6:00 A.M. This fee is called a "night premium." It is calculated in fifteen-minute increments. Payments for hours subject to the night premium for

extras are slightly different—an additional 10 percent from 8 P.M. to 1 A.M. and an additional 20 percent from 1 A.M. to 6 A.M.

- Performers are paid 200 percent of scale for weekend and holiday work. Recognized holidays include New Year's Day, Martin Luther King Jr.'s Birthday, Presidents' Day, Memorial Day, Independence Day, Labor Day, Thanksgiving Day, and Christmas Day.

TRAVEL TIME

When performers spend time traveling to or from a location, they are compensated for the time at the same rates by which they are paid for session time. Hourly or half-day rates may apply depending on the time of travel. On a travel day when no services are rendered, the talent is due a minimum scale session fee. When services are rendered on a travel day, they are paid for each quarter-hour if such work time exceeds the eight-hour work day. Travel time on a weekend is one and one-half-times scale.

CONSECUTIVE EMPLOYMENT

Performers who have traveled to location to shoot a single commercial over a series of days and cannot return home in the evening are paid for the intervening time when they are not used. For example: If performers work on Monday and Wednesday but not Tuesday, they are paid a scale session fee for Tuesday in order to hold them for performance on Wednesday.

FITTINGS/WARDROBE

Time spent by a performer in fittings is considered to be session time and is paid as such. For example: If a *principal* (primary) performer spends one hour in a fitting, the payment due would be one-eighth of the scale session fee for an eight-hour day. The performer receives a minimum of one hour's pay for a fitting. Additional time is paid in fifteen-minute units.

HOLDING FEES/EXCLUSIVITY

Advertisers must pay each principal performer a holding fee every thirteen weeks in order to retain the right to broadcast the commercial that features that performer during the following thirteen-week cycle. The holding-fee amount is equivalent to a session fee. The *holding-fee cycle* begins with the earliest date that an on- or off-camera principal works and lasts for thirteen consecutive weeks. At the end of that time the next holding fee is due if a new thirteen-week cycle is to begin.

Holding fees also provide the advertiser with *exclusivity*, meaning that as long as an actor is being *held* to a certain product or service, she may not accept work in any competitive television advertising.

When a commercial is no longer held, the advertiser loses the right to broadcast it and the performer is released from her employment contract and is free to accept competitive commercial work.

Holding fees do not compensate talent for use of the commercial. However, holding fees are fully creditable against the use fees of a commercial.

Maximum Period of Use

The life of a commercial contract is usually twenty-one months with additional use periods obtained through contract renegotiation. During this twenty-one-month period, the rights to continued airing are obtained through the payment of holding fees every thirteen weeks (as described above). At the end of the twenty-one-month use period, the performer has the right to negotiate a new rate.

REINSTATEMENT

In the event an advertiser wishes to use a commercial after the employment contracts run out, the talent agreements must be reinstated. This process includes making sure the principal talent does not have any conflicting SAG-AFTRA contracts for commercials for a competitive product or service, and negotiating a new payment agreement. If the performer has a conflict, he will not be able to enter into a new agreement. To reinstate, the minimum payment is two holding fees, one not applied.

RESIDUALS

In addition to session fees, principal performers are compensated by *residual payments* for the use of commercials in which they appear. There are as many use types as there are ways to broadcast a commercial. Different and complex rate structures determine talent payments for each type, including network use, syndication, wild spot, cable, foreign, dealer, theatrical/industrial, and Internet.

NETWORK USE. Residual payments for network use are based on the frequency of use. Performers are paid for each telecast during a thirteen-week cycle. The first network use date commences the thirteen-week network cycle. Rates are structured on a decremental scale, with the first use being the most expensive and use rates beyond the first decreasing in price per use.

WILD SPOT. Residual payments for wild spot use are based on market weightings attributed to the cities in which the commercial is being broadcast. The unit weightings are based on population. New York, Chicago, and Los Angeles are referred to as *majors*, and because of their populations, they are more heavily weighted. The presence of majors, if any, plus the unit weightings of any additional cities, determines the dollar amount due to the performer. This payment covers unlimited use of the commercial in those markets for thirteen weeks. If additional markets are added mid-cycle, the payment must be upgraded to cover additional units.

CABLE. For commercials used on cable networks, each principal performer is paid each thirteen-week cycle.

DEMOS/NON-AIR COMMERCIALS. There is no exclusivity required of performers in demo commercials. Because there is no exclusivity, no holding fees are paid. In the event a demo spot is upgraded to a broadcast commercial, the talent must be re-contracted under the appropriate scale, with conflicts cleared.

INTERNET USAGE. There are buyout payments for on-camera performers for one year or for an eight-week option. Voice-over performers are paid for one year or for eight weeks.

Voice-Over and Radio

SESSION. Session fees are fully creditable to use fees. NOTE: SAG-AFTRA does not allow agents of performers to deduct their fees from scale earnings. As a result, most radio announcers are paid at scale plus 10 percent for session fees and residuals. (LA performers' rate is usually approximately double the rate.)

EXCLUSIVITY/MAXIMUM PERIOD OF USE

There is no exclusivity for radio performers. Radio performers do not receive holding fees and are free to accept work in competitive advertising during the course of their contract. The maximum period of use or "life" of a radio commercial is twenty-one months from the session date. Additional use periods are obtained through contract renegotiation.

RESIDUALS

Payments to radio performers are made when their commercials air. As with television, there are several different use types and each type has its own rate structure. Some of the different use types are network, wild spot, and dealer use.

NETWORK. Residual payments for network radio are based on the length of the cycle. Network radio cycles can be one, four, eight, or thirteen weeks in length. During the cycle unlimited use is allowed on any network programs on any and all radio networks for a single advertiser. There is also a limited use for thirteen weeks for either twenty-six or thirty-nine uses during the cycle.

WILD SPOT. Residual payments for wild spot use are based on market weightings attributed to the cities in which the commercial is being broadcast. The unit weightings are based on population. The presence of majors (New York, Chicago, and Los Angeles), plus the unit weights of any additional cities, determines the dollar amount due the performer. The payment can be made for either an eight-week or a thirteen-week cycle. The rates for a thirteen-week cycle are slightly higher than those for eight-week cycles. The eight-week cycle is designed to give advertisers a price break for those commercials intended for a shorter term of use.

DEALER USE. This is a flat rate for twenty-six weeks (six months of use) for broadcast time contracted and paid for by the dealer or distributor of a product (versus media buys made by the manufacturer).

The next chapter discusses the pros and cons of working in regional markets and commuting for work, and how to tell when it's time to move on to a larger (or different) market.

COMMERCIAL MADE FOR INTERNET ONLY. On-camera performers are paid a buyout for one year or for eight weeks.

Voice-over performers are paid a different amount for one year or for eight weeks.

NEW MEDIA: This term designates everything on the Internet, including any and all apps for mobile applications.

WEBINARS AND WEB SERIES: This term designates any kind of lecture, presentation, or series that is made for (and plays on) the web.

14.

Working in Regional Areas

Advantages and Disadvantages of Working in Regional Areas

There are acting opportunities in commercials, radio, industrial/corporate videos, voice-overs (see Chapter 15, Voice-Overs), commercial print, Internet, film, and television, in regional markets outside of Los Angeles and New York. These opportunities vary from market to market and year to year and include national searches for lead characters in film and television. The area you live in is an important place to develop and nurture your acting career (see fig. 25).

One reason a national commercial will be shot in a smaller region is to utilize a particular location. These commercials are usually cast locally, with simultaneous casting in the larger markets such as New York, Chicago, and Los Angeles. Local actors beware: You are up against some stiff competition. Producers don't mind flying someone in from a larger market to do the job. The best man will win.

Commercials are also shot in regional areas because their production costs generally come in lower than shoots in New York or Los Angeles due to possible tax incentives and non-union crews and talent.

In every state in the country, you can now find a high degree of commercial production professionalism that has evolved from our sophisticated communications systems and mobility. In addition, many directors, producers, and ad agencies have relocated from larger

OPPORTUNITIES AVAILABLE

STATE	NEAREST MARKET	ON-CAMERA	VOICE-OVER	RADIO	CORPORATE VIDEOS INDUSTRIALS	COMM. PRINT	THEATRE	FILM	TV*
Alabama		x	x	x	x	x	x	x	x
Alaska		x	x	x		x	x	x	x
Arizona		x	x	x	x	x	x	x	x
Arkansas	GA, LA, OK					x	x	x	x
California		x	x	x	x	x	x	x	x
Colorado		x	x	x	x	x	x	x	x
Connecticut	MA, NY				x	x	x		
Delaware		x	x	x	x		x	x	x
Florida		x	x	x	x	x	x	x	x
Georgia		x	x	x	x	x	x	x	x
Hawaii		x	x	x	x	x	x	x	x
Idaho		x	x	x	x	x	x	x	x
Illinois		x	x	x	x	x	x	x	x
Indiana	IL, OH, KY	x	x	x	x	x	x	x	x
Iowa		x	x	x	x	x	x	x	x
Kansas		x	x	x	x	x	x	x	x
Kentucky		x	x	x	x	x	x	x	x
Louisiana	TX	x	x	x	x	x	x	x	x
Maine	MA				x	x	x	x	
Maryland	NY, Wash DC	x	x	x	x	x	x	x	x
Massachusetts		x	x	x	x	x	x	x	x
Michigan		x	x	x	x	x	x	x	x
Minnesota		x	x	x	x	x	x	x	x
Mississippi	LA, TX	x				x	x	x	x
Missouri		x	x	x	x	x	x	x	x
Montana	ID, UT, WA	x	x	x	x	x	x	x	x
Nebraska		x	x	x	x	x	x	x	x
Nevada		x	x	x	x	x	x	x	x
New Hampshire	MA				x	x	x		
New Jersey	NY, PA				x	x	x		
New Mexico		x	x	x	x	x	x	x	x
New York		x	x	x	x	x	x	x	x
North Carolina		x	x	x	x	x	x	x	x
North Dakota		x	x	x	x	x	x	x	x
Ohio		x	x	x	x	x	x	x	x
Oklahoma		x	x	x	x	x	x	x	x
Oregon		x	x	x	x	x	x	x	x
Pennsylvania		x	x	x	x	x	x	x	x
Rhode Island	MA, NY				x	x	x		
South Carolina		x	x	x	x	x	x	x	x
South Dakota		x	x	x	x	x	x	x	x
Tennessee		x	x	x	x	x	x	x	x
Texas		x	x	x	x	x	x	x	x
Utah		x	x	x	x	x	x	x	x
Vermont	MA, NY	x			x	x	x		x
Virginia	MD, Wash DC	x	x	x	x	x	x	x	x
Washington		x	x	x	x	x	x	x	x
West Virginia	NC, PA	x	x	x	x	x	x	x	x
Wisconsin		x	x	x	x	x	x	x	x
Wyoming		x	x	x	x	x	x	x	x

*Television includes sitcoms, Movies-of-the-Week, and/or national searches for TV series.

FIG. 25: Percentage of opportunities varies with size of the market.

markets to smaller ones because the latter better suit their lifestyles. Actors often make the same move, bringing with them new ideas, up-to-date photo styles, and a greater competitive edge.

Agents and casting directors in all markets can communicate instantaneously, and anyone who is interested can become savvy to the workings of the industry, thus becoming more competitive commercially. Casting directors get breakdowns out nationwide and in moments agents email photos or demo reels to casting directors across the nation and/or around the world.

One of the benefits of working in smaller markets is less competition, which makes it easier to get an agent, book a job, build your résumé, and get your SAG-AFTRA card. In many regions, you can keep busy if you are willing to audition in all areas of the business. One day, for instance, you might be working in a film, and the next day on a print job.

Heather Laird, a casting director at Wright/Laird Casting in Kansas City, Missouri, says, "You can gain a certain level of confidence working in a regional market. That, I think, is *really* valuable. So many people end up in the LA market with very little experience, hoping to get 'discovered.' If people have an opportunity to work in a regional market, they are going to be a step ahead of ninety-nine out of a hundred other people who just decided they want to be famous and walked out the door and went to LA."

There can be some disadvantages to working in smaller markets as well. There is less work than in New York and Los Angeles, it's harder to find good coaches and classes, and you may have to invest a great deal of time driving to auditions and scouting for opportunities to network and/or to find auditions. Savvy talent make the most of their regional market by creating their own opportunities to build their résumé and get experience and exposure.

The reality is that there may not be much happening in your area. If you love where you live and don't want to leave, you will have to find another means of financial support that allows you to go out on auditions when they arise. Many actors in New York and Los Angeles have to have flexible jobs as well to support their acting career. Be sure to set yourself up with a job that allows you time to go to auditions and do commercials.

Commuting

Another option is for actors to commute from smaller markets to larger ones. There are a lot of people commuting within local regions, i.e., from places like Milwaukee, Indianapolis, and Detroit to Chicago. Some actors travel among the Washington, D.C., Philadelphia, and Pittsburgh areas, or between Atlanta and Wilmington, North Carolina, or between Austin and New Orleans. For film and commercial opportunities, actors in Florida travel as much as four hours from Orlando to the Miami area for an audition. Actors from New York will temporarily relocate to Los Angeles for pilot season or episodic season.

By networking with other actors, you can find markets that would be viable for you. You would then want to find an agent in the other markets. It is accepted practice to have a different agent in each market. If the market you are commuting to is very close to your home region, check with your agent to make sure your agreement with him does not cover the other market you are interested in. Doing so will avoid unnecessary and potentially messy contractual issues with the agent you sign with in the new area.

It is not realistic to think that you can live in a regional area and travel as far as a plane ride away for a commercial audition. Be realistic; add up the time it takes to get to the airport and wait for the plane, the cost of airfare, and the transportation costs to and from the audition once you land. Then you may have to wait for what could be an hour to get into the audition room . . . only to be in the audition room for five minutes. After all that, you leave and travel home. If you get lucky and get called back, you will most likely get the call the night before the callback. Then you would have to take the trip all over again. If you get put on avail/first refusal you are usually not told until the day before to report to wardrobe. This scenario is not monetarily or emotionally cost efficient.

If getting to and returning from your audition is too costly, it will make the audition "too important" and put too much pressure on you. Avoid these situations.

Moving to a Larger Market

If you have reached a point where you feel you've done all you can within your base area—and if you're willing to relocate—it's time to consider moving to an area where you can get more work. The market you pursue depends on where your aspirations within the industry lie.

If your primary focus is on film and television, you will want to consider moving to Los Angeles, since that is where most of those projects are done and where there are many more opportunities to audition on a daily basis. There are national search auditions in New York, Chicago, and other places in the country, but if you *know* you want to make your living in film/TV, traditionally you should be based in LA.

Do your homework regarding regional markets as it differs year to year and city to city. Research what shows are shooting when and where. For instance, Florida may have two to four TV series, New Orleans could have a couple. TV shows that film in regional areas typically cast the main name cast of characters in Los Angeles or New York and all the day players, guest spots, and recurring roles in the local area.

Angela Peri, CSA casting director, owner/founder Boston Casting, Inc., says, "Boston is booming. Film production has escalated from a handful of movies ten years ago, to between twelve and twenty films shot in Massachusetts per year. The credit can be given in part to the production incentive established in 2007, and it has put Boston back on filmmakers' radars. As a result, Boston actors have had to step up their game in order to become real film actors. It's not just about having a Boston accent anymore. Boston talent needs to do a credible Boston accent, but they also need to be able to drop it—instantly. It's not just about getting a few background shots of the New England scenery and being an extra in the crowd. Entire films are now being shot here, and Boston has had to double for Paris, New York City, Indiana, Alaska, and Pennsylvania. Boston actors need to be adaptable and that means putting the 'r' back in their words when they need to."

If you are looking to move and your passion is theater, your base should be New York. There is also a good amount of work in film, television, and commercials in New York. Depending on the year, research what TV shows are shooting there. Chicago is a regional market that is known for good theater as well as film opportunities, and many talent searches for main characters for TV and film are conducted in that area.

There is clearly no one "right" place to be. Go where you feel most comfortable and content. It is important to balance your aspirations for your career with the rest of your life. Before making the move to a larger market, make sure you have gotten as much experience as possible in your local area.

A good time to move to a larger market could be when you have exhausted all of your options. Or, perhaps when you were going hot and heavy and interest in you has cooled off because you've become overexposed. The creatives who are making the selection decisions are always looking for the "new" idea, the "new" person.

Actors tend to move on to a larger market when they become bored with what is available to them in their home market, or they outgrow the kinds of parts they are getting and move to an area where more opportunities are available to them. They also leave for markets with more choices for training.

Missouri casting director Heather Laird adds, "People who want to be actors get involved in their regional market, and they do well so they don't stay. However, there are an awful lot of people who go to LA, get some time in, and come back to their original market. It is definitely a plus to have joined SAG-AFTRA (or become SAG-AFTRA eligible) before leaving for a larger market. Expect competition to be much stiffer.

"In New York and Los Angeles, it is not unusual to be competing against 125 other people for the same role, in comparison to 15–25 in a smaller, regional market. Also be prepared for more competition for agency representation. An agent in a larger market may not want to represent you because doing so would create competition within her own agency. They don't want too many people who, in their opinion, are too similar."

Lori Wyman, CSA casting director in the regional Florida area, who is known for casting such TV shows as *Burn Notice*, *The Glades*,

Magic City, and *Graceland*, as well as film and TV commercials, points out some of the hard realities of moving to a larger market:

"Actors are enticed by the fact that they will have more of a chance to audition for a lead in LA or New York than in Florida. But if you can't get an agent and don't get auditions, what chance do you have? Everybody comes from somewhere. Your regional market can be a great place to get your feet wet, learn the business, learn the rules.

"I have heard it said that in Florida we are the barracudas and in LA they are the great white sharks. Smaller markets are not as aggressive or as brutal. Actors get a little taste of it out here, but out there it is thrown at them. Here, a strong talent might go out on every single casting that they would be right for. In LA, that won't happen all the time. Actors come back frustrated. Now, with the financial incentives being offered in many states around the country, you can build just as strong a résumé in the Southeast as you can out in Los Angeles."

In smaller, regional areas, local TV stations, ad agencies, and film production companies do their own casting. You can look up who they are and get your photo and résumé over to them. Call and speak to an assistant or receptionist and ask how they prefer to receive this information. Write a note attached to your info telling the person what you are interested in doing. (For tips on sending out your promotional materials, see Chapter 2, Résumés and Cover Letters.)

Despite the challenges relocating to a larger market presents, if you hope to etch out a full-blown acting career, eventually you might make the move. In the meanwhile, making the most of your regional market is a valuable part of the process.

Advice from Tom Jourden

TOM JOURDEN started out with a business degree, working in sales management in a Fortune 500 company in Atlanta, Georgia. Wanting to make the transition into acting, he started studying it in Atlanta. After a year of pursuing acting in a secondary market, he moved to Los Angeles to expand his studies and opportunities in acting. He is now one of those rare actors who has a career acting in television, film, commercials, voice-overs, and hosting (Tom is well recognized for hosting more than sixty infomercials in addition to Travel Channel's *Amazing Vacation Homes*). He not only made a move successfully, but also transitioned successfully into a new career. He offers some valuable insights into the issues facing performers who are considering the move to a larger market:

> Secondary markets are great for learning about acting, studying, and getting some work under your belt. Atlanta is a perfect example. It's not as competitive as the larger markets and consistently has a lot of opportunities in the area of industrials and commercials. Bottom line—if you can't book work in a secondary market, then you probably aren't ready to make the move to a larger market. It's similar to a player who jumps from college basketball to the pros before he's ready—it will end his career quickly. The most important thing is to have a good sense of when the right time is to make the move, and it varies by person based on many factors: experience, talent, connections, savings, maturity, looks, etc.
>
> If you work in a secondary market first, you're going to understand what agencies do, what casting directors do. You're going to learn a little bit about taking headshots, hitting a mark, and how lighting works, and hopefully you'll get your union card and book some jobs. Even though it's not like the big markets, the experiences you have in a secondary market serve as training wheels. They give you a start.
>
> In a secondary market, it's much easier to book work at different levels—nice little parts in films, parts in industrials, and commercials. You might be competing against eight or ten decent people in a smaller market, whereas in a larger market, you're competing against hundreds or even thousands of actors who all look like you and might be better than you, especially if you're coming out to Los Angeles without training and experience.
>
> After doing a certain number of industrial films, local commercials, or small parts in films or TV shows, you may feel like there isn't a whole lot more you can do without simply repeating yourself. At that point it may be time to move on, take the bigger risk and challenge—to learn and grow as an actor.
>
> The worst thing that can happen in the big market is not having enough money. You end up getting to a place with great

opportunities for commercial work and training, but you can't take advantage of them because you're working as a waiter somewhere forty hours a week and you don't have the time or the money to pursue leads.

I read a lot about acting in the area before making the move, and I talked to people who either were living in LA or had been there. I've learned that it's important not to put a time frame on your success. If you say, "If I don't make it in two years . . . ," you're not really committed to staying with it for the long term, and that kind of commitment is absolutely necessary in this business.

When I first moved to Los Angeles, whenever I would go home or talk to friends, they always wanted to know either when I'm going to do something they can see or, even if I've just done something, when I'm going to be in something else. People not in the business have absolutely no idea how incredibly difficult it is just to get an audition, let alone a booking. When leaving a secondary market, you've got to expect those questions and be prepared to say, "I just met an agent . . . and that is a big deal." Make your victories a little different than they used to be.

One thing I discovered when I moved to LA was that there are a lot of *bad* actors in the big market. Yet for all the bad actors, there is an enormous amount of good actors. In some cases, I observed actors pick up three pages from an Oscar-nominated scene or an Emmy-winning scene and after twenty minutes give a polished performance. It's hard to find the same level of competence in the smaller markets. No one expects you to be that good that quick in smaller markets. But to compete in a big market, you need to be able to meet that challenge.

But, probably the biggest surprise to me was to not assume you know the exact path you will have as an actor. When I first got to town, I worked consistently in industrial films and commercials since I was right for those roles. My business background helped me to market myself more effectively than more talented actors and I quickly started working in small television roles. But then the first surprise happened. I found I had an eye for editing while creating my own demo tape and ultimately began a consulting service working with actors in creating their tapes. It was a great sideline until the next surprise happened—I booked a hosting job for my first infomercial (NordicTrack) and began working consistently as an infomercial host with more than sixty shows, resulting in close to $1 billion in sales to date. That led to reality show hosting

(DirectTV, Travel Channel, etc). And then I came full circle with my business background and began producing, directing, and consulting for infomercials with many hits now under my belt. So, whereas I moved to LA to be an actor, my bread and butter has become hosting and producing infomercials. It's given my family a great life and I get to do a little bit of everything. I really enjoy the fact that I get to reinvent myself every few years, so I am looking forward to my next act—whatever that might be.

15.

Voice-Overs

Voice-over is another area in which you can find many opportunities to develop your talent, make money, exercise your acting ability, express yourself, and have a lot of fun.

What Are Voice-Overs and Who Does Them?

A voice-over is the off-screen voice you hear in a commercial (or other filmed material). Talent fall in love with this medium because it doesn't matter what they look like, and there are significantly fewer restrictions on the talent than in other areas of the business. Women can go to auditions without makeup, it doesn't matter what kind of clothes you wear, age is not a deterrent—you can be fifty and sound thirty—and there are no ethnic restrictions. If your voice sounds non-regional, you are eligible for any and all non-regional-sounding parts.

It can be a plus for certain types of talent to be able to do funny or cartoon-style voices. A grown man can do the voice of a magic carpet or a tiger or a spoon or a shark or a clock. An adult woman can do the voice of a little boy. The voice of Bart Simpson is done by an adult woman.

Another plus is that the booking usually doesn't take all day. In theory, you can record a commercial (which usually takes two hours) and have the rest of the day to go on other auditions or do whatever else you want.

Voice-over talent for television commercials receive residuals for the run of the spot. They also tend to have less of a chance of becoming overexposed. Because on-camera actors are visibly recognizable, clients may feel reluctant to use the same people too much and will often want to choose new faces or looks for their commercials. This is not a problem for voice-over talent.

Many newcomers to the field have the misconception that having a "nice" voice is enough. This is not true. The voice is your instrument, but to become a professional voice-over talent depends on several elements—how well you play the instrument, as well as its tone and quality, your interpretive skills, your personal point of view, and your performance.

Voice-Over Markets

The three major markets for voice-over work are New York, Los Angeles, and Chicago. Secondary markets are Dallas, Florida, and Atlanta, with limited work in other states.

Voice-over talent may (and most of the more successful talent do) have different agent representation in different cities. There are no boundaries, as you don't necessarily have to live in the city or town where the audition originates or where the booking will take place. You can audition from a home studio that is as simple as a mic on your computer or iPad. In a lurch you can also record right to your smartphone. You can audition worldwide. If you book the part, a producer may be willing to rent a professional studio with an ISDN (Integrated Services Digital Network) setup in the town where you live. This system allows the production team to direct you and record you from a studio in another city.

In addition to getting your auditions from your agent, there are professional Internet sites where casting directors and producers post breakdowns directly to the talent. You can find out about these sites through Internet searches and by joining social networking voice-over talent discussion groups.

Types of Opportunities in Voice-Over

Television, radio, film, industrial and corporate films, video games, performance capture and Mocap (Motion capture), voices in toys, and the Internet all offer many opportunities for voice-over work. Other opportunities include audiobooks, voices for business applications such as automated recordings on answering devices (like those on automated answering and/or billing services for department stores and utility companies), promos for TV shows, network announcements, and trailers for films.

TELEVISION

Television offers opportunities for network announcers, promos (promoting a show), animated cartoons, sitcoms, and action voices (any voices not appearing on camera: for example, a talking parrot or voices coming out of a TV set) and ADR (additional dialogue recording), such as loudspeaker announcements in hospitals and airports or background conversations at tables in a restaurant.

In television, the picture is completed and edited first, then the creative team goes into the studio with the voice-over actor and lays down the track (records the voice-over) to the picture. At this point the voice must fit the time and mood of the finished (visual) commercial.

RADIO

Radio and television are very different media. Voices for television have the support of the visuals, whereas in radio, the voice is the only thing that conveys the message; it must create the mood and produce a reaction, whether it be humor, frustration, intimacy, or curiosity.

Radio has no visual restrictions. This allows the creative team to be more flexible in the studio. They can change ideas as they go along. Because of this, flexibility and a wider range of performance on the part of the talent are demanded more frequently for radio auditions than for TV auditions. Radio spots allow more opportunities to react and relate with other characters. Technical ability, knowing how to take direction, and having a good sense of timing are essential in both media.

FILM

In film, there are opportunities in *dubbing*–replacing the original voice of the actor with another person's voice. Foreign films, for instance, are often dubbed over with American voices. That way, subtitles are not necessary when the film is viewed in English-speaking countries. A film also may be dubbed if the dialogue needs to be changed. If the original actor is not available, a person who sounds like him or her does the dubbing. The actual technique involves watching the picture and recording the words or sentences in sync with the dialogue being replaced.

Other opportunities exist in ADR, also known as *looping*. A loop group is an ensemble of actors who record background sounds. For instance, in a huge office or crowd scene, the background noises may have to be "sweetened" (enriched) with sound effects or speaking voices or music. The actors watch the action and supply additional voices as orchestrated by a director. They have to be very clear as to what the scene is all about and technically correct to it. For example, if the scene involves a hospital, the actors may have to know some hospital jargon. They often have to know regionalisms. If the film takes place in the South, they have to speak with a Southern accent. Actors who do ADR have to be very versatile and have great improvisational skills. They must be able to think and change quickly to coordinate with the visuals.

PERFORMANCE CAPTURE AND MOTION CAPTURE (MOCAP[1])

JULENE RENEE-PRECIADO is a performance capture actor with more than ten years' experience, including work on *The Polar Express* (the first performance-capture feature film) and *Avatar*.

Performance capture is a unique style of performing, allowing each actor to truly embody the character, bringing ALL kinds of characters to life . . . regardless of individual physiognomy.

Interview with Julene Renee-Preciado

What is performance capture?
Motion capture or performance capture or "Mocap" is the technology of capturing a performance into the computer.

Since you are not sequestered within the frame of a film camera, performance capture acting is a lot like the stage or black-box theater and requires a bit more physicality then traditional film acting. You have an entire three-dimensional space in which to bring your character to life. That space is called the "volume." (Going back to those who were paying attention in geometry . . . the volume is the empty area inside a shape.) In this case, our

---

[1] MOCAP: Capturing strictly the motion of a character (walking, running, sitting, standing, walking up and down stairs, dining, background movement, etc.)

volume is our stage. Wearing a special suit (similar to a wetsuit) with markers on the body, a performance capture actor performs the scene. This performance will bring to life characters created in the computer.

Can you describe the process of performance capture?
You have a call time to arrive at the studio. Once you arrive, you get into your performance capture suit. Then you go into the "volume" for a ROM (Range of Motion). A ROM is a series of movements you capture into the computer to see where the markers are on your body for that day.

Once you are set inside the computer, then you begin to block out your scene with the director. You lay down marks in the volume of where things are in the virtual world (like doors, streets, sidewalks, trees, etc.), so when you perform you know where those things are. And then you shoot the scene.

What qualities would you say an actor needs to be in the running for this?
First, you have to be a good actor. You have to know how to bring a character to life. Second, you really need to be aware and in control of your body as you perform. This skill is not often required for those who are strictly film/TV/voice-over actors. I was a competitive gymnast and a dancer. I did sketch comedy and used a ton of physical comedy to bring my characters to life. All of those physical traits along with my acting skills are what keeps me working in performance capture. Overall, those who do well in performance capture have a positive, grateful attitude, are great actors, have wonderful physical and vocal ranges, are great at improv, and are able to switch characters quickly.

Each performance capture actor must be able to bring many different characters to life, as well as inanimate objects! Just as a voice-over actor must be a bit bigger in their voice performance, a performance capture actor must do the same with their bodies. (More on Performance capture can be found at ROM school at www.romschool.com.)

What It Takes to Succeed in Voice-Overs

In every market, there are a handful of performers with the tools to compete nationally. The right tools are training, a professional-quality voice-over demo, a website, and the marketing savvy to position yourself properly on the national scene.

The quality of delivery must be solid, sure-footed, and should be defined by the actor's personality. A voice-over talent has to know how to interpret copy and then execute it with the right sense of timing and rhythm. A good voice-over talent can take a piece of mediocre copy and make it come alive.

Your voice has its own distinction. Most importantly it's about your delivery. You need to be able to access what the client is looking for in your delivery to support their sell. Examples of delivery choices are bright, high energy, trustworthy, compassionate, or comedic. After you figure that out, your mind has to be able to direct your voice to do what you chose. You then have to have the ability to know if you have attained your choice. It is important to be able to work with subtleties and to sound connected to the material.

Comedy is a venue unto itself. The successful comedy-driven voice-over performer is original and freed-up creatively. Examples of comedy-driven celebrity prototypes referred to in casting breakdowns are Robin Williams, Ellen DeGeneres, Janeane Garofalo, Amy Poehler, Zach Galifianakis, Eddie Murphy, David Hyde Pierce, and Wanda Sykes. They have a way of looking at the world that comes through loud and clear, and there's no mistaking their personality—other people will try to be imitators, but it's never quite the same.

How to Get Started Doing Voice-Overs

The process of developing your talent and getting into voice-overs is similar in every market. You need to learn to give a good audition and to perform well under pressure. You also need a good demo to use as your calling card.

If you are already doing on-camera work, you'll have an edge. You may already have an agent who knows your work and will submit you for voice-over breakdowns, or a casting person might know you from your on-camera work and will call you in to audition for voice-over. Quite frequently comedic actors can make the transition more easily into humorous radio spots.

Training

If you are not a performer, you should take some sort of acting class so that you understand how to play and develop a character. In addition, take a good class in voice-over technique so you know what to do when you get on a microphone. It is important to find your own "voiceprint" (voice personality). From there you want to be able to execute copy with variations on the theme. After several workshops, you should know the difference between TV and radio reads, what your strengths are, how to make strong choices, and how to take direction.

Know that one three-hour workshop is not going to make a career. It's going to take a lot of practice time outside of class. You want to get to a point where you can compete with people who do this for a living every day. In order to be successful doing voice-overs, it has to be a passion for you. It can't be just a passing fancy. You have to have the kind of enthusiasm that will give you the energy to see you through the times when it is really tough. Developing a career in voice-over takes time.

Another good resource to gain knowledge from working professionals is Voicebank's Voiceregistry. Voiceregistry is an educational division of the voice industry's leading breakdown and posting service, voiceregistry.voicebank.net.

What Is a Demo?

A demo is the voice-over performer's calling card. Like the on-camera actor's headshot, it requires careful preparation. This demo should be on your computer and/or smartphone for a quick response for any demo requests. Responses to any requests for your demo materials must be immediate. The person who has their materials at their fingertips for a quick response to their agent, producers, or casting directors definitely has a competitive edge over those who don't.

To get a demo that sounds professional, you cannot have a friend put it together. Find a professional by getting references from friends who have a good demo, or call local talent agents who represent voice talent. The producer of your demo will help you choose scripts that are best suited for you and will direct you while recording the demo. They will then edit any glitches out of your demo and finish it off with the proper music.

Always ask about studio costs and make sure that cost is included in the demo production quote, as you will be charged for the time it takes to record and edit your demo. Meet the producer before agreeing to hire him. It is important that you feel comfortable with this person. Shop around before choosing a producer. Find out what the going rate is in your area for demo production. The average rates can range from $750 to as much as $1,500. Make sure most of the prep work with your producer is done before going into the studio, as studio time is expensive—from $25 to $150 per hour.

Discuss the option of a package deal that covers all the elements of producing your demo. The elements include meeting with the producer for him to know what your voice is all about, choosing copy, rehearsing copy, recording, choosing music to go behind your spots, and editing. Package design is separate, usually done by someone else.

You can reference and listen to good voice-over demos on Voicebank.net. Find your "type" and listen to all you want at no cost. A good demo will demonstrate what you do best. If you have only four good pieces and the demo is under a minute long, that is fine. You can build on it as your experience develops. The level of quality has to show that you can compete against people in the market who are working every day. The spots should be produced with music and sound effects. The spots must sound finished and ready to be put on the air.

Each commercial should not be put on the demo in its entirety. Instead, your demo producer will compile short clips of the spot cut off in an appropriate place, so that your demo moves quickly from one spot to the next. Blunt cuts with quick changes into the next piece force listeners to pay attention. Slow fades lull listeners. Your demo must start strong, stay strong, and finish strong. Don't try to bury a weak piece in the middle. The creatives want someone who can nail the job and give one hundred percent every time.

A demo is not only for the performer just entering the field; even the most seasoned voice actors have a demo. It is important to keep your demo current by upgrading it as you (and the industry) evolve.

DEMOS FOR ADVANCED VOICE-OVER TALENT

A ten-to-fifteen-second clip of a spot is plenty to get across a style. The finished demo should time out to approximately a minute to a minute and a half. The demo should show a variety and range of what you can do. Some examples of range are *real-person conversational, spokesperson, cosmetic, personality-driven, bright, warm,* and *edgy.* Some people have one identifiable style that they do very well and are booked for it. Examples of such a style are flat rasp, sarcastic, and comedically edgy. Celebrity prototypes for these styles are Zach Galifianakis, Aubrey Plaza, and Tina Fey.

There are different types of voice-overs: *commercial, promo, animation,* and *narration.* If you are proficient in more than one, your demo should have a separate track for each type. The tracks should be separated by types and quickly accessible on your computer and smartphone for easy, rapid transmission to anyone inquiring about your voice. If someone is looking for a specific style, such as promo, you would send the style they are requesting. The last thing you would want to do is send them one continuous demo with all styles mixed together. It would take too much time for the person to listen through the complete demo. You will lose their interest, and they will move on to someone else.

HOW TO PACKAGE YOUR DEMO, IMAGE, AND WEBSITE

The main means of delivering your demo is via the Internet. You might want to have a small supply of CDs on hand for the rare occasion of being asked for one.

You should work with a designer who can find an image for your website and demo CD that reflects your voice style. If your design is bold and strong with lightning bolts as part of the imagery (fig. 26), and your voice is mid-range and whimsical, you have misrepresented yourself. Even if your demo is good, the listener will be disappointed and confused by your marketing. (See figs 26 and 27 for samples of demo covers.)

Your website must be well-organized to avoid any confusion. When you are established enough to have a solid variety of venues such as commercial, narration, promo, radio, and animation, you should have a separate demo for each venue. There should be organized links available so that visitors to your site can easily navigate to the venues they want to listen to.(fig. 27).

GETTING SOMEONE TO LISTEN TO YOUR DEMO

This is a business and you are your own salesperson. You have to know exactly what your strengths are and make people aware of them. The

FIG. 26: Brett Ericson. Packaging portrays strong, intensive, driven, electrifying voice personality (voiceprint).

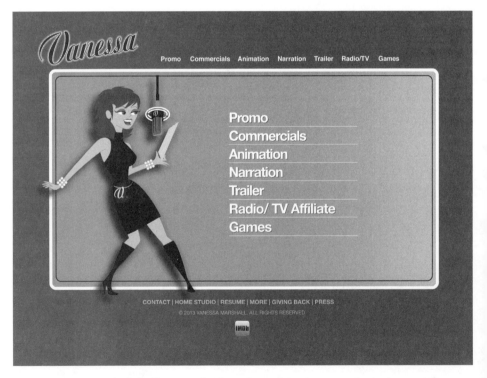

FIG. 27: Vanessa Marshall. Well-organized website that reflects the personality and type of voice.
CREDIT: Joanna Holden, Modularink.com.

more people know about you and what you can do, the better your chances of getting an audition and/or booking. Once you are trained well enough to give a professional-level performance and have put together a well-produced demo, the next step traditionally is to find an agent. There are, however, alternative ways to market yourself.

WHOM TO SEND YOUR DEMO TO

If you are in a market with voice-over agents, try to get an agent to listen to your demo. Ideally, you want agency representation. The most effective way to get an agent to listen to your demo is to have another one of that agency's clients recommend you to them. If you know a casting director, producer, or anyone else an agent does business with, ask them to refer you. Remember: When someone recommends you, it is a reflection on themselves. Generally, people in the business will only recommend you if they feel that you are competitive and will be able to book work.

Another, more independent, way to market yourself is to look up local production companies that produce industrial films, animation, video games, TV and radio stations, and any other businesses you can think of that may need a voice. Call them and ask who you may email your demo to. If you have a website, include that website link with your email. Consider an online search to find social networking websites that post legitimate jobs listings from casting directors and producers.

Marketing and Packaging Yourself as a Talent

In any profession, marketing is everything. From your résumé to the work you do on a daily basis, it's all about marketing. The fact of the matter is that you are all in business for yourselves. You are all entrepreneurs. In this particular case, the voice is the product you are offering. The product has to have a unique stand, a unique identity that's presented in your demo.

How Long It Will Take to Book Your First Job

It's hard to say. Some people hit it immediately. They take a workshop and within six months they are out there and have three or four national

TV or radio spots. Most of the time it takes years to do it. Many times, people don't make it because they don't have the desire to get out there and stay at it. They send out demos, then don't follow up with calls and networking to keep a marketing momentum going. They just sit and hope someone will contact them. You have to really make it happen. The more you work at it, the quicker you may succeed. It's a numbers game. You have to practice. You have to get the auditions. You have to be good. Sometimes it's just being in the right place at the right time.

Tapping the Regional Markets

In addition to major markets, there are voice-over opportunities nation-wide, even in the smallest markets. Wherever there is advertising of any kind, there is voice-over. Check out local radio and televison stations and companies that produce industrial films and in-house training films. As mentioned previously, it does not matter where you live to audition for voice-overs. Check out all the reputable online-submission voice-over sites and start submitting your auditions. Join social networking sites that have blog forums set up to share information.

You Finally Book the Spot

WHAT AN ACTOR CAN EXPECT AT THE ACTUAL BOOKING

The producer is one of the principal players who decide who will get booked for a job.

Barbara Goldman, a radio and television voice-over producer in New York City, takes us into the recording studio for a look at what happens during a typical voice-over session.

Generally—to start the process—the talent is e-mailed the script before the session.

Interview with Barbara Goldman

What can an actor expect when he first arrives at a session?
Depending on the climate of the session, you will either be sent right into the booth (the actual soundproof space the talent stands in to record) or you will come in and meet the client and everyone else in the room.

At a radio session, where there may be many characters in one spot, the actors may be called in at the same time to record the spot together because an overall timing and/or feeling of relationship to each other is needed for the spot. You may then be asked to step aside so the creative team can concentrate on different performances in different segments of the spot. Many times, you'll have to wait around while the team perfects all the technical aspects of the spot—it's not a reflection on how well you're doing. After the spot is timed out, the announcer might be recorded and allowed to leave; then work begins with the other actors.

Who is in the studio for a radio voice-over announcer session?

A radio recording session will run most efficiently if one person talks to the talent. This person is usually the producer, or it might be the writer. The art director, clients, assistant writer, writer, account executive, engineer, and the producer could all be at the session.

Many times, radio work is done at the last minute, so all parties involved are needed there to move the process along. Something magical can happen in the recording session, something unexpected, so it's a good idea for the client to be there. Many changes, including ones involving legal issues, can occur, and actors usually have to record over and over again to cover all bases.

The actor can expect anywhere from three to forty takes. All takes are listened to. The first take might be the one actually liked best. It would then be played back for the talent, and the actor might be asked to do it again. You are expected to understand what you did in a particular take so you could recreate a very subtle nuance of it, if necessary.

Who is in the studio for a television voice-over announcer session?

Generally, the producer, writer, art director, engineer, and, in many cases, the editor are present. Ideally, the voice is the last element that is put on the spot. After the spot is shot and edited, the music is edited, and all the pieces put together, the announcer will be called in. Ideally, one person who can convey the message clearly directs the talent.

If the director is not getting the feeling he or she wants from the actor's read, perhaps the actor will have to chime in and help figure out what is wrong. An experienced actor may suggest a solution as simple as projecting a smile into her voice. Interpretation can make or break a reading.

What is expected of the actor in the studio?

If an actor gives one or two takes and that's all he can or will give, then it is not worth having him there. It may be the greatest performance of his lifetime, but if it's not what the client wants, it's not right.

The attitude and personality of everyone involved are very important. The actor should accommodate—not get in the way. An actor may feel he can read the line ten different ways and give them all to the creatives before being asked. That would be totally distracting. On the other hand, if an actor feels a line should be read differently than directed, he can find ways to approach that without resisting or offering too much.

The actor should not feel that he has to be the center of attention. He has to sense the climate in the control room, determine whether it is playful or serious, and whether or not there is room for some levity. Sometimes it's better simply to get the job done and get out of there.

The more people in the control room, the more likely it is to be a tense situation, simply because there are more people who have to be pleased. If it is a tense control room, the actor has to go along, do what's asked of him, and finesse a way to ask, "What if I try it *this* way?"

Actors have to realize that the people in the studio are under a lot of pressure to get the right outcome. It is the producer's job to accommodate the writer and the client. After the creative team finds what they want, actors are welcome to their way of doing it. But they should bear in mind that the creative team in the control room is not thinking just about the voice. They are thinking about all the elements of the production.

What do actors tend to struggle with on their first booking?

They have the ability, otherwise they wouldn't be there, but they seem to feel insecure about the procedure and, possibly, when to talk. It is not expected for a talent to be a time clock, bringing something in exactly on time. With the new technology, performance can be sped up or slowed down to meet time constraints without any change of voice pitch. If the talent and attitude are there, the creatives will have the patience. However, accomplished voice talent have developed internal clocks and can shave or add a second to their read.

Final Tips on Studio Recording Sessions—Know How to Take Direction

Too Many Directors? Sometimes there is just one person in the control room; sometimes there is a bank of people. At some recording sessions, they all have input; at others, they just sit there. The most trying time is when five or six people on the creative team show up and each one has a different opinion of how the recording should go. These people are all part of the deal. How can you satisfy all of them? Don't try to split the difference and make everybody happy. Communicate with the people who are directing you. Explain to them that you are hearing two different pieces of direction and you are not sure what they want. Suggest doing it one way and then the other way. This business is all about communication.

Too Many Takes? Nick Omana, a voice-over talent, shares his experience of an extended taping session: "There was a time when I had sixty-seven takes. I went out to get some water during a break and the engineer said to me, 'You're doing a great job. These guys do a hundred or more takes.' Producers want to make sure they have every base covered, so they are going to work you every way to Sunday to make sure they have what they want. As talent, we are always seeking approval after two takes. That doesn't happen very often."

To do well in voice-over work, you need a lot of versatility and diversification. Once you are booked and in the booth recording, you want to get the job done right. You should learn to take direction. Listen to the creative team—right or wrong. Usually a smart director or writer will say, "Is there any other way you hear or feel this?" Then you can put it down the way you feel it should go.

Animation

There is a tremendous market in cartoons, creating expanded opportunities for voice talent. The bulk of animation is done in Los Angeles, the "Mecca of Toons."

Advice from Charlie Adler

Charlie Adler is a voice actor/dialogue director, casting director, and the voice of Starscream in Michael Bay's *Transformers* series; Modok in *The Avengers*; Cow, Chicken, and The Red Guy in *Cow and Chicken*; Buster Bunny in *Tiny Toons*; Ed and Bev Bighead in *Rocko's Modern Life*. He was Mr. Whiskers in the animated TV series *Brandy & Mr. Whiskers*, three characters in *Pet Alien*, and voices *Jakers! The Adventure of Piggley Winks* as well as over one hundred series regulars.

As a voice director with over 500 TV episodes and features to his credit, he won an Emmy for Voice Direction for *Rugrats* in addition to voice directing the *Wild Thornberrys* series, *Rocket Power*, *Me, Eloise*, *Dead Space*, and *Bubble Guppies*, to name a few.

Charlie suggests that acting for animation is like acting for the theater in that it involves a much more definitive, broader use of acting abilities than acting on camera. With on-camera acting, the actor is seen. The viewer knows if the character is tall, skinny, fat, sloppy-looking, handsome, or sophisticated. In animation, the actor has to paint the picture with his voice and carry that voice with a myriad of acting skills. Charlie says,

> This is an acting job. It is offensive when people say, "Oh, I can do a funny voice. I can do cartoons." It's not about funny voices. You need to have a great ability to act and to create characters. You need an incredible imagination and the ability to be very, very free. You must be very flexible, able to switch gears in a matter of seconds. Technically, you have to be very adept at many things.
>
> Yes, voice is important. Yes, having dialects is very important. The energy level required is extraordinary in animation. I feel like I am running a marathon every time I do a show. The ability to commit to a character and to be consistent requires some serious acting skills. Animation's not a medium for people who can't act.

HOW TO GET STARTED IN ANIMATION

There are an infinite number of ways to get into animation. For example, Charlie Adler has always considered himself goofy:

> I was often a brat at school. I was the kid who never shut up, who made fun of everybody, and lived in the principal's office. Unknown to me

before I was able to channel that energy into acting, being a mimic and a clown was a way to release that need to act. My energy was badly channeled and I was acting out! It was odd because I was great student! I just NEEDED to act!

Luckily for him, he had a talent that could be translated into acting. "I went into theater and broke into commercials very early (at the age of fifteen). I learned how to work in front of a camera, which helped prepare me for voice-over and radio."

Adler's agent got him into an audition for an animated special that came to New York. She knew he was goofy, knew he had done a lot of improvisation (including work with an Off-Broadway improv company) and that he was good at satire. He went in, landed the job, and then recorded it in New York. After going on tour in a Broadway show, he moved to Los Angeles—the hotbed of animation.

> I told the agent I got in LA that I wanted to do cartoons. I had to go in and demonstrate to her that I knew what I was doing. I wrote forty characters, three lines per character, and insisted that I audition for them. They listened to what I had to do. A week later, they got me a general audition for Hanna-Barbera using my material, my characters. I was given five minutes. I ended up doing twelve. Nobody stopped me and a week later I had Smurfs. Two weeks after that I had another series, and three weeks later another. My animation career grabbed me and never let go!
>
> There's a sense that in the voice-over world, that the same people get all the work. This is not true of animation. A casting director in animation cannot hire the same people, so there is room for newcomers in the voice-over field. There was room for me and everyone I work with! Creative teams are always looking for new actors!
>
> It may feel clique-ish because there are time restraints and budgetary restraints that don't allow the producers to take as many chances as one would hope. You do have to prove your dependability once in the door and your flexibility and versatility to sustain a career!
>
> As a casting director, it is often a mandate by my producers to find new people. If you start a career with defeatist ideas like "animation is a clique," you are really sabotaging yourself. I think you have to know your strengths and possibilities and

give it everything you have. There are enough challenges thrown at you. You don't have to hurt yourself by adding to them with negative thinking.

For every working actor there is a different story of how they got in. Everyone has their own path and their own story.

HOW TO MAKE A CHARACTER COME ALIVE WITH A VOICE

Adler goes on:

At any audition the talent should be able to see a picture of the character. If a sketch is not available, a monologue in which several actions are taking place is necessary. One should not always expect these to be cohesive.

You have to have a keen sense of the visual—of what is going on—and a very strong imagination. A director or writer tells you what the action is, and you put all that information together— what you believe from the monologue and the piece, the physical characteristics you get from the picture, and what the director and the other people in the room tell you they want in the way of sensibility and feeling.

Do they want a mischievous person? A young person? An older person? Full-bodied? Angry? Edgy? Someone who is aggressive? Shy? Neurotic? These descriptions translate into an energy and sensibility. What's the scene about? Who are you talking to? How do you feel about who you are talking to? Again, this is an acting job and an actor's medium. I am describing ideas that all actors know when acting. So if this is foreign to you, the reader, then the first point of order is to learn to act!!!

Also the style of the piece should be known to you. Hugely comedic? Satire? Saturday morning? Primetime? Fantasy? Realistic? Cinematic? All those styles require a knowledge of those styles and an ability to adjust your acting style.

Acting requires courage, a sense of freedom, a full-on commitment, the ability to lose yourself, and more than anything an ability to feel free. You have to love to act. It should be a joy and a challenge and filled with creative possibility. Acting is not an intellectual pursuit but an emotional one. The language of acting is an emotional language and very hard to articulate.

From a practical and technical viewpoint, let's say you finish a monologue or scene at an audition and the director says, "Okay, that was interesting, but this character has to be a little crankier and he needs to have a little more weight. Look at the picture—he is a little heavier. And look at the upper lip—it's very, very thick, and he has buck teeth. We want to get a sloppier sound and a more aggressive character. He is a little angrier." Then all of a sudden the writer says, "You know what? I think it would be very interesting if we went a whole different way with this guy. Let's try this: Instead of making him fat and aggressive, let's make him very thin-sounding and neurotic."

Those are two huge adjustments to make. Now you have to take that monologue and adapt it to a different personality. You have to completely switch gears, and you might have fifteen seconds to make this adjustment. You must have the ability to get an idea and fly with it—that's where improv training serves you. You have to commit to the idea and accompanying feelings and go with it. That's why I say it's very improvisational. That's how you have a strong chance to get the job.

By the way, SAG-AFTRA allows the people booking you to require you to play three characters and get one payment with a ten percent bump-up for the third character. That tells you right there that it is cost-efficient for a producer to hire somebody who is very versatile.

Let's say you are playing one character and you have two more that you are required to do. Of those two, you could have rehearsed a sixty-five-year-old Irish elf, which they have decided on ahead of time. Then, in between the rehearsal and the taping they could say, "We never had the drawing, but play him as a fourteen- year-old East Indian boy. Go!" Again and finally, your joy and passion and love of your work is everything.

Interview with Bob Bergen

Bob Bergen, the voice of Porky Pig, is another inspirational source of information for those who want to enter the world of animation.

Since 1990, Bob is one of a handful of actors who voice the Looney Tunes characters for Warner Bros. The main character voices you hear him bring to life are those of Porky Pig, Tweety, Sylvester Junior, Henry Hawk, Speedy Gonzales, and Marvin the Martian. You have also heard his voice in *Robot Chicken*, *Star Wars: The Clone Wars*, *Toy Story 2*, *Wreck-It Ralph*, *The Lorax*, *Santa Clause 2*, as well as many others.

How did you break into animation?

I wanted to be Porky Pig since I was five years old. My family moved to Los Angeles when I was fourteen and I began taking voice-over workshops. At the age of eighteen, I was introduced to a voice-over agent by another voice talent. Within a week I booked my first cartoon—*Spider-Man and His Amazing Friends*. For the next five years I paid the bills primarily working as a tour guide at Universal Studios, while slowly adding to my voice-over résumé. In 1990 I auditioned for and booked *Tiny Toons*, my first gig for Warner Bros., in which I played Porky and Tweety.

How do you suggest other people get into voice-over? What tools do they need?

Well, the first thing is that you can't get into voice-over by just doing cartoons. You have to do commercial voice-over as well. Commercials are the day-to-day work in voice-over with cartoons being the icing on the cake. Before ever taking a voice-over workshop, I recommend studying acting. Voice-over *is* acting. I'm also a *huge* advocate of improvisation. Improv trains you to get out of your head and make solid choices. Once you've studied commercial and animation voice-over, it's time for a demo. Make sure you have your demo produced by someone who produces demos for today's voice-over talent.

What makes for a good animation demo?

Your animation demo should sound like a montage of real animation clips cut together into a minute-and-a-half demo. Stay away from telling a story. Also, never repeat a voice character. Once you've established a character, move on to the next. Have contrasting voices and contrasting energies/intent next to each other. Try to have each character *doing* something, not just *saying* something, in each bite. Give them some kind of action to be doing. This will show off not just your vocal range, but also your acting range. In cartoons they are looking for actors first and funny voice people second, which means that if you are a great actor who can only do a few voices, you have a better chance of booking a job over someone who does dozens of voices, but can't act.

Your animation demo should consist of original characters with distinct personalities. Everyone can do a witch. What makes your witch different? How are your kid voices different from the *Rugrats'*? Nancy Cartwright, who does Bart Simpson, had been doing kid voices for years before booking *The Simpsons*. What makes her Bart stand out is her acting. Her personality is as memorable as his voice. Think of a script as a skeleton and you—the actor—have to give it a body.

Check out animation demos from the top Los Angeles talent on Voicebank.net, represented by some of the top talent agents, such as CESD, WME, DPN, SBV, VOX, Atlas, etc. Your demo needs to be as good or better than these. And you cannot just offer agents what they already represent. They need new. They need different. They need original. They don't need what they already have.

How do you make a character come alive?

My number one rule in creating a character is if you physically play a character, the voice will follow. What that means is you can't stand at the mic with your hands at your sides just reading the script and expect to give your best performance. From head to toe you need to physically play each character, as you would if you were on stage. The only catch is you need to stay on mic! If you are playing more than one character (and my record for one episode is seven), then each character will have not only a different voice, but different facial expressions, different body language, different gestures, etc. By physically changing along with the voice from character to character, you prevent blending voices.

A one-half-hour cartoon takes about four hours to record. The direction is fast. A voice-over performance, whether animation or commercial, is basically a cold read. You won't get much time with the copy, so you are expected to be brilliant without much preparation. In cartoons you'll get direction like, "Let me hear you run, take a leap off a cliff, and slowly get up kind of dazed and out of breath—then say our scripted line." You have to be able to remember all of that while staying on mic and in character. Plus you might be having a two-way conversation with yourself since you are hired for scale to play at least two voices in episodic cartoons. If all of this sounds easy, then you are ready to pursue it. If not, keep studying! Voice-over, especially animation, is very competitive. Each listener gives you one shot, so make sure you are ready when opportunity knocks.

16.

Models Crossing Over into Commercials

Why Models Get into Commercials

Models have broken old stereotypes and have become extremely savvy. "All looks—no brains" could hardly describe the streetwise entrepreneurs who work today's runways and appear in editorials and advertisements in major markets around the globe.

As America's baby-boomers reach maturity and approach seniority, the industry has begun to tune into their needs. Whereas models used to have a career lifespan of little more than ten or so years, now a good model can work well into her forties and beyond—a direct reflection of changing demographics relating to the aging of America.

Well before a model's career begins to wind down, she starts to invest her earnings or develop businesses of her own. Models are opening restaurants, designing clothing lines, endorsing products, and branching out into other areas of the industry. More and more models are exploring film, theater, and television, and one of the primary ways for models to get their foot in the talent end of the industry is through commercials.

Models who expand into television commercial work position themselves firmly inside the industry. An increasing number of models are taking acting classes to increase their chances of getting commercial work. As models become trained in commercial auditioning technique, they broaden their careers and fatten their bankbooks. The residual income from commercial work can come in years after the actual work was done, carrying the model through slow times and/or adding a lucrative financial base from which she can expand in both careers.

Modeling agencies recognize the fact that models cross over into other areas of the industry, and are quick to give attention to this lucrative segment of their businesses by affiliating their agency with talent agencies that represent talent for commercials and film.

How Commercial Experience Can Be a Stepping-Stone to Television and Film

Many times a beautiful person is needed in a film. Its casting director or director will see a model acting in a commercial and will trace him or her down to audition for the film.

Commercials can be a model's first opportunity for exposure outside the world of print advertising. As the first experience of acting on camera, commercial work can help models learn to take direction, deliver copy on time, follow blocking instructions, and exercise expressions and emotions on film.

After acquiring some commercial experience, a model often discovers that she likes acting and pursues it more seriously by taking dramatic acting classes. The commercial experience gives her the insight and confidence to expand her career.

How Modeling and Talent Conventions Offer Opportunities to Expand into Other Areas

From Toledo, Ohio, to Hollywood, California, aspiring models and actors vie for the opportunity to break into the business by attending one of the numerous modeling and talent conventions held annually throughout the United States. These events, running over the course of a few days to one week, draw casting directors, agents, and managers from major markets across the globe, each scouting for new faces to appear in print, commercials, television, film, musical theater, and recordings.

Talent cannot individually attend one of these events; they have to come with a modeling or talent school or agency. There can be as many as 2,000 contestants and 350 VIP model and talent agents, managers, and casting people scouting for talent, judging, and giving seminars about the business. It would be impossible to meet that many agents in five years' time with no résumé or track record, as you're trying to break into the industry.

A good convention will separate the model and talent competition events. A talent can attend events and competitions in both areas. If you are thinking of attending one of these events, check out the ratio of the number of VIP judges to contestants as well as who the VIP judges attending will be (and have been in the past). Be sure to check out their credentials. It is very easy to do this over the Internet, or by directly calling the person's office.

Go to the convention, not only to be discovered but to learn from the seminars offered and see what it feels like to have a competitive experience. The most important and positive feedback one can hear from attendees of one of these conventions is that it was a self-esteem booster and a great learning experience. Life as an actor and model is competitive. Your experience at the convention will tell you if you can take the heat.

Many minds and career paths are turned around from model to talent as a result of attending these conventions. Wannabe models have also discovered a wider range of opportunities open to them through the talent exposure at these conventions. Participants of modeling and talent conventions have signed contracts with major agents and managers in both Hollywood and New York and have appeared in national commercials as a result of attending.

Some of the models and actors who have come out of such conventions and found success are Ashton Kutcher, Katie Holmes, Elijah Wood, Jessica Biel, Joel West (contracted for Calvin Klein's *Eternity* commercial with Christy Turlington), as well as many, many others.

A good way to find a convention is to look online. Then start doing your research, calling or emailing talent or model agencies to confirm that they are indeed attending a particular convention as claimed. It is up to you to determine which size and type of convention best suits your personality and needs.

HOW DO YOU KNOW A CONVENTION IS REPUTABLE?

- **HISTORY:** How long has the convention been in business?
- **REPUTATION:** What do others in the field say about it? What is its BBB record? Is it licensed? Does it have testimonials from customers?
- **SUCCESS STORIES:** Who has found success as a result of attending this particular convention?
- **GUT FEELING:** How do you feel about what you have heard? Do you feel "pushed" or "promised" anything? Never ignore your basic good sense.

The Role of a Good Manager in Making the Transition

Talent manager Vincent Cirrincione discovered and developed Halle Berry. Halle started out as a pageant contestant while she was still in her teens. She became Miss Teen All-America and was runner-up to Miss USA. A native of Cleveland, Ohio, Halle—who is only five feet seven—moved to Chicago, where she primarily did catalog modeling for various department stores. She had intended to study acting extensively, but when she met Vincent and came to New York, he moved her acting career along so quickly that she wound up getting on-the-job training instead.

"You can't expect to live in a small town and fly to a big city and have people take you seriously, until you're a big star," says Vincent. "I never heard Halle say, 'I can't do this or that.' She just did what she had to do. There was a time after her first movie when she lived on a couch in my office to save money on rent to invest in herself. She took the money and hired a publicist. When I gave her advice, she understood and acted accordingly. Halle went out there to follow her dreams. She didn't just wait for it to come to her. There was a certain amount of strategy and serendipity."

Vincent's strategy including positioning Halle's career contrary to Hollywood's assumption that you can't act if you're a model. Up to this point, Halle had done a stereotypical part in a short-lived TV series about models called *Living Dolls* and guest-starred on weekly sitcoms such as *A Different World*. Vincent's strategy led to her role in Spike Lee's *Jungle Fever* (with Wesley Snipes), where she played an unattractive crack addict. This gave Halle a chance to show that she had more to offer than just a pretty face. One thing led to another and she got an Eddie Murphy movie and a TV mini-series called *Queen*. *The Flintstones* followed.

Halle's crossover from modeling into film was made very quickly, and she was able to bypass a television commercial career. But after becoming a Revlon girl, her career had come full circle. She got the Revlon campaign because she was successful in film and television, and she feels her background in pageants gave her the ability to talk to people and express herself well. She has since proven herself to be a truly versatile talent—able to easily transition from her cosmetics contracts to her role as a Bond girl in *Die Another Day* (co-starring with Pierce Brosnan)—with an Oscar for Best Actress for her role in *Monster's Ball* (co-starring Billy Bob Thornton). With that Oscar win, Halle positioned herself firmly as one of the industry's most respected actors.

How Fashion Print Work Differs from Making Television Commercials

In some ways, modeling for print is very similar to working on camera in a commercial spot. You have to be comfortable being in front of the camera, you have to relate to the camera as you would a dear friend, and you have to be able to take direction from the person behind the camera. You have to love the camera, and the camera has to love you.

In other ways, commercials present new challenges for a model. In print work, the photographer is trying to capture a moment. Clients wade through photos looking for a single shot or a strong series of images that will best represent the client and what they're looking for. Movements for print work are exaggerated, free-flowing and stylized, often mannequin-like. A commercial is an active medium from start to finish. For an on-camera commercial, movements and expressions are more natural, usually with more warmth and approachability.

Another consideration is space. Whereas on the runway or for print a model has ample space to move and express herself, in some commercial work she will have to adjust to the limited space of the television screen. Movements for commercials in this case will be slight, yet expressive.

In print advertising, your primary promotional book is the portfolio, consisting of a range of photographs containing your strongest images as well as tear sheets[1] from previous work. For commercial work in the United States, your primary marketing tools are your commercial headshot, résumé, and—ultimately—a demo showing samples of your work in commercials. In foreign markets, where the trend is to use pretty faces for commercial work, a model may get by without standard talent marketing tools.

Request and collect a copy of every commercial you do at the time of the shoot or soon after the shoot. You will then have the material on hand to put together a demo. This will give you the competitive edge. Post these commercials on your online submission service and your website, and have them on hand when a demo is requested.

WHAT IT TAKES TO CROSS OVER

The transition from model to on-camera actor takes more than just a great face. When the model speaks, being physically attractive isn't enough. That's when knowing how to analyze a script and to audition can expand her career.

When you see those good-looking people running down the beach in a commercial, the talent knew how to make choices and handle themselves properly. It takes a choice of energy and the same ease and comfort in front of a camera that is required in print work. Whether they are just walking down the street and laughing with a friend or playing with a young child, the talent must make a definite choice. Anything a model has already experienced through print work applies to on-camera work for commercials.

---

[1] Tear sheets are samples of a model's published work (print ads, fashion spreads, etc., "torn" from the publications to put into a portfolio.

TRAINING

Although your modeling experience may give you a slight edge, the transition to commercials will be much easier if you invest in a good commercial auditioning workshop. There is a specific technique applied in commercial auditioning. Proper training will help you get comfortable with the procedure and give a good audition. Having commercial training with a good coach listed on your résumé also shows you are serious about learning and applying the craft.

Opportunities in Foreign Markets

There are many opportunities for models, not only in the United States but in foreign markets as well. Clients from all over the world often want someone beautiful to represent their products, and not just cosmetics. European markets can become a virtual gold mine of opportunities for models with acting experience. The trend there is to use models instead of actors whenever possible. In Europe, models cost less than professional actors, which saves clients as much as 50 percent in salaries.

The trend toward using primarily models in commercials is evident in many countries. For instance, models from Scandinavia, the U.S., Canada, and England go to Barcelona, Spain, to make money in commercials—then go to Madrid to do editorials—using money made in TV commercials to finance other career aspirations.

In Milan, models can enjoy a full range of work, from high-fashion editorial print (as opposed to catalogs) to television commercials. Greece does a fair amount of commercial work, as do Australia and South Africa. England has a strong commercial market. With agents sending photos and portfolios over the Internet, models' photos can be viewed very quickly and inexpensively and decisions can be made very quickly. Worldwide searches can be done quickly over the Internet by casting directors, photographers, and agents. Be aware of Internet scams. There are, for instance, web-based companies that charge money to post your photo(s) on their site, claiming that casting people frequent and cast from these sites. Know, however, that casting directors mainly cast through agents to control the degree of professionalism that is needed by the model.

HOW A TYPICAL AUDITION IN EUROPE DIFFERS FROM ONE IN THE UNITED STATES

In Europe, all commercials are dubbed over, so it doesn't matter if you can't speak the language. If there is a script, you are given a copy anywhere from the night before to an hour before, and someone will help you translate it into English and direct your facial expressions. You are just expected to mouth the words, so that when the voices are dubbed in, the audio and visual parts go together well.

Compensation

WHAT A MODEL CAN MAKE IN PRINT AND COMMERCIALS IN THE UNITED STATES

In the United States, a day rate for catalog print modeling can range from $1,500 to $10,000. As the popularity of the model increases, so does her day rate. Top celebrity models can make up to $20,000 a day.

HOW MODELS ARE PAID FOR COMMERCIAL WORK

In each country, compensation is different. In Milan, for instance, the agent negotiates a set price for the talent, then discusses royalties. If the spot runs for many years, the agent negotiates for more and more money each year. Generally, the model is paid for the day, plus the royalty for the first year. Future royalties are paid to the model by most agencies, even if they are no longer in the country.

Most foreign markets don't have unions, at least not like SAG-AFTRA in the U.S. The exceptions would be Canada, which has a strong union, ACTRA; England, which has British Equity; and Spain, which has Premios Unión de Actores. Day rates in most foreign markets depend on the model's name and experience—and whether or not it is for a private channel, a local channel, or a national channel. In Italy, for example, day rates range from several hundred dollars for a small spot to $2,000 and up plus royalties for a national commercial.

Advice from Elle Macpherson, Carmen, Tim Saunders, and Patrick Johnson

Following are some inspirational insights and advice from professional models who have made the transition into commercials.

ELLE MACPHERSON

Elle Macpherson is an international supermodel who has done commercials for McDonald's, Biotherm (in Europe), and MCI, and has successfully transitioned into film. In addition to other companies, she has a lingerie company in Australia, where she produces her own commercials. Here's what Macpherson recalls about her start in modeling:

> In Australia I was awarded an opportunity to attend law school. But after graduating from high school, I decided to take a year off before going to college. I held a variety of jobs, including waitressing in a theater restaurant and working in a pharmacy. A friend of mine, who was a model, suggested that I try it and possibly make a lot of money. "No way," I said. "No way ever. I could never do that." My friend then bet me twenty dollars that if I went to the agency with her, they would take me on. I thought, okay, that's twenty bucks, the equivalent of three or four hours' work. So I went.
>
> When you are sixteen, you have weird perceptions of beauty. You haven't grown into yourself. I was a long drink of water, very tall. I didn't look like what I thought models looked like.
>
> I gave the agent a snapshot taken by a friend. The agency sent me to have more photographs, and the next thing I knew I was being booked for jobs. I worked for a year and a half in Australia. While on a skiing trip in America, I called an agent from Click in New York who had been pursuing me, started working for them, and never left the States.
>
> I always had more of a commercial look than a high-fashion look. I really didn't do a lot of fashion. I didn't work a lot for the magazines, except *Sports Illustrated*. I did a lot of advertising campaigns and TV commercials. I guess I work well on camera. I feel like I need to move and I'm freer when I'm moving, so I'm better on camera than when I'm in stills.
>
> I never wanted to act. It was just one of those weird things. A script for *Sirens* came to my manager's attention, and he suggested

that I read it. I didn't want to read it because I didn't want to do film. I couldn't see the point. He suggested I read it anyway. The director was in town and wanted to meet with me. He said, "I think *you* should be the one to tell the director you are too lazy to read the script. That you don't care about doing a movie in Australia about a famous Australian artist and spending two months in the mountains with Hugh Grant. You should be the one to tell him that you won't even consider it."

So I read the script and changed my mind. I thought it would be really good for me to spend a few months in Australia and do something different. Working very hard in modeling made me feel burnt out. I did the film. It led to others, and my film career seemed to propel itself. Now I love making films, and that's all I want to do.

CARMEN

Carmen is known for her longevity in the modeling world. She has been with Ford Models since they opened their doors approximately fifty years ago. Carmen has appeared in every magazine from *The New Yorker* to *Vogue* and is known for her work with Revlon and for the classic *Vanity Fair* lingerie advertisements as "the girl with no face." She is trying to help people redefine themselves at every age from fifty to seventy and beyond. Her longevity in the industry lends itself to some interesting insights. Here's what she has to say about it:

I take good care of myself. Life's a challenge as a human being, not just for models. It's a long trip. One has to have an overview of the whole trip. I eat when I'm hungry. I try to keep some balance in my life. I drink a lot of water. I am always mentally prepared. I make sure I get good nutrition and maintain a high energy level. If you stay up all night at nightclubs, it's going to come out of your hide in the long run. And smoking is the worst thing you can do for your skin. Forget smoking. You have to opt for healthy choices.

Doing commercials takes natural ability, being able to apply one's inner life and imagination to the craft of acting. So I didn't find it difficult to move from print work to commercials. I found it challenging. The timing and what I am asked to do on the set is different. Television commercial work is not as intimate as photography in a studio because there are so many people around. It is a different process. The hours are different. When you are used to one and you like the area you are moving into, you just pay attention and learn the trade.

Make sure that you keep on educating yourself because the work does not come to you. You have to keep developing your lust for life in general so that you have some inner life to bring to a job. What makes the difference between someone who gets work and someone who doesn't is the amount of passion you bring to your craft.

I would advise young people to stay in school. School really teaches discipline. It's very hard to pick up self-discipline on one's own. Reading is the single most important thing for youngsters to get into. Once you can read, you can learn by yourself.

It's very tricky for young people starting out to understand the personality of some of the people they come in contact with. For instance, if you are hired for a job and you know you are going to make some money, and the photographer is on drugs and offers or insists you take the drugs to "make you more expressive," it's important for you to remember to do the right thing. It takes a lot of guts to gracefully get out of the way of something that is self-destructive, but it must be done.

TIM SAUNDERS

Tim has been modeling with Ford Models since 1966. He got his start in London a year before signing with Ford. Tim is represented by several commercial agents in New York and has done more than 200 TV commercials, including ones for Sominex, Promise margarine, United Airlines, Cadillac, Bahamas Tourism, and Prell shampoo. He describes the differences in shooting print and television commercials:

They are very different jobs. In commercials you must be able to walk, talk, and chew gum at the same time. With print, you don't. Each print job and commercial is different depending on what you are trying to sell. With fashion modeling, you are usually selling a garment and you are trying to make the clothes look good while giving them an attitude. In modeling you either look right for the job or you don't. You don't have to go deep down to any acting abilities to come up with a special look. You were chosen for the job because you look the way you do and the client wants you to be yourself.

In television commercials, you are acting more. You are relating to either the camera or to another person you are working with.

In both, you have to have a presence. When you are booked for a print job, you are booked for a certain specified number of hours or days. With a commercial shoot, the hours never end. If you are booked nine to five, you might work nine to midnight, and you are obliged to stay until the job is done. Print is not done this way. You are very often booked for one job from two to three and another job for the afternoon from three-thirty to four. You can say your time is up and go on to the next job. Commercials very often have more down time while sets are being lighted or camera angles are being changed. You very often are shot and do your scene at the end of the day.

PATRICK JOHNSON

Patrick has done more than fifty commercials, including ones for Lever 2000, Gillette, Centrum vitamins, Head & Shoulders, Schweppes, Close-Up toothpaste, and Sears. He is also an acting coach and motivational speaker. Here he shares some of his insights into what it takes to do well in the industry:

> Growing up, I never had any real interest in modeling or acting, unlike many young people today, until a good friend encouraged me to enroll in a modeling/talent school while I was a sophomore attending Arizona State University. A few months later, the school asked me to meet with Eileen Ford, who was in town on a scouting trip. (At the time I had absolutely no idea that Eileen Ford was the owner of the most prestigious model agency in the world!) She encouraged me to find a way to get to New York to try modeling. So, in the summer of 1980, I attended a modeling convention in New York City, was awarded its Model of the Year award, and signed with none other than Ford Models. I must say that if it hadn't been for the convention, I *never* would have ventured to New York to pursue a career in modeling. The thought of going to such a big city on my own was terrifying, and the convention provided me a convenient opportunity to meet with many New York agents in just a few days.
>
> Even though I was lucky enough to sign with Ford Models and quickly get a few breaks in the modeling world, it wasn't until I discovered commercials that a passion was born. Modeling came pretty naturally. On the other hand, trying to read and perform commercial scripts was like learning a foreign language. I had no

idea how to move, speak, or even look relaxed in an audition. Thank goodness I discovered on-camera commercial classes! I learned how to give commercial directors what they wanted, learned about the commercial industry itself, and learned a great deal about me as well.

With time, I began to enjoy and relish the working environment of a commercial set. I found it more challenging and stimulating than the average modeling shoot, and commercials helped me escape the dreaded "golden handcuffs" of the modeling industry. Don't get me wrong: averaging two to three thousand dollars a day, while taking a trip halfway around the world to some exotic location, is not a bad way to spend your life. However, when you are constantly at the mercy of the modeling industry's "golden handcuffs," it leaves you with no time to explore other venues of the industry.

Commercial success was a springboard into other areas of the industry for me. My experience motivated me in co-founding a theater company, performing in late-night, primetime, and day-time shows, and working in feature films as both actor and/or producer.

Modeling got my foot in the door and, although I am not "famous," the commercial industry has kept me busy and happy for over twenty-four years. Find your source of discipline, get ready for some hard work, be prepared for any challenge, and dive into classes and workshops. If you've got the desire, you can make things happen.

17.

Kids in the Business

In commercials, kids are big business. Appearing in commercials can create scores of extraordinary opportunities for children, including:

- Significant income potential
- Business opportunities that can be carried into later life
- Personal development in communication, presentations, and teamwork
- Visibility, which can help the child move into other areas of the entertainment business

What Types of Kids Do Well in Commercials?

Carol Lyn Sher, children's agent at CESD talent agency, Los Angeles/ New York, says:

> I like to work with happy, enthusiastic kids who have a healthy look. They have fun with clothes and cameras and are able to follow directions. These are kids who like making instant friends. They are talkative, outgoing, confident, and they are having fun at the auditions and on the sets. Great qualities are a willingness to try new looks, charm, and dedication. They should be looking to improve and market themselves. Kids/parents should be interested in updating their materials to competitive and current levels. They should have good grades and be a bit ahead in school. They are memorable for their personalities and their looks. The kids in demand have a love of adults and meeting new people and going to new places. They are interested in other people.

The kids in demand have great social skills and a spark in their eyes. They would likely do well in many lines of work. Most of our kids have mastered the balance of life and school. They have the heart of a giver and do charitable works from a young age. A kid can have "it" who is quirky, and a kid can have "it" if they are meltingly beautiful. They can be wholly unique but are an ideal type. They can be the ideal good son, nerd, or soccer player. They can be a fun class clown or a slightly withdrawn thinker.

Los Angeles children's talent agent Judy Savage adds:

> The first thing I look for in a child is the passion. A child who wants to do this comes in for the interview and he's just so excited and "alive"—he *loves* the idea of being in the business.
>
> I look for size. We look for forty-two-inch six-year-olds to play four-year-olds and fifty-four-inch ten-year-olds to play ages eight, nine, and ten. We also look for twelve-year-olds who are not over five feet tall, thirteen to fourteen-year-olds who are five-one to five-two. If they're thirteen and five-seven or five-eight, they have to play fifteen- to sixteen-year-olds because they're taller than everybody. It's almost always preferable to have older children who look younger.

Children who do well in the business read well. The earlier they learn to read, the better they'll do. Child actors who are very successful are always smart. Usually, the smarter they are, the more they'll work. They also have to have charisma. Kids who are suited for the business light up the room when they come in. Even with a three-year-old, the conversation during the interview should be so interesting that you'd rather be with the child than anyone else.

NOTE: Never beg, bribe, or bully a child to get him to perform. Having to resort to such tactics indicates that the child is not interested in doing this. Children will always be better at something they enjoy doing.

Prototypes

Carol Lyn Sher says:

> Day in and day out the demand is for classic prototypes, and for "real" actors. Advertisers seek kids with experience who have

worked on sets, and who are great with improvisation. From year to year, commercial types change almost as often as fashions change. A film or TV show will connect with the broad audience and suddenly everyone wants that type, or prototype.

Commercials follow trends and hits in pop culture and are inspired by them. Zooey Deschanel was *the* prototype for a year. In the last few years, there's been demand for Michael Cera types, *Napoleon Dynamite* types, Ellen Page of *Juno*, and *Modern Family* types. Funny, though, a minute before the story writer created that successful character, these actors were out auditioning for commercials. They were unknown but they handled a wide array of roles. They weren't a "type" until the writer created that iconic character and that character is now called a "type."

We at CESD have represented several celebrity kids who became prototypes for commercials. Miley Cyrus, Jesse McCartney, Ariel Winter, and Jonathan Lipnicki all became frequently asked for prototypes after they became recognizable.

Kids who do well are capable of not only winning at the audition level, but also of really being able to focus on the work on set. The reality of this work is that it is long, hard, difficult work, and often under many wild conditions. The kids are up at 6 A.M. and could be out in windstorms. A department store shoot for winter had kids wearing parkas and mittens pretending to be cold on a 100-degree day on the Salton Sea. (The salt of the sea looked like snow.)

Current Demands

Ms. Sher continues:

> Most of my time is spent sorting through the actors on my roster to find those who are real matches to the skills requested. Reality television has encouraged reality commercials.
>
> Advertisers want consumers to connect to their message and often mold the message to be a realistic slice of life. For instance, we are often asked for cancer survivors who are sharing the message of a treatment that helped them recover.
>
> It's common for me to have to find real hopscotch players, real kids who can blow bubbles as big as their faces, violinists, gamers, real face-painting NFL fans, marathon runners, dancers

and athletes of all types, Japanese rockabillys, ballerinas, as well as real kids who could do chin-ups, acrobats, parkours[1], real families, social media experts, auctioneers, chefs, psychotherapists, real doctors, and real moms and dads with their children.

The configurations are limitless. Just like calls for adults, no longer do the directors want actors playing doctors. When they want a doctor, they want doctors who can act. They want real fire breathers, firemen, and poets. I say that everyone is needed in commercials if you just wait long enough!

But overriding all the demands for types is the ever-present need of the storyteller, the great actor. They seek young minds that are advanced beyond their peers and their years.

Getting Pictures

You need some kind of photo to show to agents when seeking representation. When children are under the age of four, agents generally don't suggest parents run out and get professional pictures done, because at that age children change so quickly. It's highly impractical to spend $300 on professional headshots of a child who will change before you have a chance to send the pictures out. To get younger children started, all you need are a couple of snapshots to have available to email to agents.

In a snapshot, agents look for the same things as in a professional headshot. You want a picture that looks like your child. No hats, makeup, big bows in the hair, Halloween masks, or food on the face—just a nice, clean picture of your child looking like a child. Make sure the face is smiling or looking like she's having a good time. Don't send "crying baby" shots.

Once the child is picked up by an agent or manager, it is time to think about a good professional headshot. A good commercial headshot is your child's most important marketing tool. Your agent or manager will suggest several photographers to you. Stay away from agents or managers who charge you for photos. The photographer should be independent of the agent or manager—and the choice of photographer

---

[1] Parkour: A game. Also called the "art of displacement"—a movement training discipline that developed out of military obstacle course training.

should be yours. The agent ultimately will submit the headshots to casting directors in order to secure jobs for the child. As with adults, your child's headshot is his calling card.

In Chapter 1, Getting Headshots, you learned how to go through the process of finding a good photographer and selecting the right shot. That process is almost identical when preparing children for the business. However, you have one additional question to ask every photographer before you go to see their work: Do you specialize in photographing children for the industry? There is a big difference between commercial headshots for the industry and pageant pictures (figs. 28 and 29).

Morgan Thrush

FIG. 28: Commercial headshot.   FIG 29. Same talent, pageant headshot.

There is a big difference between a commercial headshot (FIG. 28) and a pageant headshot (FIG. 29).
PHOTO CREDITS: FIG. 28: Rich Hogan. FIG. 29: Old School Photography.

Whereas photographs intended for commercial use are done with simple lighting, simple clothing, no noticeable makeup on pre-teens and younger kids (and very light, clean makeup if any on teens), in pageant competition photographs, it is perfectly acceptable, depending on the pageant system, to use glamorized photos using makeup at almost any age, fancy dresses, and hats and accessories; gimmicky photos (using special effects, diffusion or soft focus, and "theme pictures") are also appropriate.

Some pageants are judged by modeling and talent agents, so it is best to ask for guidelines before submitting entries. Agents and managers frown on traditional pageant pictures. Agents and managers have stereotyped views of pageant kids, seeing them as little automatons, too poised or rehearsed (lacking normal childlike spontaneity). Pageant moms have also gotten a bad rap in parts of the industry.

Know that each style of photograph has a specific purpose. You would not wear a ballerina's tutu to a rodeo audition; neither would you use a typical pageant photograph for a commercial audition. To look professional, become clear as to the uses of each type of photograph and use the right picture for each circumstance.

Not all photographers relate well to children. Try to find someone who photographs lots of kids and *loves* doing it. Meet the photographer before deciding to hire him. When you go to the interview, watch the interaction between the photographer and your child. If they don't seem to be hitting it off, it might be better to look for someone else. You're paying for these pictures and a successful outcome boosts the child's chances of getting work in the business. A great headshot is a collaboration between artist and subject; the result of the shoot depends on the existence of a very positive chemistry between your child and the photographer.

Tips for a Successful Shoot

■ *Kids look best in simple, kid-type clothes.* Denim shirts or jackets, overalls, and textured sweaters look great on kids, and they love wearing them. Stay away from busy patterns, frilly things, hats, bows, and large accessories that get in the way. Avoid distracting jewelry or props. Avoid glamorous hairstyles and don't have your child wear makeup (other than corrective). Teens should look clean (not made-up). The colors and general look should reflect the child's personality without neutralizing your child. Trust the photographer and the stylist to suggest what's best when it comes to preparing for the shoot.

■ *Make sure the child comes to the shoot well rested.* No sleepovers or late parties the night before a photo session. Do not let little ones fall asleep in the car on the way to the studio, or they will look sleepy or puffy during the shoot. (They may also get crabby if they weren't ready to wake up.) If you have a long ride, plan ahead for activities that will help the child stay alert and excited about the shoot.

■ *Bring some quiet project to keep the child occupied in the waiting room.* Avoid letting her run all over the studio, and never leave a small child unattended.

■ *If the child is not well or having an off day, call and try to reschedule the shoot.* Your child will not photograph well if he's not into it. Give as much advance notice as possible as a courtesy to the photographer. Not showing up without calling to cancel is a definite no-no.

■ *Don't bring any negative energy to the shoot.* Leave problems at home. Children absorb emotional energy, positive and negative. If you have been lecturing the child or engaging in nonproductive conversation on the ride over, or especially in the waiting room, it may affect the child's session. Commercials are happy and energetic. It is important that your child feels that way when performing in front of the camera.

After the shoot, thank the photographer and assistants. When it's time, the photographer will usually help you select the best shots to consider as your initial selections. Reread Chapter 1 for help in selecting your pictures. Typically, the agent will ask you (with the photographer) to narrow your selections down to five or six top choices in different outfits and attitudes and then print up 4×6 copies, which you will bring to the agent who will make the final selection. The agent will not have time to take hours looking through hundreds of images. It is also very hard to compare one next to the other online. The agent will look for things like particular differences in energy in your look, tension in the smile, etc., by shuffling the photos back and forth next to each other.

Résumés for Kids

Résumés for kids (fig. 30) are set up pretty much the same way as adult résumés (see Chapter 2)—a single 8×10 page (which you will attach to the back of the headshots) that summarizes your child's statistics and experience in the business.

Unlike an adult résumé, children's résumés include their date of birth (never age; it dates the résumé) and eye and hair coloring. An early résumé—before the child is union—should include a lot of training. The child's résumé should also include school productions (these show the child's interest in performing), achievements that imply drive and ambition, and any special skills the child may have. (For a three-year-old, special skills might include reading and having a long attention span; for older kids, skateboarding, roller-blading, and scuba diving may be listed as special skills.) With a little imagination, even a rank beginner can put together an attractive, interesting résumé.

Never lie on a résumé, especially about a special skill. Anything you list on the special skills portion of the résumé, you'd better be able to do and do *well*. If your child gets called into an audition and is asked to do something you listed as a special skill, then can't do it, that leaves a terrible impression. Make sure your résumé is honest.

NY/LA CESD talent agent Carol Lyn Sher says:

> Unless we are meeting a movie star and reading their extensive film credits, we read a résumé from the bottom up. At the bottom are skills. What makes this talent special? Wow, this one collects cow pie art! This one dances and is working with the Debbie Allen dance studio. This one sang the national anthem at a Dodger game. I will continue reading your résumé if your skills catch my eye.
>
> Most kid résumés read the same from the top down. You'll see the classic kid's plays: *Guys and Dolls, Wizard of Oz, Winnie the Pooh*, etc. We see the same plays on most résumés, so they aren't that meaningful. We see lots of holiday pageants and school appearances. It is good to show a history of work on the stage, but we need more.
>
> A meaningful résumé should highlight improvisation, and training with top coaches. A résumé that will stand out shows theater experience at the regional or civic level, not just *Alice in Wonderland* from a school production. Directors love to see independent films as well. Never fake a credit.

ABRAMS ARTISTS AGENCY

AARON BERGER
(SAG)

Hair: Blonde
Eyes: Hazel
DOB: 12/18/2000

Height   4' 3"
Weight   65 lbs

Domina Holbeck: Abrams Artists Agency (310) 859-0625
Cinda Snow: Snow Management (323) 620-6651

TELEVISION

Criminal Minds	Birthday Boy/co-star	Jesse Warn	CBS
Burn Notice	Brandon	John Kretchmer	USA Network
Blue Planet	Mac/co-star	Phil Zizza	
Discovery Health Network	Candid Kids		Discovery Channel
Miami CSI	Boy (under 5)		CBS
Dexter	Boy (under 5)		SHOWTIME

FILM

Turbo	Danny	David Soren
A Blue Flower	Lead	Nil Taranger
Pose Down	Lead	Erika Yeomans
Out	Lead	Nil Taranger
What is The Electric Car?	Principle	Ken Grant
Spin Cast	Lead	Breht Gardner

COMMERCIAL/PRINT/RADIO
Detailed List upon request.

Voice Over

Turbo (DreamWorks Production)	Danny	David Soren
Busch Gardens	Cheetah Hunt Roller Coaster	
Florida Lottery	Dreams	Cooper Hayes
Planet Blue	Mac	Phil Zizza

TRAINING

Janet Alhanti	Scene Study, Improv., Cold Read	Los Angeles
The ActorSite	CD Workshops, Improv, Scene Study	Los Angeles
Bob Corff	Voice Coach	Los Angeles
The Edge Dance Studio	Hip Hop	Los Angeles
Harriet Greenspan	Scene Study, Cold Read	Los Angeles
Marjorie Morhaim	Scene Study, Improv, Cold Read	Miami
Krystyna Barron	Scene Study, Improv	Miami
Karen Storms	Scene Study, Improv, Cold Read	Orlando/ LA

Special Interests: Skateboarding, Razor Scooter, Diabloing, Stilt Walking, Acting, Hip hop, Singing, Knee Boarding, Water Skiing, Fishing

9200 Sunset Blvd, Suite 1125, Los Angeles, CA 90069

FIG. 30: Sample of a children's résumé (Aaron Berger).

Once you put together your résumé, print it on good quality paper. Attach one to each of your headshots. If necessary, trim the résumé to the exact size of the headshots. (Use a paper cutter, not scissors, for a cleaner look.)

Finding an Agent

Now you're ready to start submitting your headshots to children's agents. Refer to industry listings for legitimate talent agencies. First, submit your child's snapshots or professional headshots to agencies that indicate they have a children's division. If you have a friend who already has an agent, ask if they would speak to their agent about your child. Look on the agency website and it will tell you how they like to receive submissions. The answer will be either an email address to submit to, or an address to send a hard copy to. If the website does not give out that info, call and ask whoever answers the phone how to submit your child's photo. Referrals are always the best means of introduction.

In regional areas, where the legitimacy of an agency is not as clear-cut as major markets, it's a good idea to check them out with the Better Business Bureau before you approach them. In smaller, regional markets, call community theaters and the nearest SAG-AFTRA office to find talent agents in or near your area. Be sure to include a cover letter (see Chapter 2) with each submission, requesting an interview. Generally, agents only respond when they'd like you to come in for an interview. If you don't get a response within two weeks, call each agency to make sure they received your submission.

Once you've secured an appointment, the following tips may help you and your child get through the interview/audition process:

- Review Chapter 8, What You Need to Know about Agents, Managers, and Unions.
- Make sure the child is well rested and fed before going in.
- Do not coach the child about what to do or how to behave at the interview. Let the child answer questions addressed to her and do not answer for her.
- Dress the child casually, preferably in clothes she likes. The same choices and advice given for photo shoots apply to interviews and

auditions for kids. Your child's wardrobe selections should reflect her personality. If it is part of her personality to wear bright colors or patterns, let her dress that way. The interview should reflect her personality. There is not one personality that is right, so it will be detrimental to your child to try to second-guess what the agent is looking for.

■ Resist the temptation to critique or analyze the child's performance during or after the interview.

Typical Scams

You do not want to get involved with an unsavory agent. The most popular industry scam involves a so-called agent who will only offer to sign you if you pay to take a class or use his photographer. You should be able to choose any training you want and use any photographer you want. It is common for an agent to have a list of several good photographers and classes.

If you are from a smaller, regional area with limited options for access to good industry training and photographers, do as much research as possible before deciding who to work with. (See Chapter 1 and Chapter 4 for more information on finding a good photographer and/or talent coach.) Be aware of packages and contracts that run thousands of dollars. Check out your options. Do everything possible to avoid being taken advantage of (see Chapter 5 for more information on scams). An agent should only be making a percentage of the money you make on the jobs booked through their agency.

Another scam you want to avoid is one in which a so-called agent sends you out on auditions, you get booked, the agent collects payment, then does not pay you for your services. Unscrupulous agents may dangle you on with excuses such as, "They have not paid us yet," for extended periods of time. Reporting such treatment to the Better Business Bureau would be your recourse. An agent must pay a performer who has worked on a job under SAG-AFTRA union contract within fourteen days from the day of the shoot. If they do not, the actor can report the situation to the union, and fines and penalties are involved in accordance with the situation. (See more on this in Chapter 5, Scams.)

Managers

Whether or not to hire a manager is a personal decision. For a child, having a manager can be an asset. Good managers tend to nurture and develop a child's career. For children four and over, it is the job of the manager to introduce the child and get them signed to an agent for TV, film, and commercials. However, agents do not generally sign children three and under. It is the job of the manager to have good relationships with several agents who will call the manager for audition times.

While agents work hard to find jobs for your child (and many others), they are generally too busy to educate parents and kids about the business, to monitor the child's progress, or to teach the family how to deal with frustration, rejection, or success. Many people, especially beginners, find that having someone mentor parents and child as they learn and develop is well worth paying the extra 15 percent.

Parents might consider hiring a manager at the point where the child has done many commercials and the family decides it is time to expand into film and television. The manager will guide the growth and movement of the child's career just as he would for an adult.

There are many managers who represent only children. Some handle both children and adults. Others represent infants. Many agents will not sign infants as clients because they change too quickly in looks and behavior. Another problem with representing infants is that parents often change their minds about the business when they discover the cost and time involved in launching and maintaining a child's career. An agent is reluctant to invest time and energy in a client who is not in it for the long haul. Dealing with overzealous or unmotivated parents or trying to educate them about the professional expectations of the industry can be time-consuming. Many times, rather than sign on infants themselves, the agent will contact managers who represent them.

The best ways to find a manager for a child is to ask other industry parents or your agent for names of managers in your area. Call the National Conference of Personal Managers in New York City or Los Angeles. It is not a good idea to look for managers outside of industry references.

Training

When children are young (too young to read), they can pretty much get by on their personality and charm. But by the time they can read, they really have to begin to know what they are doing. Before a child knows how to read, they can get some training in taking direction and getting used to being in an audition room. They should get used to "standing on their mark" (see adult training chapter), the bright lights, and the camera. A good teacher of young kids also works with their concentration and focus, which would include minimizing their fidgeting. It's important to keep the kids natural and their imagination flowing.

For kids that know how to read, a class or workshop in on-camera commercial technique will help your child get comfortable in front of the camera while learning to audition. You want your child to stay natural and spontaneous. Never get to the point where he is slick and polished. Training should bring out a child's individual personality and eliminate inhibitions. Training should not try to mold or change a child or, worst of all, take away from the child's natural spontaneity.

Judy Savage, owner of the Savage Agency in LA, elaborates:

> I always say that if you are an incredible six-year-old—you read, you're smart, you're small, you're outgoing, you have the personality—your competition in the whole town is only about ten other kids who are that special [at that age]. By the time you're ten, there are about two hundred competitors, and by the time you turn eighteen, there are about two thousand.
>
> What happens is that everybody who turns eighteen and has a passion for acting comes to California from all over the world to try to break into the business, and your competition absolutely magnifies. These other kids might have been taking acting, singing, elocution, speech, and every other kind of lesson you can think of since they were six years old. Also, when you turn eighteen, the competition comes from the legal sixteen- and seventeen-year-olds who have graduated from high school as well as from good-looking twenty-five-year-olds, so it's tough.

Once the child starts getting calls for auditions, on-the-job training serves as the best teacher. Exposing kids to improvisation classes, acting classes, community theater, and school drama programs can help them round out their talent and develop confidence.

Tips on Auditions

DOS AND DON'TS

Do:

- Respect your audition appointment time. Casting directors have a schedule to keep. Coming late causes confusion and creates a backup.

- Sign in upon entering the reception area. Casting directors use this sheet to call performers into the studio. Forgetting to sign in could put you at risk of losing the opportunity to audition.

- Take your child aside and begin going over the script after signing in. Resist the temptation to socialize with other parents and children in the reception area. You are better off attending to the business at hand. Concentrate on preparing your child to give a good audition.

- Have your headshot and résumé ready to hand to the casting director—even if 75 percent of the time it is not asked for because everything is done online. Have it with you for that one time.

Don't:

- Over-rehearse the script. It is important to become familiar with the material while maintaining spontaneity.

- Wait until your child is called into the audition room to begin grooming him. When the casting director calls "Next!" the child should be fully prepared to go in and give a good audition.

- Bring extra family members, friends, boyfriends, or performers to the audition.

- Put makeup on your child. *Please!*

OTHER CONSIDERATIONS

- Food auditions: Many auditions for children are for food, especially snacks, fast foods, and cereals. You will be told at the time of the audition call what the food is. If your child cannot eat the food because she doesn't like it or is allergic to it, please make sure to ask if the actor will actually have to eat the food. If the answer is yes, don't waste everyone's time by going to the call. Your child will be given the food at the audition to make sure she actually likes it. She *will* be expected to eat the product enthusiastically, take after take, and will have to eat more than the usual intake. If your child cannot eat the product, it's to everyone's advantage for you to say so *when you are called for the audition*. You may have to bow out of the audition.

■ Parents are not asked to come into the audition room. Part of the casting process is to see how a child behaves without a parent in the room. If a child is shy or insecure, or cries when his parent is not with him, he is not good commercial material. Always be nearby, however, either just outside the door or in a reception room.

Sometimes parents are allowed to "assist" when the audition calls for babies and toddlers. You should be aware that for very young children (age four and under), backup kids are always booked for shoots, just in case one or more children get tired, cranky, or otherwise unable to cooperate. Twins or triplets have good booking rates because they provide instant backup that is identical or similar in looks. Consider it a "gift" when there is a backup. It shows an understanding of the natural unpredictability of kid's behavior and it eliminates any pressure from you and your child.

Common-Sense Safeguards for Showbiz Kids

In a world where parents must take every precaution to assure their child's safety and well-being, it defies logic to watch how quickly well-meaning moms and dads throw caution to the wind when it comes to working in show business. The industry requires children to talk to people they don't always know well and to do so without their parents in immediate sight, so it's very important for families to keep their feet on the ground (and the stars out of their eyes) when making decisions that affect their child's immediate and long-term future.

Common sense is essential to guard against unscrupulous vultures who prey on showbiz kids and their families. For instance:

■ Know that a minor (fifteen years or younger) *must* have a guardian at a shoot. If there is travel involved, the production company must also arrange (and pay) for the guardian to accompany the child.

■ Be alert if you are called to hotels, unsafe neighborhoods, out-of-the-way buildings, or any location late at night. It's not that auditions are not held under these circumstances. Just use common sense when dealing with these conditions.

- If you are going to an unknown casting office, be alert to the surroundings. Are there a lot of other guardians and kids there? Are other kids coming out of the room happy? Are the people who bring the children into the room friendly to them and their guardians?

- Teenagers going to auditions alone must be alert. Females are not asked to wear less than a two-piece bathing suit at a legitimate commercial audition. No one should be asked to change into a bathing suit in the audition room. If an actor needs to change clothes, some kind of changing room should be provided. There have been instances in which Peeping Toms hid behind a two-way mirror and taped clothing changes.

- Both males and females should be aware of advances or threats by people who audition or hire them (people who seem to be in a powerful position). No job is worth compromising yourself, and no legitimate job would ever involve unsavory behavior. You would *never* have to go to a producer's house or go out on a date with him.

- *Trust your instincts.* If something doesn't feel right, *leave.*

- Check out state child labor laws and make sure the shoot is adhering to those laws.

When to Consider Commuting or Relocating to a Larger Market

Most agents and managers agree that children should get as much experience in their own market (however small) before going to a larger market. Audition, perform, and learn as many disciplines as you can before going to a larger market.

Carol Lyn Sher advises:

> I surprise a lot of people and tell new actors to NOT come for pilot season. Don't come to LA during pilot season if you don't have an ongoing established relationship with your agent and have never been in consideration for lead roles.
>
> The business in LA is most active when the traditional school year is on. A new actor has a much better shot at getting in and getting seen by casting directors and getting representation meetings during episodic season. One reason being that agents are pushed for time during pilot season because the seven-year contractual deals must be negotiated before any studio test is offered.

Agents are feverishly negotiating every detail of a seven-year contract for actors who are in the running for shooting the series' regular role. The deals are set and the network then knows they have a pre-negotiated choice of any actor in the room, so there is no monetary surprise when they announce their choice after the network test. Agents may also be weighing projects against one another and need creative time to read all pilots and to research the power behind the projects.

We do bring established talent from major markets to LA during pilot season, but we also bring them to LA and NY as needed throughout the year. Models have traditionally built careers following the sun. NY is busier in spring through autumn and Chicago is busier in the summer. Miami, Orlando, and LA are busiest in the winter. The same holds for international work. The sun dictates the busy season.

We encourage relationships with regional agencies and acting coaches. They bring us developed talent who tell new stories and are fresh to our market. These talent have learned how to Skype and do Facebook. They are masters at self-taping. We have TV or film projects that sometimes cast a wide net and have the luxury of time to cast and we get scripts out to a large number of actors from around the world and collect and submit tapes/links.

You need to be in the room to have the advantage to gain a role. Get famous and then move to a ranch. If I wanted to be the top waitress in Minneapolis, then I would, at a minimum, first need to live there, right?

Make definitive plans for your first venture to NY or LA. Write representatives in advance and tell them you'll be available for meetings from Date A to Date B. Be specific. Saying that you are "willing to relocate" won't get you far. Who wouldn't move for a starring role? When are you actually coming? Take advantage of your time, combine it with a workshop, a photo shoot, and with other meaningful activities.

Stay a week or two and test out the environment. Get representation and then come for a longer stint during episodic season. Two to three months is preferred. Avoid holidays. Christmas break and spring break are also breaks for producers. Come when business is being conducted. After a few trials, you'll get an idea of the level of activity and your propensity to have a shot at success. Most talent move here permanently after the third year of smaller trips.

Commercials do not accept self-taped auditions. The performer must be in the audition room to be coached by the session director. Tell your representatives two weeks prior to your arrival. Have your paperwork and casting systems ready and updated. This way, you can be submitted for castings starting after you arrive and you can hit the ground running. We love meeting talent from around the country and the world. We travel and scout regularly and are open to submissions from all levels, managers, coaches, and self-submissions.

The child must listen to his parents. He must be able to move swiftly and in an organized manner, getting to appointments on time. He must tolerate the tedium of traveling from one audition to the next, waiting in the reception room until it's his turn to audition. At the callback, he may be asked by the director to do something over and over again. He may walk into a callback audition and have to perform in front of six clients. The child must be willing to come in early for a booking if need be, and he must be able to handle the pressure during tense moments on the set.

The demands on children in the industry can be considerable. They range from travel demands to disappointments when they don't get the job. It is certainly not for everyone. Yet some kids love the challenges and the demands, and the rewards that come with them. Inevitably, parents of serious child actors will decide whether or not to take the child to a larger market. They need to decide which market to come to and what time of year is best. A typical time to try a new market is summer, when your child is on school vacation.

Deciding between the two larger markets (New York and Los Angeles) is a matter of personal choice. If the focus is entirely on commercials (which is a good way to get your feet wet and to get comfortable with the industry), there are as many opportunities in Los Angeles as there are in New York. Look at both lifestyles and decide which you prefer. New York is a big, congested, exciting city where you would use public transportation. Los Angeles has a more outdoorsy atmosphere, and you spend a lot of time in your car driving from place to place. Look into the costs of living in both locations. Is climate a consideration for you? One place won't have the magic answer—so do your research on both markets, then go where you feel most comfortable.

When regional kids come to New York or Los Angeles for the summer, they find themselves competing against hundreds of other kids from all over the country, some of whom have several summers under their belts. Then there are kids who live in the area you will be moving to who were practically raised in the business. If your child is booking most of the jobs she auditions for (or is consistently called back) in her own market, she may be ready for a summer in a larger market. But competition will be stiff. The better prepared children are, the more experience they have, the better their chances of bookings in places like New York and Los Angeles.

A pilot is the first episode of a potential TV series. If accepted, the show is given a time slot and the production company produces more of the series. Most of the main characters will be cast with actors who have some experience under their belt and are extremely comfortable on a set. If you are focusing on television series, it might actually be better to spend time in Los Angeles during episodic season. After a season or two of episodic season, then the actor will be a stronger contender for the pilot opportunities.

Generally, pilots are cast from January through mid-March. They are finished and delivered by the end of April to be considered for pickup, with final decisions made between May and June. Episodic season is when the television series are up and running. Casting is conducted on a weekly basis to fill all the supporting acting roles, "under fives," the co-stars, and guest stars. Episodic season runs from late July to the end of March. In May and June, television series are on hiatus, which means that no production is being done. If you are focusing on television, this is a good time not to come to Los Angeles. Cable pilots run on a different schedule, often year-round, with summer months being slow.

Sue Schacter, a New York–based manager, advises:

> Summer is the best time to come to a larger market so as not to upset the family structure or the child's life. A summer in Los Angeles or New York should be like a vacation.
>
> They shouldn't come with the intention of working. The attitude should be, "Let's go to New York for the summer and have a great time and perhaps while we're there, we'll get some work," because the ones who come with the intention and the

compulsion to work never have a good time and never get enough work. It is generally an eight-week commitment. Parents will have to find housing. I try to encourage parents to bring the other children to keep the family together. All too often, because of the money involved and whatever visibility is involved, the mother becomes focused on the one child and forgets the husband and their other children.

My first questions for the mother are, "Do you have family you can stay with in that market?" and, "Does your husband have the ability to come and visit at least once or twice during the stay?" Often the answer is that he cannot because the family is financially stressed, so it becomes difficult because the mother, of course, gets lonely. The children get lonely too, so we try to create more of a vacation atmosphere for them. But whenever possible, I always encourage them to bring the siblings.

What Parents Can Expect

Judy Savage, owner of The Savage Agency (Los Angeles), says:

> Most people come here not prepared enough, not trained enough, and with high expectations. They think that in three months of a pilot season, they're going to make it. The general rule is that it takes about three years to make it. There may be an exception. They may get a little thing here and there, but to get on a series or to get a movie, the time frame we're looking at is generally wider.
>
> The parent and the child have to become partners in this. There's never been a successful child actor without one committed parent or relative—somebody who literally has to give up her own career for ten or twelve years and devote all her time to this child (or children) because they have to be ready to go at any moment.
>
> You have to realize that it's going to be really hard on the rest of the family. You can expect not to get much respect on the set. When a child is hired, the mother has to be there, within sight and sound. They would rather have you be a mute and sit in the corner and not know you're there. I did it for fifteen years and I know the feeling. You feel like you don't belong. You feel like a vegetable. You feel like you don't have a purpose. And yet, you know in your heart that this is something your children love and it's an amazing way (for most) to be with your children, and make some money for

them. Some kids pay for their braces, cars, college, and houses. A lot of them don't stay in the business, but they have all that by the time they're eighteen or nineteen.

And whatever the time frame involved, the child always needs a parent or parents around. It's very thankless to be a show-biz mom. You have to be very organized and be able to keep many facts straight.

For instance, in New York, which is a freelance market, you have to keep track of which agent sent you out for which job, and remember that when it comes to contracts and bookings. You have to keep track of schedules and figure out if you can get from one audition to the next in time. You have to be ready to move at a moment's notice for last-minute calls. The more you are available for auditions, the more chance for bookings. An agent will lose interest in you if you are not available a lot.

Compensation

Because of the many opportunities for children in commercials, a great deal of money can be made, depending on how many commercials the child books and how the commercial runs (see Chapter 13 on talent payments).

HANDLING THE CHILD'S MONEY

It is very important to know exactly what you are going to do with the money your child earns in the business *and* what the law says you *must* do to protect the child's interests.

In California, for instance, the Coogan Law (named after child star Jackie Coogan, who wound up penniless when he came of age because his parents had spent all his money) was set in place to protect young performers from their parents' or guardians' lack of knowledge, inexperience, or outright greed. The Coogan Law mandates that 25 percent of a child's earnings must be placed in trust so that when the child comes of age, he will have something to show for his efforts.

Even if there are no specific laws governing the way a child's earnings are used, know that when children reach the age of maturity (eighteen in most states), they can ask for an accounting of the money they earned while underage. Parents risk being sued by their children for mismanagement of funds if they cannot adequately account for the money.

In cases in which a child becomes the primary breadwinner for the entire family, courts tend to look with disapproval upon parents who charge the child's estate excessively for such things as chaperoning/ chauffer fees, food, rent, and schooling. Such expenses generally fall under a parent's normal responsibilities (most folks don't expect their kids to reimburse them for such things). If a child's money is used to buy property (like a bigger house, for instance), the youngster may even be able to sue her parents for the home, since it was her earnings that paid for it in the first place.

Aside from the obvious legal and financial problems that can arise from failing to launch a sensible financial plan for a child's earnings, the emotional and psychological damage done when children are put in the position of having to sue their parents to get what is rightfully theirs is nothing short of catastrophic. Wise parents will discuss financial planning with their accountant and their agent or manager and put a proper trust/investment package into place.

Working Papers

To actually work as a child actor, the child must have good grades. To work in a commercial, a minor is required to have a work permit from the state. The state issues the work permit based on the school approving it. The state will issue the work permit if the child has a "B" average and above. In Los Angeles, the permit is good for up to six months. However, every state has its own rules regarding the length of time the work permit is good for.

How Your Child's Acting Career Coincides with His or Her Education

Interview with Alan Simon

Alan Simon is the owner of On Location Education, a company that provides tutors for children in the business while they are on the set. (Alan was previously an actor who supported himself by substitute teaching in the New York City school system.)

The education of children in the entertainment industry is important and definitely not overlooked. On Location Education provides teachers, studio teachers, and educational consultants to work with production companies employing child actors in television, film, theater, national tours, commercials, industrials, and circuses. Children who have alternative lifestyles must work their schooling around their production day. On Location Education helps them form an educational plan of action with their home schools.

Legally, at what age does the actor fall under the "child" category?
In the SAG commercial contract, the definition of a minor is fifteen years and younger, which means anyone older technically is not considered a minor, and provisions that apply to children under the SAG contract cease to apply. Local and state labor laws may have certain provisions pertaining to the needs of sixteen- to eighteen-year-olds, and those can be found through the local departments of labor.

How do parents find out about specific child labor laws?
A complete set of guidelines is available to all members of either union from the local office (ask for the SAG-AFTRA *Young Performers Handbook*, 3rd edition). Parents should check their local labor laws. No producer is going to tell you. You have to read the code or whatever information you can find for your area.

Are there occasions when you are called to give education on the set?
Absolutely. In California, education is required on the set. There must be a welfare worker present at all times. That person, called a studio teacher, functions in the official capacity of a welfare worker empowered by the state of California to speak for the child's health, education, and welfare. Welfare workers serve many roles. They are there to educate the child and to ensure that the physical surroundings are not in any way negative or harmful. They also make sure the wardrobe area is properly situated for boys and girls. If indeed welfare workers feel that a child is being worked by the production company even five minutes over the proper amount of time, they have the right to virtually stop production and call it a day on the child's behalf. In other states the parents will need to have the forethought to negotiate with the producer and request a teacher in advance.

How is education approached on the set?

There are two ways to answer this question. On Location Education or an individual studio teacher can be responsible for finding out the specifics of the curriculum at a child's home school. We contact parents and make sure the kids bring the material they are supposed to cover, be it the textbook, handouts, or whatever. But when there is no teacher provided, then it is up to the parent to get work from the school and, if necessary, hire a teacher to oversee instruction. The ultimate goal is for the child to return to school on par with his classmates.

If a child is booked with only a day or two's notice, does that give you time to set up the education requirements?

It's the nature of the beast. These things happen very quickly. Kids who work rather frequently know they have to be prepared to bring their materials with them. Parents who do this frequently are ready for it. Parents who are novices are not. Parents need to have a tutoring support network in place. They should know where to find a teacher while maintaining a positive relationship with their home school. If they are working outside of California, they should never assume a tutor will be provided.

A good agent, at the time of the booking, is always going to tell the parent, "There will be a teacher on the set. Please make sure you bring your books." We are also given the child's phone number, are authorized to contact the family, and will do whatever we have to do to ensure that the books and materials are there.

What personality traits do you notice in kids who do commercials?

Kids who are successful, who do this regularly, tend to be bright and have a lot of energy. They tend to know how to budget their time. They know what it's like to sit in that green room[2] and keep themselves occupied.

What is the crucial information parents must have before their children get into the business?

I would say that if you want to make this a career, it would be important to cultivate a good relationship with your home school. Make sure the principal knows that your child is doing this and that there are going to be periods of time when, with very little advance notice, your child is going to be called to the set and will be out. Make sure the school staff know that the child's absences

---

[2] A green room is an offstage waiting room.

are not a reflection on the teacher or the school, that you really want to work with the school, and that you will hold your child responsible for the workload missed. In fact, you will always see to it that the child is tutored on the set, a teacher will be provided, and the work will get done.

You have to look into the issue of excused absences. If your child is going to be out two days here, three days there, all of a sudden that adds up to ten days' absences; before you know it, you have reached the legal limit of absences you can have before your child is considered truant. You need to deal with these issues up front. It is very, very important.

I think most parents are overwhelmed once they get a job on location. I don't think they realize the implications that an acting career has on their kids, on themselves, and their families. For instance, if they get booked and have to travel to another location, usually a father or another parent is left behind, and maybe other siblings as well. Parents have to create a support system in order for this to work. And I think they need to know who to go to in terms of guardianship if that becomes an issue because they both work or are unable to travel. Who are they going to get to travel with their child? What kind of questions should they ask ahead of time? Who on the set will look out for their child's best interest if they are not working in a place where there is a studio teacher empowered to act as the welfare worker?

I think parents don't realize what working their child regularly means in terms of wear and tear on the family, as well as on themselves and the child.

Specific Issues and Experiences that Young People and Their Families Go Through While Working in the Industry

Parents and guardians are the ones who have the bulk of the work to do when getting their children involved in the business. The following series of interviews are with parents who know what it takes to do well in the entertainment industry. Through their experiences you will gain knowledge to help you prepare for a successful child talent career.

First, a few introductions:

DEBBIE BOYD is the mother of two children in the business: Jenna Boyd (fig. 31), who has done commercials and stars in the films *The Missing* and *The Sisterhood of the Traveling Pants*, and a son, Cayden, who stars in *Mystic River*.

JENNIFER ARENS is the mother of Cody Arens (fig. 32), who can be seen in commercials and the films *Shadow Man*, *Riding in Cars With Boys*, *Meet the Parents*, and *Anger Management*, as well as in television series (partial list) *Punk'd*, *Malcolm in the Middle*, *The Shield*, *Passions*, *Becker*, and *Sex in the City*. (See résumé in this chapter.)

KAREN TANK, mother of Hayden Tank (fig. 33), is a mom who has two kids in the business. Hayden Tank has done commercials as well as the films (partial list) *Freaky Friday*, *Momentum*, and *The Perfect Storm* and the television series *Gilmore Girls*, *CSI: Miami*, *Six Feet Under*, *Drew Carey*, and *The Young and the Restless*.

KIMBERLEE LUCAS is the mother of Jack "Bean" Lucas (fig. 34). Jack has done commercials and has had two of his own "made for TV" cooking shows called *Bean and Sugar Show* and *What's Jack Cooking*. Mom has four children. Two of the four are active in the business.

DAVID REIVERS is a working actor with four kids in the business. His oldest son, Corbin Bleu (fig. 35), has appeared in numerous commercials, with television film credits that include (partial list) *Catch That Kid*, *Galaxy Quest*, and *Mystery Men*. He also has been a guest star on *The Amanda Show*, *Malcolm and Eddie*, *ER*, and *Cover Me*. Reivers' daughter, Hunter Grey, has booked many commercials as well as co-starring in the television shows *Felicity* and *Love & Money*.

How did you get your child involved in the acting business?
DEBBIE BOYD: We started our "journey" in this business in 1995. I read an ad that was promoting a model search in the Dallas–Ft. Worth area. The ad stated that talent agents would be judging the competition. Being skeptical and fearful that this was simply another pageant, I researched and called the company that was sponsoring the competition. I asked them to specify the names of the agents. I called those particular agencies and got confirmation that they would be participating, seeking out new talent. So, I entered Jenna (age two) in the model search. That's when and where we got our first local agent. Cayden was an infant, so he

Jenna Boyd

FIG. 31: Jenna Boyd. PHOTO CREDIT: Kelsey Edwards Photography.

Cody Arens

FIG. 32: Cody Arens. PHOTO CREDIT: Studio D Photography.

Hayden Tank

FIG. 33: Hayden Tank.
PHOTO CREDIT: Shultz Bros. Photography.

Jack "Bean" Luca

FIG. 34: Jack "Bean" Lucas.
PHOTO CREDIT: Gary Tice.

CORBIN BLEU

FIG. 35: Corbin Bleu.
PHOTO CREDIT: Nancy Jo Gilchrist.

became a baby print model with little or no input in the matter. The kids worked in commercials and print in the Texas market.

My husband's work moved us to Georgia, where the kids worked with a very "connected" agent. They worked in more commercials, print, and a couple of independent films. Before long, the Georgia agent advised and arranged for us to meet an agent in Los Angeles. We did so, and as a result of that meeting, we decided to test the waters in LA. We were under the impression that we were coming for a few weeks—that was almost four years ago! We realized it would have been a waste of time and money to leave after a few weeks. The following year was torture as we went month to month trying to decide if we should stay or go.

My husband would commute and stay for long periods of time. On one of my husband's trips to LA, I made it a point to take him around, meet agents, and hear feedback. We made a joint decision to relocate to Los Angeles. Families will face the financial pressures of living in two places at one time, and for families to stay together, husbands have to have flexibility to travel and relocate if necessary.

It has been a very slow, transitional, evolving process that has led us to LA. Each step has better prepared us for the next, and while it may have been small print jobs in the beginning, I never realized it would amount to anything more. The kids have never been taught to weigh one appointment with more intensity or preparedness than another—whether it be print, film, first-call, or screen test. I wanted to do the best with what we had and did not anticipate where we are now. Each step along the way, I was determined to be educated and be creative about how we handled the business. This determination prepared me for the next step (Texas to Georgia) and that step prepared me for the next step (Georgia to LA). I was able to learn and make mistakes in the smaller markets that would save me a lot of time and energy in the major market.

JENNIFER ARENS: I got Cody involved in the business through a modeling contest in Connecticut, where one meets managers and agents, and ended up signing with a manager in New York City when Cody was six months old. Mom and Cody have now been in the business for ten years. Cody also has a younger brother and sister in the business.

There are stages of maturity/knowledge that you go through. I remember going to Cody's first audition not knowing I had to sign in and asking a million questions without trying to seem brand-new.

KAREN TANK: Not knowing anyone else who was doing this, I started off going about it in the wrong way. First, I answered a newspaper ad and paid $900 for nothing. I then did more research, read books, and got a SAG agent list, and then found an agent the correct way.

KIMBERLEE LUCAS: Jack got into the business because of a cooking show we developed and filmed. It was seen by an agent and he was interviewed.

DAVID REIVERS: Corbin and the rest of my children were exposed to the business being that I am an actor.

What is your role as a parent at an audition?
BOYD: I believe the role of a parent/guardian cannot be defined in some one-line description. I've always tried to exercise my "stage mommy" muscle at home during the coaching or preparations. Then we usually talk things through on the way, in the car. Once we enter the casting office, I've always attempted to take off my "stage mommy" hat and let our hard work come to life on its own. Obviously, I have to play the role of mom and insist that they (my children) sit down rather than run up and down the hallways. I have to remind them to focus if I believe it's necessary and I have to remind them that we are here for a specific purpose. I keep a low profile and we take care of business and we leave.

ARENS: Sign in, fill out your size card, pull your headshot and résumé, have your child's Polaroid taken, look at the storyboard, have your child learn the copy, hand the paperwork and stapled picture and résumé to the casting assistant, make sure the child's hands and face are clean, and that their clothes are neat—and after all of this, relax. Let your child make new friends and make an effort to meet some of the parents. Although intentions are often questionable, over the years I have learned that these "friendships" are not like typical ones. You learn to balance your trust.

TANK: After my son is signed in, I sit and wait and speak to other mothers. I know there are some parents who make themselves known and try to become friendly with casting directors. The fact is that I have been doing this for over eleven years and there are some casting directors that I could not point out in a crowd.

How do you prepare for auditions?

BOYD: In regards to film, my kids have spent a lot of time in acting classes in general and have worked with a lot of acting coaches. I believe there are basic skills that have to be learned. I think it is very important that a parent pay close attention to what is happening in group classes. A family can spend a lot of money on classes. Some are far more worthwhile than others. Only recently have I felt comfortable coaching my own kids. I spend time talking them through a scene (sometimes for hours) in order to paint a picture that might help them understand and better connect to the character. Often this requires me to read through a script to get a true feeling for what is happening in the sides and spend a lot of time digging beneath a single scene to try and figure out where the character is coming from.

ARENS: The day begins the night before, writing down all the auditions that your agent has given you. Not only do you need the address and time, but the attire and copy if any (fax machines by age five or six to receive copy are imperative). Then you need to pull the wardrobe for the next day. Is it PJs, baseball, business, geek, etc.? We have nerd glasses and cool glasses, cowboy to casual attire. Bring quiet games to keep kids occupied while waiting to audition. Gameboys, hangman, tic-tac-toe, and drawing are the quiet games of choice.

Before the child is reading independently, you have to sit and help them memorize the script. It could be as little as one line (one word even) or several pages. In commercials you get the copy when you arrive at the audition. In film and television, you normally get a day's notice, so it is not much time. You want your child to learn their script while keeping it fun and fresh in the process. You don't want them to stress out because then it's not fun for anyone.

By age seven, you can normally hand off the script to them. I normally will read a couple of times with them after they are off-book just to make sure they understand the dialogue and are portraying the character description appropriately. As with any parent/child dynamic, it is often difficult for a child to hear constructive criticism from their parent. And truthfully, often what the parent thinks the writer/director is looking for is wrong.

Having your child coached is expensive, but very helpful in assuring that your child is on track and limits anger/resentment between parent and child. However, it is important that you find a reputable coach that is referred to you by your agent or by several parents in the business. I have found it important to get referrals from several parents, as one may steer you to a coach who has not worked well nor gotten positive results.

As far as preparing babies and toddlers for auditions—as with any outing—you want to make sure that you have extra outfits, diapers, clean blankets, snacks, and quiet toys. Don't forget to bring a snapshot. You do not normally need professional pictures until around age four as a child's look changes so rapidly before then. Try to coordinate naps so that they are at their best for the audition. You don't want them auditioning just after they have woken up or are ready for a nap. Also try to acclimate your child to different situations between auditions. They should be comfortable with strangers, abrupt noises, water, and animals, just to name a few. Arrive early so that if your child is fussy when you get to the audition, you can reverse their mood, change diapers, feed them, etc., before being seen.

LUCAS: Preparation for film can take more time than showing up for a commercial audition. For one, film projects often ask for several pages of a script to be memorized. Some roles might deem the need for a coach. Seeing a coach benefits your kid in knowing they understand the character and refined the audition.

My son will spend time memorizing and adapting the role to a given character, then the family has to spend time listening to those lines. I recommend not acting them out with him. It is best to sit on the couch and let the actor stand. It plays more realistic in terms of how the child will experience it in the actual session. If he needs to spend more time, try encouraging him by saying, "Really good! Keep going. Spend fifteen minutes and we'll take a break." It keeps making it more his. It takes more time, but he is still working on his skills.

TANK: Most commercial auditions have no preparation. You can drive an hour to the audition and have your child in the audition room for thirty seconds. A theatrical audition usually has dialogue that your child must learn prior to their audition, so there is more preparation.

Now that your child is successful auditioning for film, television, and commercials: How do you juggle and prepare for it all?

ARENS: For film auditions there are sides (lines) to learn and coaches to see. You will become more emotionally connected. As with any audition, if you are lucky, you will get twenty-four hours' notice. Twenty-four hours' notice for a commercial is a piece of cake. If you have several auditions miles apart (which can happen often), you have to get them to the auditions and fit in school, homework, rearrange play dates, and find time for whatever lessons they have to learn, rehearsals, and games they had planned.

In addition, and most important of all, is making sure they are well fed, rested, and happy. All this can make the most seasoned auditioning parent feel as though they are teetering between sanity and lunacy. Often there may be several films, or TV shows, with pages of scripts and different character dynamics on top of commercial auditions—or worse yet, callbacks on the same day. Obviously you can't do it all, so you need to prioritize. Although it is a thorn in their side with many parents and managers calling agents with similar issues all day long, you can ask your agent to work on trying to arrange times and sometimes even dates to better accommodate your schedule. Often it is impossible and you will miss out on some auditions. It is hard to swallow, but just know that if you are that busy, your agent and a multitude of casting directors love your child, and it is a good position to be in.

BOYD: Having two kids in the business has made for logistical nightmares on more than one occasion. Fortunately, my husband's job is somewhat flexible and we have minimized this as much as possible. Be good and gracious to your family and friends.

TANK: In order to be able to pursue this as an option, you need to have support at home, especially if you have other children not in the business. It can feel like a full-time job, and without the support of others, it would be very difficult. There are times you will have to choose which audition you are going to make. Callbacks are first priority and theatricals are second priority for our family.

LUCAS: Juggling the auditions is really about what my agency can work out for us. If I am double-booked, I notify the agents. The agent knows the casting houses and should make the arrangements. Always! A parent should not call the casting house to change an appointment. I always have everyone with me, so if I am called on the road, I will be able to make it. I like to take advantage of car time. We play games, talk about issues, dreams, plans, parties to attend, places and people to go and see. Singing your hearts out and just good old-fashioned joke-telling are such memorable times. The times we are juggling auditions can either be miserable or we can make it a good time that we are all together.

Being "on the road" does not help get things done at home. Sometimes we stress about dinner for ourselves and the rest of the family. Stock up and cook ahead of time. Use weekends to plan and prepare a few crock-pot meals for the coming week. I enlist my kids to help around the house when asked. The deal is we have to ask. But our motto is, "You are not passengers on the flight; you are crewmembers and we need you!" A sense of belonging is felt.

REIVERS: Time management does become a very large task when you are trying to coordinate everyone's schedule. You need total cooperation from both adults and kids. When it comes to children in the business, there are many times that they will have to miss out on participating in sports and dance. The desire to be in this business must be met with the flexibility to give up other things. There must always be an adult available to run with a child to an audition at any given moment. Since my wife is a stay-at-home mom, we are able to balance this task between the both of us. When many things start going all at once, we seek outside help. Things can definitely get a little crazy. An example being, my daughter got booked on a job that shoots either the seventeenth or eighteenth of the month, she has elementary graduation on the sixteenth, her senior school party is on the seventeenth, and I then booked a job on the eighteenth. Here's where we call upon our resources of babysitters, friends, and family.

If I have a booking at a location away from home for an extended period of time, I try to come home during the weekends. If it is one of my children, my wife travels with them and, depending on my schedule at the time, we may hire some help to be at home with the other children.

There is actually a set-sitting service that has been developed due to situations of families not having enough help with numerous kids in the business. This service provides a responsible adult to accommodate the child on the set.

What is it like for a parent on a commercial set?

TANK: You must learn how to blend into the background. You never want to interfere and get in the way. Directors do not want you as a distraction in any way. As the parent you must make a point to be there for the protection of your child, to make sure nothing is happening that you feel is inappropriate, but you must be there in an invisible way.

LUCAS: I am there to be supportive and informative. Aside from school time and recreational time, my child should grow with a sense of ownership in the project. I will give you the analogy of a baseball player: If you want to play ball, you watch great ballplayers and you practice and get involved in every aspect of that sport. All this to say, if your child is on the sidelines waiting to be on deck, teach him to be an observer. Spend time getting into the environment provided for his role, which allows your child to be a part of it all. So far, every director has spent time showing Jack equipment and playbacks because of his interest in the filming process. Some actually had Jack shadow them for the time he was on set. A child who is out of control and thoughtless to the surroundings of the set is a nuisance and trouble to the crew and to themselves.

Set your rules before you go on set. We have a no-soda-or-candy-until-we-leave-the-set rule. No running on set. Explain why before you are on set, not later. Give them a sense of having a job by teaching them how people handle jobs. Discuss people you know and the businesses they are in. "Can Dad go running around the office screaming and jumping on the furniture?" Do not drag down or embarrass your little actor on the set, but prepare them for the things they can look forward to experiencing when they arrive there.

ARENS: As a parent you automatically feel as though you are in the way, no matter how nice everyone is to you. And if you don't, you should. It will keep you out of trouble. Arrive early and you can catch breakfast from craft service. Have all of your child's paperwork with you (I-9, Coogan and work-permit paperwork, and your child's schoolwork). Keep quiet and out of the way. However, while your child is shooting, you have the right to view them either via a monitor or off camera. For toddlers, they let the parent be right near them while shooting, and a treat can be given to them as leverage and reward between takes. Be careful that their hands and face do not get messy. Also make sure that the treat is not too big, or it will stick in their teeth. Be aware of foods that will color their tongue such as an Oreo or a colored lollipop or popsicle.

Sometimes they will be able to run to you; other times you will be able to run to them. This is a question for you to ask your chain of command. For older children, limit their visits to craft services.

School-aged children have schoolwork to do on set. Bring their schoolwork. Younger children should have quiet toys to keep them occupied during down time. Laptops are helpful for educational games. Bring a book for yourself.

When you leave the set at the end of the day, make sure you sign out. Also make sure you ask for a call sheet. This will have the commercial name and ID as well as the client and ad agency information so that you can inquire about a copy of the commercial (which you can receive only after it has aired). It will also have talent names and phone numbers in case you want to keep in touch.

What is the chain of command you should follow on the set?

ARENS: The studio teacher is there to teach, but also to ensure the welfare of the child. This is the first chain. The second chain you may talk to is the second AD (assistant director). *Never* speak directly to the first AD, director, producers, or ad-agency members. Always go through your chain of command. The only exception is if they speak to you first, or when you are leaving and want to thank them for the opportunity.

What is the difference between being on a commercial set and a film set?

BOYD: The time difference (or lack thereof) to make relationships. In the case of a commercial or short-term commitment, everyone understands that "we're working together for a very short time and then we may or may not ever work together again." For that reason, it's very "business." A child doesn't always understand that, and it sometimes comes across as impersonal and indifferent. Children get attached quicker than adults, and my kids have struggled with this on occasion.

We work very hard to be prepared before going on the film set. If there are questions, we try to get them answered at the lowest level possible. There is no point in me asking the director a question that the PA (production assistant) can answer. I go to great lengths to give the directors, producers, etc., their space. I want the relationship to be between my child and them. I do not want to be the buffer between. My ultimate wish is for our hard work to pay off, for my kid to shine, and for the project to be a huge success. In order to increase the likelihood of that, I invite and encourage the decision-makers to feel free to discuss how "this scene or that" might be improved and what my child should or shouldn't be doing to help in that process.

This is not about me, and I usually go to great strides to make sure that set people see that I recognize that. If I notice that a particular adjustment should or could be made to improve the performance, I may or may not say something. There are times I have asked to speak to the director or my child, but those instances are far and few between—and typically not before a basic level of respect has been established. I do not advocate that you sit back and turn your head if rules are being broken and your child is being taken advantage of. Those rules, and how to handle the bending or breaking of rules, should be discussed between parent and the set teacher/welfare worker. I usually have a conversation early on so that the set teacher/welfare worker understands that I am not there as one who will "sacrifice anything and everything" in the name of work. I believe in the team concept, and we are all there to work together for a common goal. However, I will not do so at the expense of jeopardizing my child's protection and the laws that were put in place as a direct result of abuse by the system.

How do you deal with jealousy issues between siblings?

LUCAS: We encourage our children by exposing them to their strengths and let that direct their steps. We cannot measure ourselves against another's success. We are successful in so many ways every day. We are about getting behind each other and helping them to be effective human beings. We have to example that and live it. On the flip side, we need to be gracious when we are given an awesome opportunity. We want to have our brothers and sisters happy for us. We need to tell our working actor how he/she can enlist the help of the other siblings. Even offering to bring back some goodies from the craft service table will help them feel like the brother/sister cares for them. Encouraging an individual's success is a team effort. Parents need to help the other sibling, if there's a problem. They need to be supportive and cheerful for the child.

TANK: You have to point out that even though one may be working a little more now, the other has also had great accomplishments at another time. Other achievements need to be stressed and commended like sports and school achievements.

REIVERS: We, as a family, are very supportive of each other. The children have been taught from a young age that the success of one is the success of all. When one person's career seems to be moving slow, we always take time to make sure they are involved in something that they love to do and feel is their own. That way no one feels forgotten and we can all be proud of each other's accomplishments as well as our own. We have been blessed as a family to have had success in this business while still being able to keep in perspective what is most important, each other.

What advice would you give in handling "rejection"?
BOYD: I believe this is a situation that must be handled delicately. I do not compare my two children in any aspect of their lives. I have taught my children to focus on their own personal best and not the end result. We have emphasized the things we can control, and minimized the things we cannot. We have treated "positive feedback" as a victory in and of itself. I celebrate my children's differences. We also try to celebrate success as a whole family and celebrate each other's victories. We're in this together, we've achieved success together, and we've all had to make sacrifices for such. It's a team effort. I have never fretted over the status of a project—at least not in front of the kids. I focus forward. I do not assume or pretend that either child is "right" for every project. Your handling rejection will have *everything* to do with how your kids handle the rejection that is sure to come.

TANK: I was fortunate as Hayden was never a child to ask about an audition after it was over. He never asked if he got a callback or if he booked the part. When we were fortunate enough to book a job, I would let him know and it became an exciting moment. We always realized that you have to go on many auditions before booking something, so we just waited until it was Hayden's turn.

LUCAS: The disappointment is met with understanding, but also with our faith. Jack knows his job is to give 200 percent to every opportunity. He does. He has no regrets and does not take it personally when he is not chosen. Looking back at some of the things he had set his heart on, he realizes they may not have been for him, considering what he was able to go off and do instead. You know the saying, "When God closes a door, He opens a window."

How do you find time for your child to have activities outside of working in the industry?

ARENS: The longer you are in the business, the more your children will replace their school friends with friends who are also auditioning. Since it is hard for children and their auditioning parents to make play dates, it is nice to have spontaneous play dates with other auditioning children and parents after an audition. There are opportunities to go to a park and play, a movie, or dinner.

REIVERS: Due to the nature of this business, extended vacations always become difficult to plan. We have learned that spontaneity and short weekend trips work very well. There are many times that we don't have any idea what we are going to do or where we are going to go until that morning. For us, having fun doesn't involve a long thought process.

What advice would you give other parents?

BOYD: Get educated as quickly as you can. No one has all (if any) of the answers for success. If any one agent, manager, casting director, acting coach, director, or producer had "the" answers, we would only need one agent, manager, casting director, acting coach, director, or producer in Hollywood. Through time, effort, and education, each of these may bring an educated opinion to the table, but you should regard it as just that. None should be expected to work harder for your kids than you do. None will care about your children like yourself, and none will be willing to make the sacrifices that you may or may not be willing to make. Therefore, your opinion or input should be added to the "pool of opinions" that are sure to flood you. The only way that you will ever feel comfortable and confident about trusting your own judgment and intuition is if you have worked to educate yourself. Read, ask, discuss, experiment, explore, evaluate—do whatever it takes to get educated as quickly as possible.

TANK: Make sure your child truly has an interest. I truly believe that you cannot make a child who does not want to be doing it succeed at this. It is a lot of work if it is not fun. Also, keep trying. We know many people who went years without any success, only to have big success later on.

LUCAS: It takes commitment from the parent. Starting with a support system of family, extended family, or friends will be very helpful. Be prepared to drop what you are doing—with a good attitude—or call part of the support team to get your kid to the audition. It is important to understand that the casting houses are the ones requesting your child to come in. A good agent works hard to facilitate information flowing back and forth to get you on the casting schedule. Do not take these two entities lightly. Casting houses do not appreciate no-shows, and agents can work years to get your child exposed to this industry for next-to-no pay. Treat them with respect and kindness and do your best never to say, "Sorry, I can't make it." It could take a month or it could take a couple of years to really have your child doing good, solid auditions, showing ownership of role development, and getting jobs. As the kids engage in the aspects of auditioning and working, along the way we learn life lessons.

REIVERS: The Screen Actors Guild is a great place for a parent to start for information. Make sure the child understands the entire process and the length of time it could take before actually booking their first jobs. Teach them that they should go over their scripts and always be prepared for every audition. Also, teach them to always focus on getting the next audition and not to worry about the last one. Remember, they are still children, so make it all a fun experience. Otherwise, it's not worth it.

Thank you for your continued support in recommending
Breaking Into Commercials as a resource guide for talent.
We are proud of the positive results this book has had in
launching and moving forward the careers of working actors.

Terry Berland and Deborah Ouellette are excited to announce
the updated 3rd edition of their industry go-to book and
wanted you to have the enclosed complementary copy.

Breaking Into Commercials, 3rd edition is now available in
bookstores (brick-and-mortar and online) or directly from
Silman-James Press at www.silmanjamespress.com.

Best,

Gwen Feldman
Silman-James Press
3624 Shannon Road • Los Angeles, CA 90027
(323) 661-9922
www.silmanjamespress.com
info@silmanjamespress.com

Breaking Into Commercials, 3rd Edition:
The Complete Guide to Marketing Yourself, Auditioning to Win,
and Getting the Job
by Terry Berland and Deborah Ouellette
$16.95 paper, 254 pages, 978-1-935247-09-8
Published April 2014

SECTION 3

WRAPPING IT ALL UP

18.

What It Takes to Make It in Commercials

Congratulations! You're nearing the end of what we hope has been a wonderful journey through the process of breaking into commercials. To wrap things up, we've summarized tips from agents, managers, coaches, talent consultants, and casting people from all over the country. Their combined wisdom and experience could be instrumental in propelling you toward a successful career in the commercial industry.

We interviewed more than seventy-five industry professionals in every state in the United States in the course of researching this book, asking what they looked for in an actor, what misconceptions newcomers have about the business, what their "pet peeves" about talent are, and what words of advice they could offer. Below are the results of our findings:

What Do Agents and Casting People Look For in an Actor?

- First impressions are important. The personality, the drive, the motivation, the talent, the look—*must* be presented.

- Your personality should be pleasant and outgoing (but not domineering).

- Charisma, determination, energy, and a solid work ethic are requisites for the successful actor.

- Integrity is essential. You *must* present yourself honestly at all times.
- Quality headshots and résumés.
- Good training.
- How you handle yourself at interviews.
- If you are nice and easy to work with.
- If you are easy to direct.
- Availability/flexibility.
- Confidence (but not arrogance).
- Magic in the eyes (expressive, animated, with an obvious love for the industry).
- Eager to work hard.

Common Misconceptions Newcomers Have about the Industry

- This is not work. It can be done as a hobby.
- You can suddenly be "discovered"—as the tabloids imply.
- Agents will be able to get you every job.
- Being "pretty" is all it really takes.
- It doesn't take time, persistence, and a lot of hard work.
- If you work hard, sooner or later you're going to get what you want.
- Newcomers underestimate how much competition there is in larger markets, as well as:
  - How impersonal it is outside a smaller, regional market.
  - How tough it is to get a decent agent in a larger market.
- Newcomers also think:
  - That they are eligible for every part that comes up.
  - That it's going to happen overnight.

Pet Peeves

WHAT THINGS ABOUT TALENT ARE REALLY IRRITATING?

- Being overly fussy (appearing difficult or uncooperative).
- Not being available (especially after indicating you would be).

- Obvious retouching of photographs.
- Not listening.
- Old photographs that don't look like you anymore.
- You think you know it all.
- You talk incessantly.
- Not being prepared for an interview (not having headshots, résumés, and/or demo CD out and ready to give to the agent or casting director).
- Padded résumé that's not realistic or believable.
- Not having your résumé attached to the photo when you hand it in to the agent or casting director.
- Not having your photo, résumé, and demo online and ready to send to anyone at a moment's notice.
- A lack of patience.
- Not being realistic about what can be achieved in a given period of time.
- Not following directions.
- Big egos and prima-donna attitudes.
- Wearing perfume or cologne.
- Not showing up on time for an interview, audition, or shoot.
- Not being knowledgeable about the industry and/or not conducting yourself in a professional, businesslike manner.

Words of Advice

- Have a sense of humor.
- Be prepared.
- Take classes.
- It's a business. Treat it as such.
- You are the product.
- Don't expect your agent to get work for you. They get you auditions; you get the job.
- Get everything you can out of your regional market before moving on to a larger one.

- You can't take no for an answer. Be persistent in your efforts.
- Learn the language of the industry.
- Keep active in workshops and other opportunities to train and network.
- Have your professional tools together.
- Theater is very valuable to your development as an actor.
- Know your strengths and work toward them.
- Be careful of scams.
- Get into productions and showcases.
- Have good headshots—and keep them current.
- Set realistic goals. Be willing to adjust them as necessary.
- Actively market yourself.
- Be as objective about your abilities and limitations as possible.
- Be open to criticism.
- Be persistent, honest, and hardworking.
- Know that it's not a business for everyone.
- Be willing to pay your dues.
- Have some kind of trade you can fall back on.
- Develop a philosophy that will take you through the hard times.
- Be willing to go the extra mile.
- Expect the unexpected.
- If this is something you really, *really* must do, then GO FOR IT!
- Realize that success is built on a concerted effort over an extended period of time.

Whew! That's a lot of wisdom to take in at once. We hope that you've learned what it takes to make it in the business, and that we have been able to make your transition into it a little bit easier. You know how to prepare a winning promotional package, how to prepare for and give a great audition, and how to follow through after you book the job. By reading this book and acting on the principles herein, you have taken great strides in creating a successful, lucrative career in the exciting world of commercials. Congratulations on completing a journey with us that will enrich your life for years to come.

Here's wishing you a long and prosperous career in the business!

ONLY ONE LIFE
THAT SOON IS PAST,
ONLY WHAT'S DONE
WITH LOVE WILL LAST . . .

Glossary

- **Account executives** – The liaisons between the client and the advertising agency.
- **Action** – Director's command to start.
- **Actor's Equity Association (Equity)** – The union governing performers and stage managers in live theater.
- **AD** – Assistant Director. The person in charge of the crew; the person who runs the set.
- **Ad lib** – Speech or action that has not been scripted or specifically rehearsed.
- **Agent** – The person who functions as a salesperson with *you* as the product. In exchange for finding you work, the agent is paid a commission (usually 10 percent of your earnings).
- **American Federation of Television and Radio Artists (AFTRA)** – The union with jurisdiction over live and taped television shows and commercials, soap operas, and disc jockeys and other radio performers.
- **Apple box** – A wooden box, the size of an apple box, that is used for various purposes on a set. For example, if the camera is too high, the cameraman will stand on an apple box.
- **Art Director** – The person who visually conceives the ad and makes it come alive through drawings and visuals. The art director is responsible for the entire visual concept of the commercial—the way the commercial will look.
- **Assistant Director** – See "AD."

- **Audition** – A tryout or chance to perform for the people who are in a position to give you a job.

- **Avail** (*or* **first refusal**) – A handshake agreement among the actor, agent, and casting director in which the actor guarantees that the client will have first option on his time on the specific dates set aside for the commercial shoot.

- **Barn doors** – Metal flaps in front of lighting instruments that control the direction of the light beam.

- **Beat** – A moment when an actor changes attitude, emotion, or physical movement.

- **Blocking the shot** – Carefully working out the movement and actions of actors and mobile camera equipment. (Directors determine the blocking of shots.)

- **Booth** – Enclosed, soundproof area equipped with a microphone. This is where the talent record their words. It is separated from the creatives by a glass window.

- **Cable** – Specifically for cable TV usage.

- **Callback** – Request for an actor to read again for (usually) the director, producer, art director, and writer.

- **Camera left** (*or* **right**) – Directions given from the camera's point of view, facing the audience or the camera.

- **Camera rehearsal** – Full rehearsal with cameras and other pieces of production equipment.

- **Casting director** – A person who selects and auditions the actors they feel properly fit the criteria of a character description. The casting director does not work for the actor and does not receive commissions from actors.

- **Catch lights** – Reflections in the eyes caused by the photographer's lights.

- **Cattle call** – An audition in which hundreds of people may try out for a part on a first-come, first-served basis.

- **Cheat** – To angle the performer or object toward a particular camera; this is not directly noticeable to the audience.

- **Client** – The executive(s) who represent the product that is being advertised.

- **Close-up** (**CU**) – A shot of the product, actor's face, hands, etc., taken at close range.

- **Cold reading** – An audition at which the talent is asked to act out a script without having adequate time to rehearse.

- **Conflict** – Being under contract for two conflicting products (such as Tide and Wisk detergents). This is prohibited for union commercials. An advertiser would never want one person on the air advertising both his product and a competitor's.

- **Coordinator** – Assistant to the line producer.

- **Cover letter** – A letter of introduction.

- **Craft service** – Food set up all day long on the set.

- **Creative director** – Person responsible for the work of all creatives in the advertising agency.

- **Creative supervisor** – Person who oversees the activities of the art director, writer, and producer.

- **Creative team (the creatives)** – The producer, art director, creative supervisor, creative director, director, account executive, and client(s).

- **Cue** – Signal to start, pace, or stop any type of production activity or talent action.

- **Cue card** – Card with the script written on it in large letters. It is placed near the camera lens so actors don't have to memorize copy.

- **Cut** – Director's command to interrupt action.

- **Dailies** – The film of each day's shoot. This film is developed and printed at the end of each filming day and is usually seen the following day. Also referred to as "rushes."

- **Director** – The person who directs the ad.

- **Dissolve** – Short double-exposure between two scenes, in which the first scene is replaced slowly by the second scene.

- **Dolly** – Wheeled tripod on which a camera is mounted and can move about.

- **Dry run** – Rehearsal without equipment during which the basic actions of the talent are worked out. Also called "blocking rehearsal."

- **Dubbing** – Replacing one voice with another.

- **ECU** – Extreme close-up.

- **Fade** – *Fade up* means coming from black and fading into a scene. *Fade down* means fading out of a scene into black.

- **Fitting** – Trying on of clothes.

- **Flap (mouth flap)** – In animation, this refers to the movement of the mouth. If the talking stops and the character's mouth keeps moving, an actor will be called in to add words so that the mouth flaps match the rhythm of the speech.

- **Gaffer** – Chief electrician.

- **Gaffer's tape** – Electrical tape used to hold things together on a set.

- **Generic look** – Neutral, classic, all-American look.

- **Gofer** – Person who does (goes for) odd jobs, such as getting coffee, running errands.

- **Grain** – In film, the tiny dots that make up the image. This is generally accentuated by overexposure or overdevelopment of the film. (High-speed films are naturally grainy.) NOTE: The digital equivalent of grain is referred to as "noise."

- **Green room** – Waiting area (historically painted green).

- **Grip** – Crewmember who moves equipment.

- **Headshot** – An 8×10 photograph that serves as your commercial calling card.

- **Hero** – The best-looking product on the shoot.

- **High hat** – The lowest platform on which to place a camera, usually about floor level.

- **Industrials** – Promotional films used either to educate employees or to promote companies. They can be produced strictly for in-house use or to be shown at promotional events such as trade shows.

- **"It's a wrap."** – Statement signifying the end of a shoot.

- **Line producer** – Director's producer who generally manages day-to-day set operations.

- **Lip-sync** – Synchronization of sound and lip movement.

- **Load** – A technical way to put gum in the mouth for a commercial.

- **Long shot** – A shot from far away or framed very loosely (widely).

- **Loop group** – Group of people who work together providing additional dialogue for a scene.

- **Manager** – A talent representative who guides the talent's career.

- **Martini shot** – Last shot of the day.

- **Master shot** – A wide shot that shows the scene in its entirety.

- **Meter reading** – Light measuring with a light meter.
- **Milk-her-down** – Use dulling spray to get rid of unwanted reflections.
- **MOCAP** – Capturing strictly the motion of a character via digital means. (This might include walking, running, sitting, standing, jumping, etc.)
- **MOS** – A silent take (from a German director's mixed-language instructions "mit out sound").
- **Network** – Broadcast all over the country, including the three major markets (New York, Los Angeles, and Chicago).
- **On bells** – When shooting sound, a bell rings to indicate there should be quiet on the set.
- **PA** – Production assistant. Does odd jobs.
- **Pan** – Horizontal turning of the camera.
- **Parent union** – The first performing artist union you join.
- **Parkour** – A movement training discipline that developed out of military obstacle course training.
- **Pilot** – The first episode of a potential TV series.
- **Playback** – To replay (on a monitor) scenes that were shot.
- **Print it** – Director's designation for a filmed scene that is good enough to be developed and printed.
- **Producer** – Person responsible for putting together all the elements that make up the production of a commercial, including budgeting, selecting the director, coordinating all decisions of the people involved, and making sure the production, including final editing, is on schedule.
- **Production assistant** – See "PA."
- **Props** – Short for "properties." Furniture and other objects used for set decoration.
- **Read-only CD** – A read-only CD allows you to view the CD contents, but you cannot make copies of it.
- **Residuals** – Payments made to the talent every time an ad runs.
- **Résumé** – A one-page summary of your vital statistics, experience, training, and special skills. It is used to attract the interest of an agent, manager, or casting director.

- **Retouching** – Work by a photo artist (retoucher) on commercial prints to minimize minor flaws in the image by "touching up" temporary blemishes, stray hairs, and scratches or dust spots (white spots caused by dust on the negative).

- **Right to work** – Non-union. In a right-to-work state, companies cannot refuse to hire someone because he does not belong to the union or does not want to join the union.

- **Room tone** – The ambient sound on the shoot in total "silence" (i.e., when no hum or mechanical sounds are being made).

- **Rough cut** – The first edit of the filmed scenes.

- **Run-through** – Rehearsal.

- **Screen Actors Guild (SAG)** – The union governing actors in film. This includes motion pictures (whether shown on television or in movie theaters) and television commercials.

- **Script supervisor** – Crewmember who reads and times the script as it is shot. The script supervisor helps maintain shot-to-shot continuity by taking notes of each scene's details.

- **Seasonal** – Shot specifically for a particular holiday or season that must be identified as such in the commercial. For instance, if it is going to be run during the Christmas holiday, some Christmas decorations or a Christmas tree would be in the scene. There are no conflicts for seasonal commercials.

- **Set** – The arrangement of scenery and properties in the space (in a studio or on location) where something is filmed.

- **Slate** – (1) To identify verbally and visually each take before it is shot. (2) A little blackboard (or white board) upon which essential production information is written (such as title, scene date, and take number).

- **Slugging** – Inserting.

- **Speed** – Designates that the camera is running properly, i.e., up to speed.

- **Standard contract** – Contract used as written with no alterations or amendments.

- **Stand-in** – A person or product used only for testing the lighting before shooting starts.

- **Statistics (stats)** – On a résumé, your name, union affiliation and agent (if applicable), height, weight, eye and hair colors, and a phone number (cell phone, service, machine, or pager) where you can be reached quickly.

- **Sticks** – Tripod on which the camera can be mounted in a stationary position.

- **Stylist** – Wardrobe designer or purchaser.

- **Sweeten** – To enrich the audio background, often with music or sound effects.

- **Sync sound** – Sound captured in sync with the picture.

- **Taft-Hartley** – A waiver that allows you, as a non-union worker, to work on as many union jobs as you want within a thirty-day period, after which you must join the union. This means that you must be prepared to join the union for the next job you get after the thirty-day waiver.

- **Take** – (1) Each time you shoot a scene, it's a "take." (2) An actor's reaction.

- **Teamster** – Union people hired to drive trucks and to load and unload equipment. Member of the International Brotherhood of Teamsters.

- **Tear sheets** – Samples of a model's published work (print ads, fashion spreads, etc.) clipped from the publications in which they appeared and put into her portfolio.

- **Teleprompter** – Electrical device that displays the script in large letters that roll by in front of (and usually a bit below) the camera lens at the speed of the actor's delivery. This is an electronic replacement for cue cards.

- **Test** – A commercial that will run for a limited time in a specific market to test a product's recognition. The time of usage would be agreed upon at the time of booking the talent.

- **Thermal print** – Black-and-white still photograph taken directly from an image coming from a video camera. It prints on thermal paper.

- **Trailer** – Advertisement of a film that usually previews selected scenes from the film.

- **Two-shot** – Framing of two people in a camera shot.

- **Under five** – Speaking role of less than five lines.

- **Voice-over (VO)** – The actor's voice recorded off camera.

Index